The Complementarity of Women and Men

The Complementarity of Women and Men

Philosophy, Theology, Psychology & Art

Edited by
Paul C. Vitz

The Catholic University
of America Press
Washington, D.C.

Copyright © 2021
The Catholic University of America Press
All rights reserved

Library of Congress Cataloging-in-Publication Data
Names: Vitz, Paul C., 1935– editor.
Title: The complementarity of women and men : philosophy, theology, psychology, and art / edited by Paul C. Vitz.
Description: Washington, D.C. : The Catholic University of America Press, [2021] | Includes bibliographical references and index.
Identifiers: LCCN 2021006201 | ISBN 9780813233888 (paperback)
Subjects: LCSH: Theological anthropology—Catholic Church. | Women—Religious aspects—Christianity. | Men (Christian theology) | Femininity—Religious aspects—Catholic Church. | Masculinity—Religious aspects—Catholic Church. | Catholic Church—Doctrines.
Classification: LCC BT701.3 .C6632 2021 | DDC 233/.5—dc23
LC record available at https://lccn.loc.gov/2021006201

I dedicate this book to Timmie,

my wife of more than fifty years,

my three daughters, Rebecca, Jessica, and Anna,

my daughter-in-law, Ann,

and my many granddaughters.

They have taught me a great deal

about complementarity.

CONTENTS

List of Figures and Tables   ix

Introduction: Women and Men and
Their Complementarity: The Rationale
and Evidence | 1
PAUL C. VITZ

1. The Meaning of Sexual Differences | 9
J. BUDZISZEWSKI

2. Gender Reality vs. Gender Ideology | 35
SR. PRUDENCE ALLEN, RSM

3. Woman and Man: Identity, Genius,
and Mission | 89
DEBORAH SAVAGE

4. Michelangelo and the
Shrine to Complementarity:
The Sistine Chapel | 132
ELIZABETH LEV

5. Men and Women:
Their Differences and Their Complementarity;
Evidence from Psychology and Neuroscience | 182
PAUL C. VITZ

Bibliography   217
Contributors   235
Index   237

FIGURES AND TABLES

Figures

4-1.	Overview Image, Sistine Chapel Vault, *photograph copyright © Vatican Museums*	134
4-2.	Diagram of Sistine Chapel, *licensed with Cc-by-sa-3.0*	135
4-3.	Creation of Man, Sistine Chapel, *photograph copyright © Vatican Museums*	140
4-4.	Detail of Creation of Man God/Eve, Sistine Chapel, *photograph copyright © Vatican Museums*	141
4-5.	Creation of Eve, Sistine Chapel, *photograph copyright © Vatican Museums*	142
4-6.	Temptation and Fall of Man, Sistine Chapel, *photograph copyright © Vatican Museums*	144
4-7.	Eritrean Sibyl by Bernardino Pinturicchio, Borgia Apartments, *photograph copyright © Vatican Museums*	149
4-8.	Eritrean Sibyl, Sistine Chapel, *photograph copyright © Vatican Museums*	150
4-9.	Libyan Sibyl, Sistine Chapel, *photograph copyright © Vatican Museums*	152
4-10.	Jeremiah, Sistine Chapel, *photograph copyright © Vatican Museums*	153
4-11.	David and Goliath, Sistine Chapel, *photograph copyright © Vatican Museums*	155
4-12.	Judith and Holofernes, Sistine Chapel, *photograph copyright © Vatican Museums*	156
4-13.	Eleazar's Wife, Sistine Chapel, *photograph copyright © Vatican Museums*	165

4-14. Meshullameth, Sistine Chapel, *photograph copyright © Vatican Museums*   169

4-15. Mary and Jesus of Last Judgment, Sistine Chapel—Detail, *photograph copyright © Vatican Museums*   181

Tables

5-1. Developmental Gender Differences and Tendencies   189

5-2. Important Developmental Differences   190

5-3. Proposed Masculine and Feminine Psychological Strengths and Weaknesses   214

The Complementarity of Women and Men

Introduction

Women and Men and Their Complementarity

The Rationale and Evidence

Paul C. Vitz

"Men and women are fundamentally equal." "Men and women are fundamentally the same." These two sentences are not equivalent. In the past two centuries, secular Western thinkers, especially most feminists, have pressed for the essential sameness of the sexes out of a desire for equality among men and women. Others, including some feminists, have responded that the sexes are both equal *and* different—that is to say, they are complementary. The concept of complementarity has been especially promoted by the Catholic Church, although the implications of this view have not always been spelled out in great detail, which has left room for both scientists and theologians to elaborate upon it. From the early twentieth century to the seminal writings of Pope John Paul II to the warnings of Pope Francis against "gender ideology" and his calls for "a theology of woman," the church, for about the last hundred years, in spite of some earlier positions, has remained firmly on the side of the complementarity position of collaboration between the sexes rather than "battle of the sexes" or a false sameness position.

The purpose of this book is to carry out what we see as the urgent task of exploring and elaborating the complementarity of the sexes from both a psychological and a theological point of view. Its central claim is that theology, far from providing a constricting set of artificial impositions on reality (as many have argued), is actually a light clarifying the difficult and complex realities of masculinity and femininity. Empirical science is neither a substitute for nor an enemy of sound theological reasoning—the two constitute mutually supporting approaches, enabling a clearer understanding of the whole.

Before we begin briefly discussing the individual essays, it is worth asking: is the conflict between those who claim there are no important sex differences and those who claim that important differences exist and complement each other merely one of ideology? Are these two irreconcilable orthodoxies? Or is there empirical evidence showing that there are important differences, differences grounded in reality, differences that are not merely an imposition of culture?

In fact, there is strong evidence. Despite the political and cultural winds that blow against those who assert the existence of real sex differences, psychologists and neuroscientists have not stopped addressing the issue in methodologically rigorous studies—and the evidence clearly points in the direction of difference, not sameness. Much of this evidence will be summarized and referenced in chapter 5; but here let us explore briefly a few of the findings in depth to show what the researchers were testing for and what they found.

For example, research conducted by Ingalhalikar et al., 2012,[1] shows that very different brain activity patterns exist in healthy men and women. The researchers used 428 males and 521 females from ages eight to twenty-two and mapped their neural connections. (Neural connections represent a kind of roadmap of a person's brain.) The basic finding was that there was a big difference between these roadmaps in male and female brains. In particular, men's neural activity was mostly in one brain hemisphere, and connections were stronger between front and back. Women, with a larger corpus callosum—the structure connecting the two hemispheres—were highly connected across the left and right hemisphere. Significant conclusions were that men's brains were wired for perception and coordinated actions and women's brains were mapped for social skills and multitasking. One coauthor noted, "It's quite striking how complementary the brains of women and men are."[2]

---

[1]. M. Ingalhalikar et al., "Sex Differences in the Structural Connectome of the Human Brain," *Proceedings of the National Academy of Sciences of the United States of America* 111, no. 2 (2014): 823–28.

[2]. Ruben Gur, quoted in "Male and Female Brains Wired Differently, Scans Reveal," by Ian

Much research shows the greater interpersonal skills of women compared to men. This difference begins in infancy, where studies have found in female infants a greater response to faces, a greater response to other babies' cries, an early and greater empathy for others, and, throughout life, a greater involvement in relationships. Often these female interests are related to hormone effects, such as greater oxytocin in women.

In contrast, men show more involvement in objects and in systematic understanding of them. Men also demonstrate more risk taking and more aggression and hostility to others. All these characteristics are observed in boys starting at very young ages. Many of these effects are often linked to greater testosterone in men.

The reader may be aware that a common counterargument to male-female differences is the observation of overlap—most traits identified more strongly with one sex or the other can commonly be found in both, and a particular individual man or woman may show a sex-linked trait more or less strongly. All the chapters in the book note this issue, and it is given particular attention in my own chapter, chapter 5. Nevertheless, every chapter challenges the common assumption that there are no important differences between men and women that can be generalized. Every chapter also provides a case for complementarity as well.

Chapter 1, by renowned philosopher J. Budziszewski, sets the stage for the subsequent chapters by providing a Socratic dialogue that provides a rational case for sexual differences. *The Socratic dialogue has long been used to introduce a conceptual understanding to a student, and students are a major audience for this book.* Budziszewski's case often uses the different but complementary roles of parenting that he draws from typical examples of family life. To say that manhood and womanhood are truly different is not at all to say that this difference is simple or all-encompassing. Because men and women are not different species, but corresponding sexes of the same species, each is defined partly in terms of the other. When necessary, they can even step outside their

---

Sample, *Guardian*, December 2, 2013, http://www.the guardian.com/science/2013/dec/02/men-women-brains-wired-differently.

roles in some ways, can become partners in some of the same tasks, and can even tone down some of their differences. None of this means they are identical! For even when men and women do step out of their roles, they tend to have different motives for doing so. Even when they do share tasks, they tend to view them differently. And even when they do tone their differences down, the most common reason is that they have taught each other something. How is it that they have something to teach each other? Because they are not the same. This opening salvo explains how they are different.

In chapter 2 Sister Mary Prudence Allen, the foremost expert on the history of the philosophy of woman, examines contemporary gender theory and offers a philosophical defense of gender reality.[3] Drawing on philosophy and theology, she refutes the "gender ideology" position and makes a case for sexual differences. Gender ideologies hold that human beings fall along a continuum of three, five, or even fifteen different loose groupings of genders. They are based on revisionist metaphysics (rooted in neo-Platonism or Cartesianism) and a deconstructionist approach to the human person as a collection of qualities, attributes, or parts. Gender reality holds that human beings are "always or for the most part" women or men, female or male. It is based on a descriptive metaphysics (Aristotelian- and Thomistic-grounded) that integrates science into a view of the human being as an integral soul/body composite.

The chapter uses a philosophical methodology to answer the following questions:

What is the conflict between gender reality and gender ideology? How did sex and gender ideologies begin? What are the characteristics of sex and gender ideologies? How did gender ideology "go viral"? Who mapped the virus of gender ideology? How can gender reality be ransomed?

The answers to these questions draw upon the work of a number of Catholic philosophers, including Thomas Aquinas, Dietrich von

---

3. See her landmark studies in Sister Prudence Allen, *The Concept of Woman*, vols. 1–3 (Grand Rapids, Mich.: Eerdmans, 1997, 2002, 2017).

Hildebrand, Edith Stein, Jacques and Raissa Maritain, Gabriel Marcel, Bernard Lonergan, Emmanuel Mounier, M. A. Krapiec, and Karol Wojtyla/John Paul II. Together the work of these philosophers provides a vigorous defense of gender reality.

Philosopher and theologian Deborah Savage continues Allen's approach in chapter 3. She explores John Paul II's thought and extends his theory of complementarity to include a more comprehensive framework within which both the particular "genius" of woman and of man can be understood. Savage develops a lengthy theological defense of sexual differences. She ends with an analysis of the complementarity of women and men as exemplified in the lives of the Virgin Mary and St. Joseph. The chapter has a twofold purpose: to extend John Paul II's theory of complementarity to include a more comprehensive framework within which both the genius of woman and the genius of man can be understood; and to provide a clear and unambiguous affirmation of the gifts that men have made and continue to make to the creation of human civilization and the sustaining of culture and of families.

Her proposal is grounded in both scripture and the philosophical foundations of the Catholic tradition. She demonstrates that a proper understanding of Genesis 1 and 2 provides us with a point of departure for a more complete understanding of the nature of woman in relation to man as well as the particular "genius" attributable to both. We will see that man and woman are both "equal" and different and that they each bring distinct gifts to the tasks of human living. She shows that her account is confirmed both by the story of the fall in Genesis 3 and, perhaps most surprisingly, by science.

This chapter is intended as the starting place for what we might call a "theology of complementarity." Her hope is that this account will enable men and women both to understand themselves more fully and to find a way to work together more intentionally in realizing their shared mission to return all things to Christ.

Chapter 4, by art historian Elizabeth Lev, offers a surprising further exploration of these themes. She examines the art of Michelangelo in the Sistine Chapel, which John Paul II called "the sanctuary of the theology of the body." Lev identifies previously important unnoticed ways in which Michelangelo's work in the Italian Renaissance provides examples of sexual differences and especially of complementarity.

Although "complementarity" as an ecclesiastical term describing the relationship between men and women is relatively recent, the concept is not new, as evidenced in scripture, spirituality, theology, and even art. Coined in a certain sense by St John Paul II during his catecheses on the theology of the body, complementarity has become an essential part of Catholic language, able to express the complex nature of God's design for marriage, family, and salvation. But while the language may be new, its greatest visual expression is half a millennium old. The Sistine Chapel, arguably the most male-oriented space in Christendom, paradoxically contains perhaps the most complete compendium of complementary images of men and women in the entire history of art. Michelangelo's astonishing frescoes on the vault not only pair Adam with Eve from the very creation of man, but continue to complement male Jewish prophets with female sibyls for the Gentiles, to flank heroes with heroines, and, most surprisingly, to portray a mother for every father listed in the genealogy of Matthew.

This chapter looks at Michelangelo's striking artistic insistence on the presence of women alongside men in the history of salvation and specifically notes the variety of figures, active and contemplative, busy mothers and preening wives, youthful leaders and older mantic (prophetic) women, that the artist represented in the 6,000 square feet of the vault. Technical analysis demonstrates his varied stylistic approach from figures that took weeks to fashion to other images that are the equivalent of a candid photograph in fresco. This illustrated history of complementarity reveals its true matrix in Michelangelo's painting of the Last Judgment, where Mary, gentle and quiet, becomes as one with the thunderous Christ the judge.

Therefore, the art of this chapel reveals an age-old meditation on complementarity, even if not always defined in those terms, which is a fundamental part of the church from its origins and was given its most compelling expression by that genius formed in the heart of the church, Michelangelo.

After the preceding rational and humanistic support for differences and complementarity, chapter 5 provides a psychological interpretation of complementarity based on the available scientific evidence. It is theologically informed but with a focus on significant support from psychology and neuroscience. Its theological basis is largely derived from the work of Sr. Prudence Allen, who posits that the two sexes are equal in dignity and worth, but that each sex has significant differences from the other. These differences are complementary and through positive synergy can lead to greater flourishing for both. Keeping in mind that there is always some overlap, important differences in abilities and interests between men and women are presented; these are demonstrated by much psychological and neuroscientific research and are commonly interpreted by evolutionary theory. The most important psychological differences are men's greater abilities in dealing with the external world and objects and women's greater abilities in dealing with persons and interpersonal relationships. The differences begin in infancy and continue through adulthood. A list of ten personality differences between men and women is proposed and briefly discussed, showing how each difference has strengths and weaknesses and how the differences show a complementarity and imply the possibility of positive synergistic effects. In short, this chapter argues that the "no important differences" position is simply not scientifically correct. I also provide many examples of how the sexes complement each other and point out that evolutionary theory strongly implies that sexual specialization in different roles increases the success of raising children.

It is important to emphasize that sexual differences are not grounds for claiming that one sex is superior to the other. All chapters emphasize men and women as having equal dignity and worth. This important view is derived from scripture, primarily Genesis, and from its theological interpretation, especially in recent Catholic writings. This is a central issue throughout the book, especially in the chapters by Allen, Savage, and me. But the theme of equal dignity also receives support in the chapters by Budziszewski and Lev.

Embracing the complementarity model means two things for contemporary society. First, it means *embracing a common and very significant truth and its interpretive framework over what is mostly a political ideology*. There is strong and growing scientific evidence that there are major and reliable sex differences. To deny these facts is simply to deny an important part of reality.

Second, it means finally overcoming the evils of male domination over women and establishing a fruitful collaboration between men and women. Despite generations of feminists, we have yet to purge modern society of the sinful attitudes that men use to take advantage of women. But when it rejects the complementary aspects of masculinity and femininity, ideological feminism is doomed to fight not only the evils of sin but also the pull of human nature itself toward fruitful difference; in the process feminists often make enemies of those in society who value both tradition and scientific truth. The complementarity position resolves the tension between the differences and transcends that tension in ways that lead to mutual support and flourishing.[4]

---

4. I would like to thank my colleagues at Divine Mercy University, especially Edward Moran, for their support of this book. Thanks also go to DMU students for their helpful comments.

CHAPTER 1

The Meaning of Sexual Differences

J. Budziszewski

How many more colors there are in the world because there are two sexes and not just one! How amusing they are to each other, and yet how baffling! Mutual perplexity can be part of the fun, a fountain of mirth, making the shimmering hues of strangeness sparkle all the more. In our day, though, perplexity isn't so amusing; it has an edge to it. We see all those colors all right, but admitting to the sight is considered shameful and offensive. Just as some ages have held it loutish to work with one's hands, so our time holds it crude to make use of one's eyes. So we make ourselves a little blind. We squint, throw dust in our eyes, and try not to look at things straight on.

A well-socialized young woman whom we may call Carissa had been reading some of the classics for the first time. One day when we were talking, she asked a question that all well-socialized young women who are reading the classics for the first time are expected to ask these days. Why did those bygone writers speak as though men and women are different?

"Maybe because they are different," I said. "Don't you think so?"

Plainly annoyed by my answer, she demanded, "Weren't those old views just prejudices?"

"Well, it's not easy to disentangle the prejudices of one's own time

---

This chapter previously appeared as chapter 3 of *On the Meaning of Sex*, by J. Budziszewski (Wilmington, Del.: ISI, 2012). It appears here with the permission of the copyright holder, ISI.

and place from universal truth. Maybe none of those writers did disentangle them perfectly. Still," I said, "aren't certain differences between men and women acknowledged everywhere?"

"But men and women *aren't* different."

"Then why do you think every culture supposes that they are?"

"Oh, I know the sexes *end up* different everywhere," she said. "But that only happens because boys are *raised* differently than girls."

"Let me be sure I follow you. You don't deny that some sex differences are universal—"

"No."

"—but you say they aren't natural. The only reason for them is differences in how boys and girls are brought up."

"That's right."

"Let's think about that. To produce the same differences between boys and girls everywhere, those differences in upbringing would also have to be the same everywhere, wouldn't they?"

"Yes. Boys are *always* raised differently than girls."

"And yet you think these differences in upbringing have no basis in human nature."

"Right, because they don't."

"If they have no basis in human nature, then why are they universal?"

"What do you mean?"

"If they are merely arbitrary, wouldn't you expect them to vary from culture to culture?"

"No, because cultures *influence* each other."

"You mean cultures that raise boys and girls differently influence other cultures to raise them differently?"

"Of course."

"Why shouldn't it be the other way around? If it's all because of culture, then why don't some cultures raise boys and girls the same and influence other cultures to follow *them*?"

"I don't understand you."

"To put the question another way," I asked, "if the pattern of upbringing has no basis in human nature, then why is it so persistent?"

The Meaning of Sexual Differences | 11

Carissa dodged the question, instead protesting an opinion I hadn't expressed. "Aren't men and women equally human?"

"Equally human, sure, but not the same. Complementary variations on the same musical theme. Different voices singing in polyphony."

"Tell me *one* fundamental difference between men and women," she demanded.

"That's easy. I could never bear a child. A woman can."

"Not *all* women. Aren't some women infertile?"

"Sure, but you're confusing essence with accident," I said. "A fertile woman can bear a child, but not even a fertile man can pull off a feat like that."

By now Carissa was thoroughly exasperated. Hurling down her trump card, she exclaimed, "I know men's and women's *bodies* are different, but *in their brains* they're just the same."

The details fade from memory, so I may have slightly misquoted some of Carissa's words. Not the words of her final sentence, which have echoed in my mind ever since. This chapter is not about brain science. Nonetheless, let us pause to consider what is known about men's and women's brains.

"In their brains," it turns out, men and women are different after all. According to neuroscientist Larry Cahill, the differences are marked, pervasive, and consistent.[1] The cliché that variation within each sex is greater than variation between the sexes is simply false. Moreover, the contrasts between men and women are evident not just in a few extreme cases, but across the whole distribution, and they involve not only the activity of the brain, but also its organization and development. Doreen Kimura, another brain scientist, remarks that although environment certainly influences us, the differences in brain organization occur "so early in life that from the start the environment is acting on differently wired brains in boys and girls."[2]

How many are these differences in wiring? Legion. To mention

---

1. Larry Cahill, "Why Sex Matters for Neuroscience," *Nature Reviews: Neuroscience* 7 (2006): 477–84. See also Cahill, "His Brain, Her Brain," *Scientific American* 292, no. 5 (2005): 40–47.

2. Doreen Kimura, "Sex Difference in the Brain," *Scientific American* 267, no. 3 (1992): 119–25.

just a few: Large parts of the brain cortex are thicker in women than in men. Ratios of gray to white matter vary, too. The hippocampus, which plays a role in memory and spatial navigation, takes up a greater proportion of the female brain than of the male brain. On the other hand, the CA1 region of the hippocampus is larger in the male. A variety of neurotransmitter systems work differently in men and women; neurotransmitters are the chemicals that carry nerve impulses across the synapses. Sex hormones, obviously different in men and women, influence not only the excitability of hippocampus cells, but also various aspects of their structure. The right and left hemispheres are more interconnected in female brains than in male ones, and the corpus callosum, which links them together, is larger. The amygdala, involved in emotion and emotional memory, is larger in men, but the deep limbic system, which is also involved in emotion, is larger in women. Across a spectrum of different functions, which side of the amygdala controls which function is reversed in men and women. Sex-related differences between the hemispheres exist for other brain regions as well, including the prefrontal cortex, involved in personality, cognition, and other executive functions, and the hypothalamus, which links the nervous system with the endocrine system and has some connection with maternal behavior. External circumstances, such as chronic stress, act on male brains differently than on female. Brain diseases also diverge in men and women, not only in their frequency, but in their age of onset, duration, and the way they manifest themselves. Even the neurological aspects of addiction differ between the two sexes.

Although not all neurological differences are associated with behavioral differences, the differences between male and female brains affect numerous aspects of behavior, including "emotion, memory, vision, hearing, processing faces, pain perception, navigation, neurotransmitter levels, stress hormone action on the brain, and disease." Cahill says that "the picture of brain organization that emerges is of two complex mosaics—one male and one female—that are similar in many respects but very different in others. The way that information is processed through the two mosaics, and the behaviors that each produce, could be identical or strikingly different, depending on a host of parameters." He concludes with a quotation from a report of the medical branch of the National Academy of Sciences: "Sex does matter. It matters in ways that we did not expect. Undoubtedly, it matters in ways that we have not yet begun to imagine."[3]

So Carissa had it exactly backward. It seems that our brains are even more different than the rest of our bodies.

Why is it so hard even to discuss the differences between the sexes? I think because we miss four large truths.

One of these large truths might be called the *duality of nature*. Manhood and womanhood reflect the same human nature, and with equal fidelity and dignity, but they reflect different facets of it. There are two ways to get this matter wrong. One way is to think that because the two sexes are different, they must be unequally valuable—woman an inferior version of man, or man an inferior version of woman. The other way is to think that because the sexes do have equal worth, they must be exactly the same.

Another large truth is the *duality of path*. The developmental trajectories of men and women are different at both ends—not only in what they start with, the susceptibilities and tendencies that each sex must discipline and prune, but in what they end with, what each sex ripens into when all goes as it should. Some people miss the point by ignoring the difference in starting points, as though the difference between the raw materials from which maturity is built were unimportant. That is like thinking that a house can float above its foundations. Others miss the point by paying attention *only* to the difference in starting points. For instance, they may say that men have a stronger desire for sex (which may or may not be true) and then draw the conclusion that a man who beds as many women as possible is more manly than a man who is faithful to his wife (which does not follow).

The third truth is *body and soul unity*. Human beings aren't one thing but two things together, composites of physical body and rational soul, each element equally personal and equally part of what we are. Again, there are two opposite ways to miss the mark. One way is to

---

3. Cahill, "Why Sex Matters for Neuroscience."

think that the true self is nothing but a body, so that the soul or mind is merely one of its activities, like the secretion of bile.[4] The other way is to think that the true self is nothing but a mind, a nonbodily person mysteriously occupying and using a nonpersonal body.[5] By the way, readers who are suspicious of religion need not feel jittery about the word "soul." It was used even by the pagan philosopher Aristotle to refer to the formal principle of an embodied human life, the pattern the presence of which makes the difference between a living human body and a human corpse. The pattern "informs" the matter but is not itself matter. People of my religious tradition would of course say *more* than this about souls, but one who rejects that "more" can still speak of souls. One more thing. "Mind" and "soul" do not mean the same thing. The soul is the pattern of an embodied human life; the mind is one of the powers that this pattern possesses or exercises.

The final large truth is *polaric complementarity*. Men and women aren't just different, but different in corresponding ways. They are complementary opposites—alike in their humanity, but different in ways that make them natural partners. Each sex completes what the other lacks and helps bring the other into balance. One way to reject this insight is to deny its second element, complementarity, so that the contrast between men and women seems to make them strangers or enemies. The other way to reject the insight is to deny its other element, polarity, so that we can't see the contrast in the first place. Both kinds of denial produce the same result, a kind of solipsism in which each sex views itself as complete and whole just as it is, with no need to be balanced by the other.

I hope it is clear that repudiating any of these four large truths is asking for trouble. By ignoring the duality of nature, we make it impossible for men and women to honor each other for what they really are. By failing to understand the duality of path, we persuade them to

---

4 The statement that "the brain secretes thought as the liver secretes bile," often attributed incorrectly to the eighteenth-century physician and lawyer Pierre Cabanis, is apparently that of the nineteenth-century physiologist Jacob Moleschott.

5. I borrow this crisp formulation from Robert P. George, *The Clash of Orthodoxies* (Wilmington, Del.: ISI, 2001), 42, who in turn borrows it from Luke Gormally, *Euthanasia, Clinical Practice and the Law* (London: Linacre Center, 1994), 111–66.

view themselves as either male and female beasts or sexless angels. By denying body and soul unity, we confuse them by making their bodily differences seem either irrelevant or all-important. By denying polaric complementarity, we undermine their union and destroy their human solidarity.

Where was Carissa in all this? Obviously, she denied the first, second, and fourth large truths—the duality of nature, the duality of path, and polaric complementarity. Convinced that any difference between the sexes would make them unequal, she insisted that they were just the same. She denied not only the difference in the ore from which manhood and womanhood are refined, but also the difference in the steel that results. Finally, her rejection of the polarity of the two sexes left no room to acknowledge their mutual need for each other.

Paradoxically, the notion that men and women are identical works against the very equality that it tries to uphold. The same, are they? The same as what? Though with some dissimulation, identicalists almost always answer, "The same as men." Not only do men who despise women take this line; it is also taken by those so-called feminists who detest everything feminine, regard womanly women as traitors to the cause, and insist on an ideal that is supposedly indifferent to sex, but is actually masculine. From the same root spring those strange male fantasies about worlds of the future in which women lead armies, command starships, gun down enemies, and are ready for sexual intercourse at any moment. The underlying wish is that both sexes would be men, but that some of these men would look like women. Considering how things have been going lately, I wonder why no one imagines a different future, in which the institution of marriage has disintegrated and women raise children in matriarchal herds, like elephants—the men occasionally drifting in to mate, then drifting out to roam with other men. But I digress.

I was saying that Carissa denied the first, third, and fourth large truths. To pick up the thread of the story, it is pretty clear that she denied the second large truth, too, body and soul unity, although her remark about the brain was ambiguous. Probably she was an inconsistent materialist, who identified her true self with a part of the body, her brain, while considering the rest of her body beneath notice. But I may be mistaken. She may have been a muddled angelist, who said "brain" although she really meant "mind," and who thought mind is the only thing that matters. Then again, she may have viewed her brain as non-bodily, divorced from its material conditions. It is hard to tell.

Perhaps it does not matter much whether she was a materialist or an angelist, because, in an odd way, materialism and angelism leave us equally in suspense. If we are nothing but bodies, then it is difficult to avoid reducing ourselves to our anatomical processes, so that men are but dispersers of seed, women but receptacles and incubators. If we are nothing but minds, then it is difficult to see what our bodies have to do with us at all. On this hypothesis, when a mother kisses her baby, she is not actually kissing, and the baby is not actually being kissed; she is only manipulating her husk, which is not really her, to kiss the baby's husk, which is not really the baby. Some ancient angelists reasoned that since our bodies are not our true selves, we ought to have as little to do with them as possible. In their view, we should be extreme ascetics, regarding even marriage and childbearing as evil. Other angelists reasoned that since our bodies are not our true selves, it makes no difference what we do with them. We may as well be libertines, they thought, and even whoring and dissipation are blameless. None of these views, whether materialist or angelist, makes sense of what we are: ensouled body and embodied soul together, both of them at once.

Why then do we fall for such strange views? Some say, "It's all ideology." That is no answer; what we are asking is why absurd ideologies seem attractive. Others say, "It's all because of disordered family life." That explanation is a little better; when dad flies the coop to nest with his secretary, or mom shacks up with her boyfriend, their relationships with their children are certainly thrown into chaos. Should we be surprised if these children carry confused thoughts and resentments about themselves, their parents, and the sexes right into their grown-up life? Wrongheaded sexual ideologies undermine families, and ruined families generate a readiness to accept wrongheaded ideologies. Even so, this answer is not fully satisfying, either. There have always been strange ideas and broken families. Why should the vicious

The Meaning of Sexual Differences | 17

circle be especially vicious in our own time? We simply don't know the answer.

But let us leave that aside. Is there a more adequate way to speak about men and women and a more honest way to understand their differences?

On the assumption that nothing should be taken seriously until it has been counted, some think the path to honesty and clarity lies in the quantitative analysis of cross-cultural psychological surveys. As we paused to consider what men and women look like to brain scientists, let us take time out to consider what they look like to survey researchers.

It turns out that interpreting the results of psychological surveys is more difficult than one might expect. For example, according to one widely used personality assessment, the Myers-Briggs Type Indicator, or MBTI, men are more likely to report a preference for thinking over feeling, women a preference for feeling over thinking.[6] No doubt such a result measures something—but what? It is simply impossible that it could measure what it purports to measure. Why? Because it makes no sense to "prefer" thinking or feeling. Everyone is both feeling and thinking at every moment, and the actions are inseparable. Not even having wandering thoughts is the same as not thinking; not even having calm emotions is the same as not feeling. I cannot say one time, "Now I will feel," and at another time, "Now I will think." Indeed, what I think affects how I feel, and what I feel affects how I think. If I believe you have cheated me, I will probably feel indignant toward you, and if I feel sympathetic toward you, I will probably try to think of you in the best possible light. Yes, of course, we can integrate feeling with reasoning in different ways. We can even train ourselves to integrate them in one way rather than another. Characteristically, men and women do integrate them differently; it is no accident that men find it easier to feel objectively and women find it easier to think compassionately. But we cannot choose between thinking per se and feeling per se, so there is no sense in asking people, "Which do you prefer?"

6. See, for example, Center for Applications of Psychological Types, "Estimated Frequencies of the Types in the United States Population," http://www.capt.org/mbti-assessment/estimated-frequencies.htm.

Once I offered these reflections to someone who wanted to administer the MBTI to me. She expressed the thought, "That just shows that you prefer thinking to feeling!" I have a clear recollection of experiencing unusually strong feelings about the matter.

Although the MBTI requires impossible choices, most survey researchers try to avoid putting their respondents in such impossible positions. Instead of recording what they say when confronted with a small number of preconceived false alternatives, as in the MBTI, they ask all sorts of different questions, trying to get at as many personality traits as possible. Usually they look for patterns of covariation, tendencies for people who have high scores on certain traits to have high scores on other traits, too.[7] What such research finds is that there are numerous patterned differences between the sexes. Considering that men and women belong to the same species and share with each other the nature of human beings, we would not expect them to differ significantly on every measure, or even on most measures, nor do they. In general intelligence, for example, men differ more from other men and women differ more from other women than men and women differ from each other. But the many sharp differences that do exist between the sexes hold consistently across countries, educational levels, ages of respondents, and years in which the studies are conducted.

Guess what? These differences correspond closely with traditional views of the differences between men and women. Not only that, but the differences in views about the sexes turn out to be just as universal as the differences between the sexes. In other words, not only do we find the same differences everywhere, but we also find much the same views *about* these differences everywhere[8]—even in countries like ours, where confessing to such views is branded as prejudiced and ret-

---

7. For example, see Robert R. McCrae and Oliver P. John, "An Introduction to the Five-Factor Model and Its Applications," *Journal of Personality* 60, no. 2 (1992): 175–215. A "factor" is a statistical construct reflecting a pattern of covariation among a large number of other quantities.

8. See Alan Feingold, "Gender Differences in Personality: A Meta-Analysis," *Psychological Bulletin* 116, no. 3 (1994): 429–56; Paul T. Costa Jr., Antonio Terracciano, and Robert R. McCrae, "Gender Differences in Personality Traits across Cultures: Robust and Surprising Findings," *Journal of Personality and Social Psychology* 81, no. 2 (2001): 322–31. Costa et al. perform new research that broadens Feingold's conclusions about sex differences to a wider range of cultures and personality traits.

rograde. Mark it up as another victory of quantitative social science: We can now confirm by counting that what everyone used to know without counting is really true. We can even confirm that although we feign ignorance, some of it is still really known. How surprising, how unexpected, and—in the view of some of us—how disturbing.

True, the differences between men and women, taken as groups, are stronger in some cultures than others. Ever, the cross-cultural pattern is not what one would guess. One would expect these differences to be more pronounced in poor, traditionalist countries and less pronounced in wealthy, individualistic countries. According to Paul T. Costa Jr., Antonio Terracciano, and Robert R. McCrae, they are actually stronger and more pronounced in the latter and less pronounced in the former. No one really knows why. Perhaps the explanation lies in the fact that life is simply harder in poor countries, so that women are more likely to be forced by circumstances to take on unfeminine roles they would rather not assume. Costa et al. do not consider this hypothesis, but they do take up and reject several others. Their own best guess is that perhaps the survey results have been skewed by differences in how women describe and report their own behavior. In countries where sex roles are strongly emphasized, women may be more likely to say, "This is what one does," while in individualistic cultures, they may be more likely to say, "This is how I am," even though in both cases they are behaving in much the same ways.[9] The jury is still out.

In any case, women everywhere tend to have much higher survey scores than men in nurturance or tendermindedness, trustfulness, and anxiousness. In various ways, they also show greater sensitivity to emotion. (I hasten to add that this is not the same having a "preference" for emotion over thought—it is really about how feelings are experienced and how thoughts and feelings interact.) Women experience both positive and negative emotion more strongly and vividly. Moreover, they are more likely to show their emotions in their faces, and they are better at deciphering nonverbal cues about what other people are feeling. Perhaps because of this sensitivity, they are also more vulnerable to moods and mood swings, more likely to show signs of depression, and

---

9. Costa, Terracciano, and McCrae, "Gender Differences in Personality Traits," 329.

more susceptible to stress. On the other hand, they are warmer, more talkative, more gregarious, and more agreeable or compliant. They also differ from men in the way they consider potential mates. In particular, they care much more than men do about ambition and socioeconomic status, somewhat more than men do about intelligence, and somewhat more than men do about moral virtues, like honesty and sincerity.

Men show the opposite patterns. Moreover, on average, they have much higher scores in assertiveness, they are more open to new ideas, and they are more interested in excitement. Some studies suggest that they have higher opinions of themselves: To use the more polite phrase, they have greater self-esteem, and to use the less polite one, greater self-conceit. They also tend to be better at mechanical reasoning and in spatial visualization. In comparing potential mates, they care much more than women do about physical attractiveness. They are also much more likely to engage in sex without personal relationship, a category of behavior that includes both casual and solitary sex.

The fundamental problem with such methods of investigation is that although they accurately measure how men as a group differ from women as a group, they do not really get at the difference between man as such and woman as such. To put the point another way, although they describe numerous differences between men and women, they do not get at the underlying difference, of which all those other differences are mere effects. So-called factor-analytic models, which analyze patterns of covariation to reduce large numbers of observed differences to a smaller number of "dimensions" or "factors," are sometimes said to dig deeper. But not even these get down to the underlying causal reality, the essential difference between men and women; they merely describe the effects of that reality in a more efficient and economical way.

Moreover, although such statistical methods are helpful in one way, they are unhelpful in another. If there really is an essential or underlying difference between men and women, then it holds for every man and every woman. Needless to say, the statistical generalizations hold only for some men and women; they are merely averages. Women are in general more talkative, but any given man may be more talkative than most women. Men are in general more assertive, but any given woman may be more assertive than most men. This may be one of the reasons identicalists like Carissa deny that there is any underlying difference between man as such and woman as such. From their point of view, if you want to describe any given person, Q, you should simply tally Q's various traits. Is Q talkative? Assertive? Tender-minded? Mechanical? Compliant? Once you have done that, you are finished; you know all there is to know. Except for a few purely biological purposes, nothing is added by asking, "Is Q a man or a woman?" True, whether the other person is a man or a woman is the first thing we notice upon meeting. Yet on the identicalist view, that is just one of our quirks. Whether someone is a man or a woman is really unimportant.

There is something odd about this view. If we really believe only in individuals—if we really deny the importance of categories like "man" and "woman"—then why not be consistent? Why stop with sex? Why not apply the same way of thinking to, say, species? If it is true that once you know a person's traits, nothing is added by asking whether he is male or female, then by the same token, shouldn't we say that once you know any being's traits, nothing is added by asking whether it is human or nonhuman? Shouldn't this question be equally unimportant?

As a matter of fact, a fair and increasing number of people do think so. That unimportant question is deeply offensive to them.[10] It generates a feeling of grievance.

Now to feel such a grievance, one must view reality in a certain way. I do not say that he must be conscious of viewing it that way; I only say that to be offended, he must be viewing it that way. First, he must believe that nothing exists but individual things. In other words, he must take the view that the way that we classify beings is purely arbitrary; "natural kinds" do not exist. He may believe that Mary, Claire, and Felicity are real individuals, but he may not believe that there is

---

10. Am I exaggerating? Isn't this view *outré*? On the contrary, quite a few philosophers and legal scholars, perhaps the majority, now take it as axiomatic. They may distinguish among animals with different functional capacities—just as they distinguish among humans with different functional capacities—awarding "personhood" to some and denying it to others. However, they consider the distinction between humans and nonhumans per se as arbitrary, prejudicial, and invidious. As I discover in my own teaching, they pass on this view to their students, most of whom swallow it whole.

any underlying basis in reality for the category "woman." Second, he must view all existing individuals, including individual humans, as just clusters of properties. From this point of view, there isn't anyone deep down whom these properties describe. Claire is simply the sum of qualities like "sings," "has long hair," and "balances her own checkbook." Subtract all these qualities, and there is no Claire; the self who gives rise to these qualities, the subsistent being of whom these qualities are true, does not exist.

Against these two premises I maintain an older view. Individuals are more than just clusters of properties. Human individuals have personal identities; they belong to the natural kind "humanity"; the members of this natural kind are fulfilled in the activities of knowledge, work, and love; and the terms "man" and "woman" express a real division of it. On this account, the difference between men and women is not invented or constructed, but simply recognized. It lies in the nature of things. Yes, of course, cultures try to nuance the difference between men and women in different ways, but that does not make the difference itself just a product of culture. And yes, not all women are more nurturing than all men, not all men are more assertive than all women, and so on. Even so, the fact that *most* women are more nurturing than *most* men is much more than an accident. It arises from a genuine difference in the underlying reality, the difference between womanhood and manhood as such.

To say that there is a real difference between manhood and womanhood as such is not at all to say that this difference is simple or all-encompassing. Because men and women are not different species, but corresponding sexes of the same species, each is defined partly in terms of the other. When called upon to do so, they can even step outside their roles in some ways, they can become partners in some of the same tasks, and they can even tone down some of their differences. None of this means they are the same! For even when men and women do step out of their roles, they tend to have different motives for doing so. Even when they do share tasks, they tend to view them differently. And even when they do tone their differences down, the most common reason is that they have taught each other something. How is it that they have something to teach each other? Because they are not the same.

Another aspect of the paradox is that although men and women are capable of the same virtues, they tend to practice them in different modes. Both men and women can be wise, honest, temperate, and so on—and they should be. Yet each sex "inflects" the virtues differently.[11] Consider the task of raising good children in a world that threatens to corrupt and unravel them. Because a woman wants to nurture, she conquers her fear of the threat, developing the courage to be a mother. Because a man wants to do hard things, he meets the threat as a challenge, developing the tenderness to be a father. Though she learns courage, her courage is a good deal different from his; though he learns tenderness, his tenderness is a good deal different from hers.

Even more confusing is the fact that men and women are influenced by their masculine and feminine differences even when they defy these differences. From time to time newspapers report cases of young women who have concealed their pregnancies, given birth in secret, then done away with the babies. You will say, "That is not nurturing," and you will be right. Nothing less feminine, nothing more opposed to nurturance, could be imagined. Yet consider *in what ways* these young women do away with their babies. How often they place them in trash cans and dumpsters, still alive! You will say, "That is not nurturing either," and again you will be right. But why don't they just kill them? That is what a man usually does if he wants to do away with a child. Perhaps a young woman imagines her baby resting in the dumpster, quietly and painlessly slipping into a death that is something like sleep. Or perhaps she imagines a fairy tale ending in which someone finds her baby in the dumpster and brings him up as her own. No, the act is not nurturing, but the inclination to nurture hasn't precisely been destroyed; under the influence of other urgent motives, it has been perverted.

I daresay that such data are not captured by our psychological instruments. It is not enough to count things with a survey. One must see with the eyes of the heart.

Perhaps most confusing of all, the underlying realities of the sexes

---

11. I borrow the grammatical analogy from Darrell Dobbs, "Family Matters: Aristotle's Appreciation of Women and the Plural Structure of Society," *American Political Science Review* 90, no. 1 (1996): 74–89. He is not responsible for the use I make of it.

are never perceived *directly*. For that matter, neither is any underlying reality, but for some reason this case seems to puzzle us more. With my eye, I can gaze at any number of women, but all I see is particular women. Not with my eye, but only with my mind, can I see the universal essence, womanhood. Nevertheless, womanhood, like manhood, is real; it is known through its effects. The light of the universal shines through its particular instances, even if only through a fog. Even now, even today, confused and disoriented, the overwhelming majority of men do not think of themselves simply as Frank, Steven, or Abdul. They think of themselves as men and want to be recognized as masculine. Nor do the overwhelming majority of women think of themselves simply as Mary, Claire, or Felicity. They think of themselves as women and want to be recognized as feminine.

If we do need to appeal to underlying causal realities, why not just say "DNA"? Because even though our bodies are truly part of us, we are more than bodies. Our DNA is not simply what we are, any more than our eye colors, bone densities, or brain mosaics are what we are. Then is our DNA irrelevant to what we are? Not that, either. Just as a song, a love story, or even a flawed book like this speaks to our minds about what we are, perhaps the information encoded in our DNA speaks to our flesh about what we are. Flesh holds converse with flesh, mind holds converse with mind, and mind holds converse with body.

But this raises another question. I said that the light of essential manhood and womanhood shines out, but only through a fog. How can that fog be dispersed? How can the realities of manhood and womanhood be conveyed to minds like ours, which have such difficulty seeing them? How can they penetrate eyelids that are almost squinted shut?

Would it be possible to break through simply by defining the two sexes? Would that be too simple? One never knows until one tries, so let us try.

Then again, people have different ideas about definition. One supposed method of definition is to break things down into simpler parts and then put them back together. For example, I might say that a watch has a spring, a dial, two hands, and a variety of other pieces, connected in a certain way. Such information is nothing to sneeze at; it is useful for watchmakers. However, it is not what I am calling a definition, because it doesn't tell us what a watch actually is. Still less can such an approach tell us what a man or woman is. I might correctly point out that a woman normally has a head, limbs, and a variety of other organs, all connected in a certain way. But so much might also be true of a woman's corpse, and this doesn't tell us the difference between a woman and her corpse. Nor does that kind of information make sense of the fact that a woman who is missing a part, say one of her arms, is still entirely a woman. At most, such information describes a woman's body. But she is more than a body; the personal reality that is she has an immaterial aspect, as well. Very well, can we break down this immaterial aspect into parts, as we break down the body? I don't think so. Does it even make sense to speak of souls as having parts? Her brain has various parts, but that is not the same thing. Her immaterial soul has various immaterial powers, such as reason, memory, and imagination, but powers are not parts; they are not portions of her self, or divisions of her self, but capacities that are exercised by her one and undivided self. Besides, she shares all these powers with men. Don't they too have reason, memory, and imagination?

Is there then a better way to define things? There is. Consider the watch again. Instead of breaking it down and putting it back together, we can say that it is a machine for telling time. This sort of definition explains what watches are by relating them to other kinds of things. It identifies the broad category to which they belong, machines, along with the essential characteristic that distinguishes them from other machines, the fact that they are used for telling time.

Can we define womanhood in that way? We can. We can say that a woman is a human being of that sex whose members are potentially mothers. The broad category here is human beings; an essential characteristic that distinguishes some human beings from others is the potentiality for motherhood. So let us begin here.

I say, "begin here," rather than "end here," in part because the idea of "potentiality for motherhood" needs explanation. One reason is that potentiality is often confused with physical possibility. Consider a woman who is infertile. Perhaps, by mischance, an infection has scarred her fallopian tubes. Although it is physically impossible for her to be a mother, we should not say that she lacks the potentiality for motherhood. She has that potentiality as a woman, even though her potentiality cannot be physically realized because of the scarring. It is just because she is a real woman, just because she is naturally endowed with the potentiality for motherhood, that the block to the physical realization of the potentiality is such a loss to her, such an occasion for sorrow.

Another reason the expression "potentiality for motherhood" requires explanation is that although bearing children is the most characteristic expression of motherhood, it is far from its only expression. A woman might even physically bear a child yet fail in the greater perspective of motherhood, because after she carries the child in her womb and brings him into the world, she neglects him; she fails to nurture him with that mother's love that only she can give because it is different from a father's love. When I speak of such failure, by the way, I am not speaking of giving up a child for adoption. In some cases such an act may be profoundly maternal, for if a mother is unable to raise her child, then it is an act of sacrificial love to give her child up to a woman who can. My point is that potentiality for motherhood includes more than potentiality to give birth. That is why the woman who accepts the child is in that respect a true mother, too.

We can carry this line of reasoning still further. A potentiality is something like a calling. It wants, so to speak, to develop; it demands, so to speak, a response. Of course, this is figurative language because a potentiality has no will of its own. Yet it really is directed to fruition. The potentiality for motherhood is like an arrow, cocked in the string and aimed at the target, even if it never takes flight. It intimates an inbuilt meaning and expresses an inbuilt purpose that cannot help but influence the mind and will of every person imbued with them. A woman may be unaware of this secret influence, and she may even fight against it. But she cannot destroy it. This is why Alice von Hildebrand has remarked that even though not every woman is called to marry and bear physical children, "every woman, whether married or unmarried, is called upon to be a biological, psychological or spiritual mother." A woman knows intuitively, von Hildebrand insists, the profound importance of caring for others, suffering with and for them, "for maternity implies suffering."[12] Although this knowledge is intuitive, in a well-functioning society it is deepened and made explicit by the traditions that mothers pass on to their daughters, generation by generation.

Obviously, I cannot speak from inside experience of womanhood, because I am a man. Yet even a man can see that it is a very different thing to be a woman than to be a man. This is true at every stage of life, but it is especially true in the childbearing stage. What women say about themselves confirms my judgment. A man may deeply love his child, but he has not carried the child in his body for nine months before his birth or nourished the child with milk from his breasts. These experiences connect the mother with her child in an intimate, physical bond that we men can easily recognize, but that we cannot experience. In subtle ways they condition her emotional responses not only toward the child, but also toward herself and even toward everyone else.

They also make sense of certain other differences between men and women, differences for which women are sometimes wrongly criticized. For example, are women in general more conscious of their bodies than men are? Of course, they are. Are they more protective of themselves physically than men are? Yes, certainly. But considering their potentiality for motherhood, this heightened physical awareness is entirely appropriate. It may present temptations to vanity, yes, but in itself it is not vain, and to cowardice, yes, but it is not cowardly. Women need to be like this. There would be something wrong if they were not like this. Men, by being men, are not more virtuous; their most characteristic temptations are merely somewhat different from a woman's, and their virtues have different inflections.

The other sexual differences make sense in this light, too. As Edith Stein reminds us,[13] men are more prone to abstraction and women more prone to focus on the concrete. Men don't mind what is imper-

---

12. Interview with Alice von Hildebrand, Zenit News Service, November 23, 2003, http:www.zenit.org/article-8793?1=English.

13. Edith Stein, *Essays on Woman*, 2nd ed., trans. Freda Mary Oben, vol. 2 of *Collected Works of Edith Stein*, ed. Lucy Gelber and Romaeus Leuven (Washington, D.C.: ICS, 1996).

sonal; women are more attuned to the nuances of relationships and to what is going on in other people. A man tends to be a specialist and a single-tasker; he develops certain qualities to an unusually high pitch, using them to do things in the world. A woman tends to be a generalist and multitasker; she inclines to a more rounded development of her abilities, using them to nurture the life around her. The woman's potentiality for motherhood ties all her qualities together and makes sense of her contrast with men. Consider just that multitasking capacity. In view of what it takes to run a home, doesn't it make sense for her to have it? A woman must be a center of peace for her family, even though a hundred things are happening at once.

Although men gravitate to careers and women to motherhood, not all women will pursue an exclusively domestic life. Even so, the potentiality for motherhood explains why women who do pursue a career, and who have free choice of career, tend to choose careers that allow them to give the first place to caring for their children. It also explains why they tend to choose careers that give greater scope to maternal qualities. Let us not forget that well-balanced women who do choose traditionally masculine careers also tend to perform them in ways that give scope to maternal qualities. A male lawyer tends to focus on the properties of the task itself. This is worthy, but it is all too easy for him to lose sight of the humanity of his clients. Can he learn to remind himself of their humanity? Of course, he can, but he is more likely to need the reminder in the first place. A female lawyer may find the abstract quality of the law, which is necessary, somewhat alienating. On the other hand, she is much less likely to forget that she is dealing with human beings.

A quick caveat before going on: The things I have just written are true only when women are allowed to be themselves. Under the spell of identicalism, they may not be allowed to be themselves. If they are punished for their feminine qualities, or if they self-censor them to beat men at their own game, they may think they don't want to be themselves. Feminism has brought about a terrible fear and hatred of everything womanly.

These few paragraphs about womanhood may have given the impression that men are to be defined negatively. Someone reading them might suppose that if a woman is a human being of that sex whose members have the potentiality for motherhood, then a man is simply a human being of the sex whose members *lack* the potentiality for motherhood—making the man a sort of incomplete woman. On the contrary! A man, like a woman, is correctly defined only when he is positively defined. He is a human being of the sex whose members have a *different* potentiality than women do: the potentiality for fatherhood. Just as motherhood is broader than biological motherhood, so fatherhood is broader than biological fatherhood. Just as not all women are called to marry and bear children, so not all men are called to marry and sire children. Yet just as all women are called to motherhood in a larger sense, so we may say that all men are called to fatherhood in a larger sense. And just as extended motherhood is well understood only when motherhood as such is well honored, so extended fatherhood is well understood only when fatherhood as such is well honored.

I say this in earnest, yet it is much more difficult to speak about fatherhood than motherhood. Perhaps because the father's connection with his children is not mediated by his body in the way that the mother's is—or perhaps because paternal absenteeism and other forms of masculine failure are so conspicuous in our day—most of us have a dimmer idea of fatherhood than motherhood. Open mockery of fathers has become a fixture of popular culture.

The difference between fatherhood and motherhood, hence between manhood and womanhood, involves a difference in the male and female modes of love for their children, but there is much more to it than that. The difference is both greater and deeper. Manhood in general is outward-directed and womanhood inward-directed. This is no cliché; the distinction is quite subtle. Outward-directedness, for example, is not the same as *other*-directedness, for many men prefer dealing with things. Inward-directedness is not same as *self*-directedness, for the genius of women includes caring for the local circle. If the contrast between outward- and inward-directedness sounds like a dig at male vanity or sexual promiscuity, or for that matter at female narcissism or emotional dependency, it isn't that, either. Characteristics of those sorts are not the essence of the sexual difference; they are merely vices that result from the indulgence of temptations to which the two sexes are unequally susceptible. In speaking of outward- and inward-directedness, my intention is not to call attention to the corruptions, but to the good things that are sometimes corrupted. It is a good thing that an unmarried man pursues the beloved, whereas an unmarried woman makes herself attractive to pursuit; that a husband protects the home, whereas a wife establishes it on the hearth; that a father represents the family and oversees it, whereas a mother conducts the family and manages it.

Although the directive geniuses of the father and the mother are not the same, both truly rule the home. We may compare the father with a king reigning over a commonwealth, the mother with a queen. These potent archetypes express nobility, glory, and self-command. Men joke about their wives telling them what to do. The joke would have no point unless two things were true: On one hand, they would not want their wives to be kings; on the other hand, they know they are really queens. It would not be absurd to suggest yet another analogy. The father and mother share and divide the different aspects of sovereignty between themselves in much the same way that the directive functions are divided in corporations. Does this seem to be a new idea, an accommodation to current fashion? Far from it. In a first-century letter from one of our oldest wisdom writers, St. Paul, to a young man he is grooming for leadership, we find him using a curious pair of words—a verb, *proistemi*, and a noun, *oikodespotes*—one of them for what a husband characteristically *does*, the other what a wife characteristically *is*. Both words indicate authority. The former has a range of meanings that include standing before, presiding, superintending, protecting, maintaining, helping, succoring, and acting in the capacity of a patron—very much like a chairman of the board. But the latter means "ruler of the house"—very much like the chief executive officer. So the idea is really very ancient.[14]

---

14. The verb is applied to the husband in 1 Tm 3:4, 3:5, 3:12; the noun is applied to the wife in 1 Tm 5:14. Literally, *oikodespotes* means "house despot," which is even stronger than the rendering I have offered, "ruler of the house." Other glimpses of St. Paul's view of the thoroughly mutual subordination of man and woman, husband and wife—equal in dignity, yet with different places in the dance—are found in 1 Cor 11:11–12 and Eph 5:21–32.

When all goes well, fathers and mothers also exemplify and specialize in different aspects of wisdom. A wise father teaches his wife and family that to love you must be strong; a wise mother teaches her husband and family that to be strong you must love. She knows that even boldness needs humility; he knows that even humility needs to be bold. He is an animate symbol to his children of that justice that is tempered by mercy, she a living emblem of that mercy that is tempered by justice. Each of them refracts a different hue from the glowing light of royalty. A wise father knows when to say, "Ask your mother," a wise mother when to say, "Ask your father." When they do this, they are not passing the buck, but sharing sovereignty.

Today it is almost embarrassing to read prose like the patch I have just written. Comparisons of fathers and mothers with kings and queens seem naïve, sentimental, and exaggerated. They make us squirm. There are strong reasons for this reaction, but they are bad ones. How many parents have lost their regal dignity, disbelieve in their authority, and confuse the proper humility of their office with being self-mocking and ironic? We have turned husbands and wives into androgynous "spouses," fathers and mothers into interchangeable "parent figures." We approach having a child like acquiring a pool table or widescreen TV. Would it be fun? Would it be tedious? Would it be worth the expense? Fathers and mothers have need of recovering their sense of regal calling, taking up their ball and scepter, and ruling their dominions with love for their precious subjects. It is not for nothing that the king of a commonwealth is called "Sire"; humanly speaking, of the callings of fatherhood and kingship, the deeper and more primordial is fatherhood.

May it be needless to say that mothers and fathers must also recover the conviction of their need for each other. This they must do not only for their own sakes, but for their young. Every child needs both a mother's and a father's love. It is not enough to provide an intermediate love that is half motherly and half fatherly or an inconsistent love that is motherly at some times, fatherly at others. Nor is it enough to give one kind of love for real, while giving only a pretense or simulacrum of the other kind. Even though the two loves resemble each other, they are distinct, and neither can be imitated by anything else. It may be true heroism when through no fault of one's own, a father or a mother raises a child all alone; yet it is better not to be alone. No woman can fully take the place of a father, nor can any man substitute for a mother.[15]

Though I have been speaking of fatherhood and motherhood in relation to the family, these matters actually reach much further. For men, growing up is like joining a brotherhood. Our grasp on this fact is attenuated by the fact that we have lost our rites and customs of apprenticeship and coming of age. Men naturally desire to be something like knights, who not only do hard things, but in firm and fatherly manner train squires who attend them so that these young men can learn to do hard things, too. As I was in earnest before about the calling of all men to extended fatherhood, so I am in earnest now about the chivalric element in this calling. A man will more readily aspire to manhood if he can taste it; his life must have the flavor of valor. This is true of how he carries himself not only toward other men, but toward women. The fashion of the day is to think of medieval knights not as valiant but as cruel. Many were, yet even in that day, knighthood was more than a veneer for oppression. It was a great and noble ideal that did much to civilize a society still governed by a warrior caste and too often running with blood. Like the members of our own ruling class, different as it is, the members of that caste sometimes fought for the wrong things, fought in the wrong ways, or committed atrocities. All such perversions should be condemned. Yet let us not abuse the members of that caste just because they liked to fight. Are there not plenty of things to fight for in this world, and plenty of evils to oppose?

After all, most men do not *simply* like to fight; they are too lazy for that. They like to fight when there is something worth fighting for. True, they sometimes make up things worth fighting for just to be able to fight for them, and one of the tasks of becoming a man is learning to resist the temptation. Yet there are plenty of noble things to fight for without making them up. One must war against temptation, capture the citadel of virtue, contend for just laws, defend and protect sound traditions, attack lies and fallacies with the weapons of frankness and

---

15. See, for example, David Popenoe, *Life without Father* (Cambridge, Mass.: Harvard University Press, 1996).

reason, and even, yes, make gentle war for courtesy. By the way, if it is right at times to fight, then it is also right to enjoy fighting, even though it is also right to grieve the evils incidental to the struggle and to try to minimize them.

A certain militancy and a certain vigilance are essential parts of manhood, and a man's great project is not to do away with his impulse to fight, but to learn to fight nobly and generously—to refine the raw ore, burn away its dross, and make it into purified steel.

This is an ideal to which any man may aspire. It is wholly independent of what he does for a living, of how much education he has had, or of whether he is muscular or athletic. Medieval knights engaged their enemies physically, and there is always some need for that; in our time we have armies and police. Yet there are many ways to fight besides the physical. One may fight through a word in season, a clap on the shoulder, a quiet admonishment or commendation. One may wage war by bearing witness, by lifting the fallen, by refusing to countenance evil. One may do battle by admonishing idlers, by encouraging the fainthearted, by helping the weak.

Unlike the achievement of biological maturity, the achievement of manhood is hard work, labor that requires a firm hand with the desires and devices of the heart. Alas that the carving and shaping of these impulses are so unfashionable. We have not yet got over teachers like Freud, who called such noble woodcraft "repression," considering it, though necessary, unnatural. His doctrine was deluded and false, because the nature of a thing is set not by its beginning but its end; the fact that our impulses resist being carved and shaped takes away nothing from the fact that they need all that carving and shaping to realize their inbuilt purposes. The truth is that *not* to endure being carved and shaped well is unnatural and a source of numberless miseries. The best instance of an oak is not a gaudily decorated acorn, but a tree; in the same way, the best instance of a human male is not a glorified, walking packet of urges, but a man who, for the sake of the highest and greatest goods, commands himself, strengthens his brothers, and defends his sisters, regarding even the meanest of women as a lady.

Once upon a time the differences between men and women were

not thought so strange. We have a long quest and a difficult journey before we can speak of them again with ease and gaiety. There are so many sweet and lovely things that our ears can no longer hear without odium, so many blameless things that can hardly be discussed without scandal. Just imagine the din that would erupt if I were to praise and extol that great activity that comes so much more readily to the woman and is slandered under the false name of passivity: *Fiat mihi secundum verbum tuum!* And if I were to compound the offense by pointing out that every last one of us, both man and woman, is feminine with respect to—but I have promised not to speak of that yet, and I will keep my vow.

When we do attempt the journey back to the commonwealth of sense, we will meet trolls and enchanters on the way. They will obstruct passage, demand tribute, and try to lure us into byways and bogs. But why should that discourage us? We are already begrimed and bewitched. The first thing to do is open our eyes, grasp hold of the nearest branches, and pull ourselves out of the ooze. Odd knights we! Having made ourselves muddy and ridiculous, we may as well journey with a smile.

CHAPTER 2

Gender Reality vs. Gender Ideology

Sr. Prudence Allen, RSM

St. Thomas Aquinas, Doctor of Humanity, Pray for us
Holy Mary of Guadalupe, Intercede for us

This chapter is divided into three main sections: first, a description of the origins of sex ideology and gender ideology; second, a mapping of the rapid spread, or "going viral," of gender ideology; and third, arguments drawing upon the work of Catholic philosophers for a vigorous defense of gender reality.[1] Much of the material in the first two sections of this essay is disturbing to read; it is even more distressing to realize how many innocent persons have been and are being harmed through a combination of intentionally deceptive research methods and reporting of results. Thus, it is important that it be brought into the light so that remedies and counterarguments can be developed that are based on the truth about the real identities of women and of men.

Thomas Aquinas, in his *Commentary on the Letters of Saint Paul to the Corinthians*, repeats chapter 2, verse 14: "But thanks be to God, who in Christ always leads us in triumph, and through us spreads the

---

1. Versions of this lecture were given at the American Catholic Philosophical Association Conference in Marina del Rey, California (November 3, 2012), the Gender Colloquium, University of Notre Dame Australia (July 2, 2013), and as Plenary Address for Conference on Thomas Aquinas: Teacher of Humanity, Pontifical Academy of St. Thomas Aquinas, Center for Thomistic Studies, and John Paul II Forum, Houston, Texas. A fuller development is in Sr. Prudence Allen, RSM, *The Concept of Woman: Search for Communion of Persons*, vol. 3, 1500–2010 (Grand Rapids, Mich.: Eerdmans, 2016).

fragrance of the knowledge of him everywhere."[2] Thomas then describes how to spread the fragrance of the knowledge of Christ everywhere:

> Here it should be noted that preachers of truth should do two things: namely to exhort in sacred doctrine and to refute those who contradict it. This they do in two ways: by debating with heretics and by practicing patience toward persecutors.[3]

Debating well demands knowledge of the sources and arguments of one's opponents. It also helps us to practice patience toward those with whom we strongly disagree. I hope that this presentation will help us toward this goal.

What Is the Conflict between Gender Reality and Gender Ideology?

The present conflict between what I call "gender reality" and "gender ideology" is the result of two different views of the human person. Gender reality holds that human beings are "always or for the most part" women or men, female or male. Gender ideology holds that human beings fall along a continuum of three, five, or even fifteen different loose groupings of genders. Gender reality is grounded philosophically in a descriptive metaphysics (rooted in Aristotelian and Thomistic thinking), and gender ideology is philosophically grounded in a revisionary metaphysics (rooted in neo-Platonic or Cartesian thinking).[4] Finally, gender reality depends upon a *hylomorphic* (soul/body composite unity) understanding of a human person, woman or man; gender ideology leads to a deconstructionist approach to the human person as a loose collection of qualities, attributes, or parts.

---

2. Thomas Aquinas, *Commentary on the Letters of Saint Paul to the Corinthians*, ed. J. Mortensen and E. Alarcón, trans. F. R. Larcher, OP, et al. (Lander, Wyo.: Aquinas Institute for the Study of Sacred Doctrine, 2012), 427.

3. Aquinas, *Commentary*, 428.

4. This distinction between descriptive and revisionary metaphysics comes from Peter F. Strawson, *Individuals* (London: Metheun, 1961), 9.

How Did Gender Ideologies Begin?

Neo-Platonic Reification of Masculinity and Femininity

In distinguishing between the concept of gender and the word "gender," it is helpful to notice that neo-Platonism has historically been associated with making masculinity and femininity into cosmic reified entities like forms that tend to reduce the significance of the individual man or woman. For example, the neo-Platonist Nicholas of Cusa (1401–64) introduced a theory in which the concept of gender as cosmic masculinity and femininity operated within a "coincidence of opposites" with reified independence from bodily distinctions of male and female.[5] In 1620 Reform England, also influenced by neo-Platonism, a satirical mismatching article and noun, entitled *Hic Mulier*, was answered by another satire reversing this play on words and engendered characteristics, *Haec Vir*.[6] In this text, the concept and word "gender" merged together when the satire focused on culturally gendered masculine clothing and characteristics ascribed to a woman and culturally gendered feminine clothes and characteristics ascribed to a man: "For since the days of Adam women were never so masculine; masculine in their *genders* and whole *generations*, from the mother, to the youngest daughter; masculine in number, from one to multitudes; masculine in case, even from the head to the foot; masculine in mood, from both speech, to impudent action; and masculine in tense: for (without redress) they were, are, and will be still most masculine, most mankind, and most monstrous."[7]

Three hundred years later, the neo-Platonic text *The Cosmographia* of Bernardus Silvestris is commonly thought to have been the source for C. S. Lewis's *Perelandra* and other texts in his *Space Trilogy*. In *Perelandra*, the narrator (who is thought to be Lewis himself) separates gender as a higher cosmic masculine and cosmic feminine reality from

---

5. See "Nicholas of Cusa," in Allen, *Concept of Woman: The Early Humanist Reformation*, vol. 2, *1250–1500* (Grand Rapids, Mich., and Cambridge: Eerdmans, 2007), 761–88.

6. "Hic Mulier," A3, in *Half Humankind: Contexts and Texts of the Controversy about Women in England, 1540–1640*, ed. Katherine Usher Henderson and Barbara F. McManus (Urbana and Chicago: University of Illinois Press, 1985), 265.

7. "Hic Mulier," 265.

sex. In his words, "*Gender* is a reality, and a more fundamental reality than sex. Sex is, in fact, merely the adaptation to organic life of a fundamental polarity which divides all created beings. *Female sex is simply one of the things that have feminine gender*; ... The male and female of organic creatures are rather faint and blurred reflections of masculine and feminine."[8]

These three examples of neo-Platonic approaches to reified masculinity and femininity and cosmic gender reveal a certain tendency to devalue the concrete individual human being, man or woman, in comparison with some abstract "real" form. This is not to suggest that C. S. Lewis especially ignores concrete women and men in his other works or to argue that he or Nicholas Cusa would have agreed with the radical gender ideology that has become so evident in the twentieth and twenty-first centuries. However, a neo-Platonic approach to the human person, especially as it influenced the Reform traditions, which accepted and built on Descartes's metaphysical dualism, ended up rejecting the Aristotelian/Thomistic concrete *hylomorphism*, or foundational soul/body composite identity, of an individual woman or man. And it is this rejection that has led to the radical gender ideology of the present time.

Sex Ideology: Proactive Reduction of
Sex Identity to Sex Acts

Dr. Alfred Kinsey (1894–1956), an entomologist, earned his Sc.D. from Harvard University in 1919 studying gall wasps. His original orientation toward animals, and particularly insects, framed his attitude toward human beings as simply another kind of animal.[9] Raised in a Methodist Reform family, Kinsey totally rejected God and the view that the human

---

8. C. S. Lewis, *Perelandra: A Novel* (New York: Macmillan, 1944), 214.

9. See Lionel Trilling, "The Kinsey Report," in *An Analysis of the Kinsey Reports on Sexual Behavior in the Human Male and Female*, ed. Donald Porter Geddes (New York: Mentor, 1954), 213–29. Trilling observes that while comparisons with animals are explicitly made throughout his two volumes on males and females, "Professor Kinsey is a zoologist and he properly keeps us always in mind of our animal kinship, even though he draws some very illogical conclusions from it"; 218.

soul was both form and spirit.¹⁰ Subsequently, when he became part of an interdisciplinary course on sexuality and marriage at Indiana University, he studied sexual activity as a human animal "outlet," to use the word that characterized all his research.¹¹

Kinsey decided to *quantify* all aspects of a man's, woman's, and child's sexual "outlets" by age, the size of organ, and frequency of "outlets" without being concerned whether the so-called "outlet" occurred with the person alone, with members of the same or opposite sex, with animals, or with children. He included in his classification systems of men any and all who would agree to give their sexual history in a detailed interview. The groups included serial rapists in prison, pedophiles, single men, married men, male prostitutes, and so on. Kinsey included in his classification systems of married women and women in common law relations, as well as female prostitutes living with their handlers.¹² Kinsey's data samples were contaminated, and his work was actually more "pseudo-science" than the hard science he claimed.

When the volume on *Sexual Behavior in the Human Male* was published in 1948, with its initial claim of being based on interviews with "12,000" males, and the volume on *Sexual Behavior in the Human Female* in 1953, with its claim of being based on interviews with "nearly 8,000 females," it had the force in the popular culture of authority of numbers. Even though Kinsey revised his numbers down by claim-

---

10. Wardell B. Pomeroy reports the following incident with Kinsey's four- to five-year-old son Bruce when he said, "'Look at the pretty flower, Daddy, God made it.' 'Now Bruce,' Kinsey said gently, 'where did that flower really come from?' From a seed,' Bruce admitted. He had learned his father's lessons well"; Pomeroy, *Dr. Kinsey and the Institute for Sex Research* (New York: Harper and Row, 1972), 29.

11. Consider just the titles of his chapters in Alfred C. Kinsey, Wardell B. Pomeroy, and Clyde E. Martin, *Sexual Behavior in the Human Male* (Philadelphia and London: W. B. Saunders, 1948), part 2, "Factors Affecting Sexual Outlet": chapter 6, "Sexual Outlet," chapter 7, "Age and Sexual Outlet," chapter 8, "Marital Status and Sexual Outlet," chapter 9, "Age of Adolescence and Sexual Outlet," chapter 10, "Social Level and Sexual Outlet," chapter 12, "Rural-Urban Background and Sexual Outlet," and chapter 13, "Religious Background and Sexual Outlet"; and part 3, "Sources of Sexual Outlet," xii–xv.

12. See Kinsey, Pomeroy, Martin, and Paul H. Gebhard, *Sexual Behavior in the Human Female* (Philadelphia: W. B. Saunders, 1953); Gebhard and Alan B. Johnson, *The Kinsey Data: Marginal Tabulations of the 1938–1963 Interviews Conducted by the Institute for Sex Research* (Philadelphia: W. B. Saunders, 1979); and John Money, "Hermaphroditism," Ph.D. diss. (Harvard University, 1952).

ing that he "scientifically conducted" interviews with 5,300 men and 5,940 women, it was widely received in the broader culture as describing the truth about human sexuality separated from any context of love, marriage, or human good. The first volume became a bestseller, and it promoted the theory that the greater the quantity of so-called sexual outlets the healthier the man or woman. According to Pomeroy, "By the time Kinsey died there had been eleven printings of the Male volume..., and the book was translated into French, Spanish, Swedish, Japanese, Italian, Dutch and German."[13] Kinsey's report of the "usual numbers" of sexual outlets in various population groups had a proactive influence on a hyper-eroticism not only in the United States, but throughout the world. It redefined what had been considered "normal" sexual activity and encouraged counselors, psychologists, and others to push his new version of normal. Kinsey's single-minded promotion of amounts of sexual activities without regard to human relations eventually took on the qualities of a cultural sex ideology.

The French philosopher *Michel Foucault* (1926–84) thought that sexuality ought to displace sex identity in any analysis of this aspect of human life. In *The History of Sexuality* he claimed that "sex ... [is] an imaginary point determined by the deployment of sexuality."[14] Foucault argued further that sex identity was completely a social construct and that the "anchorage points" of "the body, anatomy, the biological, and the functional" should be eliminated in favor of "sexuality."[15] Here we see the elimination of the human being per se and its replacement by an experience.

In Foucault's deconstructionist approach, the metaphysical foundation of the human being as composite substance or *hylomorphic* union of soul/body is jettisoned for floating "I think" or "I feel" sexual pleasures. In the spring of 1975 Foucault plunged passionately into

---

13. Pomeroy, *Kinsey and the Institute*, 274. An immediate critique from the perspective of broader human values and sexual activity with respect to the Kinsey reports can be found in Donald Porter Geddes, ed., *An Analysis of the Kinsey Reports on Sexual Behavior in the Human Male and Female* (New York: Mentor, 1954).

14. Michel Foucault, *The History of Sexuality*, vol. 1, *An Introduction* (New York: Vintage, 1980), 152.

15. Foucault, *History of Sexuality*, 156.

San Francisco's gay community, attracted especially by the consensual sadomasochistic eroticism that flourished in a number of bathhouses in the Bay City at that time. In *History of Sexuality*, he argued that sex as maleness and femaleness is an illusion, while at the same time he chose to seek purpose or intelligibility of his own identity in its multiple sexual acts.

Foucault's rejection of sex identity had been preceded by his prediction in *The Order of Things* (1966) of the disappearance of man, the human being from Western culture. Stating that "man is a recent invention" and "one perhaps nearing its end," Foucault speculated that if structures of language crumbled, "one can certainly wager that man would be erased, like a face drawn in sand at the edge of the sea."[16] Foucault's deconstructive approach to the human being and his reduction of one's sex identity to maximization of sexual pleasures gained many adherents among intellectuals throughout the world. It also began to become a cultural sex ideology.

Gender Ideology: Proactive Fragmentation of Gender Identity

Margaret Mead (1901–78) earned her Ph.D. in anthropology from Columbia University, New York, in 1929. She soon revolutionized methodologies that anthropologists used to study primitive cultures. Mead described her early goal: "So, in 1931, my problem, which I had declared to be central to the research I was undertaking, was to study the different ways in which cultures patterned the expected behavior of males and females."[17] Her articulation clearly emphasized how a man's or woman's identity resulted from what other persons expected of sexually differentiated behaviors. Mead concluded later that her research project to identify "how culturally attributed contrasts in masculine and feminine behavior differentiated the character structure of men and women,

---

16. Foucault, *The Order of Things: An Archaeology of the Human Sciences*, ed. R. D. Laing (New York: Vintage, 1970), 386–87.

17. Margaret Mead, *Blackberry Winter: My Earlier Years* (New York: Touchstone, 1972), 196.

seemed to have yielded very little."[18] She reoriented the field of anthropology away from any consideration of essential differences between the sexes and toward a relativism of "sex styles."

During her research in south Asian primitive cultures Mead also rejected her familial Episcopal religion for an attitude of cultural relativism. By 1949, in *Male and Female*, she claimed that sex-roles and sex-styles were simply culturally learned. In one example she argued, "Characteristic after characteristic in which the differences within a sex are so great that there is enormous overlapping [between males and females] are artificially assigned as masculine or feminine."[19] Mead's conclusion about the relativism of sex roles and sex identities flowed over into a reflection on the word "gender" itself. She introduced the *word* "gender" in a discussion about polygamy when she posited the difficulty a person has to imagine contrasts in other societies. In her words, "We know by sad experience how difficult it is for those who have been reared within one civilization ever to get outside its categories, to imagine, for instance, what a language could be like that had *thirteen genders*. Oh, yes, one says masculine, feminine, and neuter—and what in the world are the other ten?"[20] In her framing of this hypothetical question, Margaret Mead set the world stage, perhaps unknowingly, for a mutation of gender ideology to begin. Toward the end of her life, at a conference they both attended, Dr. John Money reported that Margaret Mead encouraged him to continue his work breaking sexual taboos related to incest and adult-child activities by telling him that "this is something he has to do."[21]

*

Dr. John Money (1921–2006), as a young man in New Zealand, likely knew of Mead's anthropological research in his area of the world. Traveling to the United States for graduate studies, he completed a doctorate in psychology in 1952 at Harvard University on the study of

---

18. Mead, *Blackberry Winter*, 200.

19. Mead, *Male and Female: A Study of the Sexes in a Changing World* (New York: William Morrow, 1949), 373.

20. Mead, *Male and Female*, 13. Emphasis mine.

21. John Money, *Love and Love Sickness: The Science of Sex, Gender Difference and Pair-Bonding* (Baltimore: Johns Hopkins University Press, 1980), introduction.

hermaphrodites. Shortly after its completion, Dr. Money was hired at Johns Hopkins University Medical School to join a medical team in a newly formed gender clinic. In 1955, Money published an essay arguing directly from the study of 131 intersexed individuals to a conclusion about normal males and females—namely, that gender identity is environmentally caused during the first two years of life.[22] Money later called this time-frame of approximately two years from birth to the settling of one's gender identity a *gender gate* or *gender window*.

Twenty years later, in 1975, Dr. Money continued to argue from the exception of hermaphrodites to the rule of all infants: "Convincing evidence that the gender identity gate was wide open when you were born and stayed open for some time thereafter can be found in matched pairs of hermaphrodites.... But is the gate also open for those who were sexually normal at birth? Transsexuals give the answer—yes."[23] Dr. Money's gender-gate theory claimed that all children have a period of approximately two years from birth within which they could develop as either a male or a female. Money's fixed attitude toward the fluidity of all infant-children gender identity soon became a cultural gender ideology.

What Are the Characteristics of Sex and Gender Ideologies?

In order to highlight specific characteristics of sex and gender ideologies, this presentation will focus primarily on the work of Kinsey and Money with occasional references to similarities in Foucault and Mead. It will also go back and forth between Kinsey and Money in further elaboration of common elements in their arguments, research practices, and consequences. There is no doubt that Money was well aware of Kinsey's research and that Mead personally encouraged Money's con-

---

22. Money, "Hermaphroditism: An Inquiry into the Nature of a Human Paradox," Ph.D. diss., in John Colapinto, *As Nature Made Him: The Boy Who Was Raised as a Girl* (New York: Harper Perennial, 2000), 33–34.

23. John Money and Patricia Tucker, *Sexual Signatures: On Being a Man or a Woman* (Boston and Toronto: Little, Brown, 1975), 90–91.

tinued research. It is also likely that Foucault was well aware of Money's research on hermaphrodites. Gender ideology developed mostly within the social sciences and pseudo-science under the radar of traditional philosophy and theology. Only recently have its corrupt roots and serious consequences come under rigorous philosophical and theological critique. In the next section, six erroneous aspects of sex and gender ideologies are identified.

Faulty Arguments

Arguing from the Exception to the Rule
The first error of reasoning that we encounter in John Money's method is to argue from the exception of hermaphrodites to the rule that gender development is fluid and able to be changed in all children for a period of two years. Money argues from the fact that some children born with ambiguous sex identity could, with medical intervention, become either male or female to the conclusion that *all children with normal sex identity from birth could become either male or female in gender*.

Michel Foucault made a similar error of reason when he analyzed the personal diary of Alexina-Herculine Barbin (1978). Identified as female at birth in 1838, Barbin developed male anatomy and physiology after puberty. Changing her civil status to male led to depression and suicide in 1868. Arguing from this exceptional case to a rule, Michel Foucault asks in the first paragraph of his text, "Do we *truly* need a *true* sex? With a persistence that borders on stubbornness, modern Western societies have answered in the affirmative."[24] Foucault instead answered negatively. His error was to reason from the exception of hermaphrodites to the rule that *no* children should be labeled male or female.

---

24. Michel Foucault, *Herculine Barbin: Being the Recently Discovered Memoirs of a Nineteenth-Century French Hermaphrodite*, trans. Richard McDougall (Brighton, UK: Harvester, 1980), vii.

Gender Reality vs. Gender Ideology | 45

Arguing from Multiple Parts (Sexes and Genders)
to the Whole

As early as 1955 John Money described "the sexuality of the individual [as] a cumulative composite of [six] separate sexes."[25] The six separate sexes were called: chromosomal sex, gonadal sex, physiological sex, morphological sex, behavioral sex, and psychological sex (gender-role/identity).[26] In 1972, Money and Anke Ehrhardt continued this pattern by sequential categories in their book: "Terminology and Nature of Hermaphroditism"; "Chromosomal and Gonadal Sex"; "Gonadal, Hormonal, and Morphologic Sex"; "Fetal Hormonal Sex, the Nervous System, and Behavior"; "External Morphologic Sex and Assigned Sex"; "Differentiation of Gender Identity"; and "Gender Identity and Pubertal Hormones."[27] By 1975 Money introduced the concept of "forks" in the road, which were detours "selected" prior to birth, in the space and time between some of the earlier named sexes: chromosomal sex, gonadal sex, and external genitals, before the letter "m" or "f" is put on his or her birth certificate.[28]

The question that a philosopher must ask is, "What guides this sequential and multivariate process?" In other words, how can an unborn human being, as a collection of different sexes, take a detour or fork when there is no organizing principle within the being? Money has no principle comparable to a substantial form that actualizes potentialities within the developing fetus.

---

25. John Money, "Hermaphroditism, Gender and Precocity in Hyperandrenocorticism: Psychological Findings," *Bulletin of Johns Hopkins Hospital* 96, no. 6 (2005): 253–64. As summarized by David Crews, "Functional Associations in Behavioral Endocrinology," in *Masculinity/Femininity: Basic Perspectives*, ed. June M. Reinisch, Leonard A. Rosenblum, and Stephanie A. Sanders, Kinsey Institute Series (Oxford: Oxford University Press, 1987), 91.

26. Crews, "Functional Associations," table 6-2, p. 91.

27. Money and Anke A. Ehrhardt, *Man and Woman, Boy and Girl: Gender Identity from Conception to Maturity* (Northvale, N.J.: Jason Aronson, 1996), in chapter 1, 6–25. In subsequent chapters further categories included internal genital, external genital, brain dimorphism, and gender dimorphic traditions: 41, 44, 95, 248–49, and 130ff.

28. See Money and Tucker, *Sexual Signatures*, 48–49.

Arguing from Artificial Division Gender-Identity/Role
(G-I/R) to Fractured Identity

In 1972 Dr. Money artificially separated "gender identity" as *private to an individual* from "gender role" as *public expression to others*.²⁹ Using a forward slash (/) to keep this artificial distinction clear, he introduced the anagram G-I/R to represent "gender identity/role."³⁰ In this context he used "masculinity" and "femininity" to characterize *proportions* within a person who is more or less masculine or feminine in "vocational and domestic role" and "role as an erotic partner."³¹ By 1980, in *Love and Love Sickness*, in a chapter entitled, "Gender Identity/Role (G-I/R)," Money described the mind in Cartesian terms: "Herein lies the issue of solipsism. Oneself, alone, is privy to what goes on in one's own mind. In the absence of its being overtly transmitted to other people behaviorally, that is to say, either in words or in body language, the content of one's mind remains forever covert and unknown to others." Frank A. Beach raised an important question about Money's division between "the introspective component *gender identity*" and his "defined *gender role* as a social script"³² in an essay entitled, "Alternative Interpretations of the Development of G-I/R." Beach stated, "Somewhere in the argument the distinction between gender role and gender identity gets lost. I understand that sociologists consider gender role as a script imposed on the individual by society. But what happens to gender identity? Is it relegated to Immanuel Kant's category of innate ideas?"³³

Arguing Directly from Animal Behavior to
Human Behavior

Turning to another more serious error, the entomologist Kinsey began to erroneously draw direct conclusions concerning human behavior from insect sexual behavior. Kinsey concluded that early sexual activity

---

29. Money and Ehrhardt, *Man and Woman*, 4,300–301.
30. Money and Ehrhardt, *Man and Woman*, 153.
31. Money and Ehrhardt, *Man and Woman*, 153.
32. Money, *Love and Love Sickness*, 15.
33. Frank A. Beach, "Alternative Interpretations of the Development of G-I/R," in *Masculinity/ Femininity: Basic Perspectives*, ed. Reinish, Rosenblum, and Sanders, Kinsey Institute Series (New York and Oxford: Oxford University Press, 1987), 30.

in children was a better preparation for successful adult sexual activity in human beings, and, conversely, the lack of early sexual behavior would inhibit capacity for successful adult sexual behavior. A recent essay by Judith A Reisman et al. in the *Ave Maria International Law Journal* has demonstrated the direct link between Kinsey's arguments and SIECUS (which supports early sexual education and freedom for children's sexual expression) as well as UNESCO (which promotes international sexual education and freedom of children's sexual expression).[34]

John Money was fascinated with lower forms of animals and fish. In his 1987 article on "Propaedeutics of Diecious G-I/R," he introduces the theme of "diecious fishes," or fish who sometimes breed as males and other times as females. Money concluded that "once science uncovers the secret of hermaphroditic versatility of sex-changing fish and parthenogenetic lizards, then on the criterion that today's science fiction becomes tomorrow's science, it will undoubtedly be applied to mammals. Thus, one can envisage a future when sex-irreducible G-I/R will no longer be fixed and irreducible, but, by a process equivalent to reverse embryogenesis, it will be sex reversible."[35]

Money considered that "the chief source of empirical data on juvenile erotosexual rehearsal play is the Wisconsin Regional Primate Center where juvenile rhesus monkeys have been studied."[36] In this study both female and male monkeys deprived of sex play in early life proved unable to mate in later life. From this Money drew the conclusion that "it [early sex play] may well play an extremely influential role as a critical-period phenomenon wherein nature and nurture merge to establish future erotosexual health, male and female."[37] He began to introduce pornography into his therapy sessions in the gender identity

---

34. Judith A. Reisman, Mary E. McAlister, and Paul E. Rondeau, "Global Sex Deviance Advocacy: The Trojan Horse to Destroy the Family and Civil Society; A Report on UNESCO and International Planned Parenthood Federation," *Ave Maria International Law Journal* 1, no 2 (Spring 2012): 231–63.

35. Money, "Propaedeutics of Diecious G-I/R," in Reinish, Rosenblum, and Sanders, *Masculinity/Femininity*, 18–19. See Frank Beach's argument that Money's theory about the dimorphic brain schemata present in both males and females implies an erroneous leap from the general to the particular, "because his list includes both human and animal behavior ... in several cases [where] no such implication appears justified," in "Alternative Interpretations of G-I/R," 33.

36. Money, "Propaedeutics of Diecious G-I/R," 26.

37. Money, "Propaedeutics of Diecious G-I/R," 26.

clinic with young children and to give lectures on the so-called positive uses of pornography in the home and school.[38]

Power, Deception, and Harming the Innocent

In this next section further aspects of Kinsey's and Money's research methods and promulgation of research results that came to light over time will be described. Here we begin to discover the pernicious effects of their ideologies on people.

Abuse of Power to Promote the Ideology

Kinsey required anyone who wanted to hear a lecture by him or have some other favor from him such as employment to agree to give an interview sex history.[39] The interview techniques involved frequent use of what philosophers call "the fallacy of a complex question"—that is, "trying to support a proposition with an argument in which that proposition is a premise."[40] The interviewer would ask, "When did you start ___ sexual activity?," and this question would be repeated frequently, even when the person denied he or she had ever done that particular act. Kinsey's associate Wardell Pomeroy later on described it this way: "We also never asked *whether* a subject had ever engaged in a particular activity; we assumed that everyone had engaged in everything, and so we began by asking *when* he had done it."[41]

The abuse of power in this technique eventually wore down the re-

---

38. Money, "Pornography in the Home," in *Contemporary Sexual Behavior*, ed. Joseph Zubin and John Money (Baltimore: Johns Hopkins University Press, 1973), 410.

39. For interviewing techniques, see Kinsey, Pomeroy, and Martin, *Sexual Behavior in the Human Male*, 35–62; Gebhard and Johnson, *Kinsey Data*, 11–24; Pomeroy, *Dr. Kinsey and the Institute for Sex Research*, 97–137; for a critique of interviewing techniques, see Judith A. Reisman, *Kinsey: Crimes and Consequences; The Red Queen and the Grand Scheme* (Arlington, Va.: Institute for Media Education, 1998), 28–31, 58–63, and 211ff.

40. See David Kelley, "Fallacies," in *The Art of Reasoning* (New York and London: W. W. Norton, 1988), 133.

41. Pomeroy, *Dr. Kinsey and the Institute*, 112. This fallacious approach to interviewing was pursued indefinitely. For example, Pomeroy adds, "If a subject was of low mentality we might pretend that we had misunderstood his negative reply, and ask another question as though he had answered affirmatively; for instance, 'Yes, I know you have never done that, but how old were you the *first* time you did it?' To make it as easy as possible for subjects to correct their answers, we ignored contradictions, accepting the correction as though it were a first reply"; 113.

sistance of the person being interviewed until many would make up an answer to just get over the process. Kinsey also told his university audiences that he would not agree to speak unless *everyone* in the audience would be interviewed. This brought peer pressure onto the young women or men to complete the interview. Finally, the content of the interview involved specific mention of every conceivable sexual act, and the interviewee would often use slang words for these acts that would be commonly understood by the group to which the person interviewed belonged. The overblown statistical results, whether true or not, ended up promoting sex activities under the implication that "everyone did it." At the time of Kinsey's gathering of his data, some individuals protested, but most people did not realize what was happening.

Another abuse of power in Kinsey's work was his use of persons as "objects" rather than subjects of sexual activity. This obvious utilitarian use of the person reduced him or her from a loved "someone" to a used "something."[42] Kinsey's reports made no connection between sexual activity, married love, the generation of children, and a woman's experience of maternity. The reports also seemed to encourage sexual activity outside of marriage, breaking promises of fidelity to have experiences with prostitutes, homosexual partners, and the spouses of others. It suggested that adults "need" this kind of variety for their "sexual outlets."

John Colapinto, a journalist who gained the trust of the members of a family who had been clients of John Money's gender identity clinic, has left for posterity a detailed record about how his abuse of power was directed toward individual persons.[43] After Money's research method of arguing from hermaphrodites to normal male and female children was criticized by a medical research team from Kansas in 1958 and another one from Toronto in 1959,[44] Money thought he found "a perfect controlled experiment" to prove his gender identity theory: two normal identical male twins, one of whom could be brought up as a boy and the other as a girl. A Canadian couple from Winnipeg had identical twin

---

42. See Robert Spaemann, *Persons: The Difference between "Someone" and "Something,"* trans. Oliver O'Donovan (New York: Oxford University Press, 2006).
  43. Colapinto, *As Nature Made Him*.
  44. Colapinto, *As Nature Made Him*, 44–46.

boys, Bruce and Brian Reimer, born in 1965. The parents consulted at Johns Hopkins Gender Identity Clinic for help because one son (Bruce) had lost his penis through a poorly performed circumcision. So Dr. Money recommended bringing up the wounded son as a girl surgically, medically, and socially; and he insisted that this not be revealed in any way to either of the twenty-two-month-old children.

Consequently, the wounded child's name was changed to Brenda, and he was castrated in 1967. Mrs. Reimer and Mr. Reimer were told to constantly reinforce typical (that is, stereotyped) behaviors of girls and boys in every possible way. In spite of Money's projected goal of helping this normal male child grow up as a "normal" female, Brenda fought the change continuously. Even with hormonal displacement and continuous reminders about what girls do and what boys do, by 1970, Brenda was not adjusting well to being told he was a she. He was a normal active boy, a physical fighter, hitting and attacking others, and actually defending his brother on occasion. He adjusted poorly to school and suffered a great deal.

During annual visits of the Reimer children to the clinic, in a clear abuse of power, Dr. Money encouraged sexual play between the two, with one being the girl and the other the boy, and he photographed the children in these positions. During a later interview by John Colapinto the twins said that Dr. Money "would show us pictures of kids—boys and girls—with no clothes on . . . ; and showed them pictures of adults engaged in sexual intercourse. He'd say to us, 'I want to show you pictures of things that moms and dads do.'"[45] Dr. Money even suggested that Mrs. Reimer walk around nude at home and that the parents allow their children to observe them having sexual intercourse. They refused to comply with this latter suggestion.

In 1978, at the annual visit of the Reimers to Johns Hopkins University, Dr. Money wanted to convince thirteen-year-old Brenda to have further sex-change surgery. He introduced Brenda to an adult transsexual, and the adolescent patient fled his office, never to return. Two years later, through the help of Dr. Mary McKenty, a psychiatrist in Winnipeg, the Reimers were encouraged to tell their fifteen-year-olds

---

45. Colapinto, *As Nature Made Him*, 86.

the truth about what had happened so many years ago. In March 1980, as soon as Brenda learned the truth, she immediately made the decision to revert to the biological male sex of her birth and to take the name of David. In spite of the complete failure of John Money's Baconian experiment, he always publicly claimed it was a success.

Deception in Research Methods, Results, and Ignoring Facts
The Kinsey Institute, located in an elegant house near the campus of Indiana University, provided a veneer of respectability to the project of the study of sexuality and also to those who worked at the Institute of Sexology. Only much later has it become known what actually happened at the institute. It is now known that behind the walls every conceivable kind of sexual activity was occurring in multiple combinations of people who worked there or who were specially invited and that much of this activity was being filmed.[46] Thanks to the work of Judith Reisman and others, it is also known that many of these activities included children from birth to eight years whose parents offered them for the experiments.[47] The Kinsey Institute not only deceived those whom they interviewed, it also deceived governmental agencies and members of the public about the nature of their research and about whether the facts did or did not support their exaggerated claims. As the truth began to trickle out, funding was withdrawn, and toward the end of Kinsey's life the institute was no longer able to continue as in the past. By that time, however, sex ideology was launched through media and journalism, and it began a new life of its own in willing hosts.

A similar result came to John Money's project of reconfiguring gender. In 1972, a shift from academic professionals to broad public audiences occurred when Dr. John Money published, through the Johns Hopkins University Press, *Man and Woman, Boy and Girl: The Differentiation and Dimorphism of Gender Identity from Conception to Maturity*. In this book, intentionally deceiving the public, he proclaimed the "great success of his twins experiment" in spite of the fact that he knew it was

---

46. Linda Wolfe, *Kinsey: Public and Private* (New York: New Market, 2004), 15–80; Pomeroy, *Dr. Kinsey and the Institute*.
47. Reisman, McAlister, and Rondeau, "Global Sex Deviance Advocacy," 252–61. Reisman, *Kinsey*, 51–90,140–86.

failing. Sprinkled through the book Money states proudly, after describing his successes in gender identity-differentiation among human hermaphrodites, "A similar extraordinary contrast has been observed even when a child born as a normal male was surgically reassigned as a female.... In gender behavior, she is quite gender-different from her identical twin brother."[48]

This new book of Money's was praised on its cover by the *New York Times*: "The Brilliant New Landmark study of human sexuality.... The most important work since the Kinsey Reports!" *Time Magazine* soon followed. The claim most often repeated was that sex and gender identity were more because of environmental factors than because of genes, anatomy, hormones, and other natural factors from conception, birth, and puberty. Money himself "made the case the centerpiece of his public addresses, rarely giving a speech in which he did not mention it."[49]

In 1975, Dr. Paul McHugh was appointed as psychiatrist-in-chief at Johns Hopkins Hospital. McHugh requested a systematic study of those who had gender identity changes at the gender clinic. After two years he realized that "we in the Johns Hopkins Psychiatry Department eventually concluded that human *sexual identity is mostly built into our constitution by the genes we inherit and the embryogenesis we undergo*."[50] In 1979, McHugh closed down the gender identity clinic at Johns Hopkins Hospital and soon after moved Dr. Money's office off campus and limited his teaching. However, John Money continued to publish his false claims about the gender gate and his so-called proof for changing a normal male to female gender.

Even though Dr. Money and the general public continued to herald Money's "twins experiment," Dr. Milton Diamond from Toronto had published serious doubts about "the twin" case in two journals, and he "never deviated from his conviction that sex reassignment of a developmentally normal infant was impossible."[51] Around this time, the BBC

---

48. Money and Ehrhardt, *Man and Woman, Boy and Girl: The Differentiation and Dimorphism of Gender Identity from Conception to Maturity* (New York and Scarborough, Ontario: New American Library Mentor, 1972), 19. The text also refers the reader to further details in this case in chapter 7 of the text.

49. Colapinto, *As Nature Made Him*, 71.

50. Paul McHugh, "Surgical Sex," *First Things* (November 2004): 4.

51. Colapinto, *As Nature Made Him*, 45ff, 166 ff, 174ff.

Gender Reality vs. Gender Ideology | 53

had discovered where the Reimer twins lived and went to school to film for a program called "Open Secret" on medical scandals. After the BBC's report in 1979, Dr. Money just went silent on the Reimer case, but by then it had become part of a "gender ideology" that had its own trajectory.

Harming the Innocent

It is a characteristic of ideologies that in addition to ignoring facts and abusing power, they also tend to harm innocent persons. Beginning with Kinsey we already noted his focus on children's sexual activity and his promotion of it as healthy even when initiated by adults. His reports contained clear sections of data that quantified sexual arousal in children from zero to eight years, citing that they were stimulated by an adult. Even though Kinsey was careful to mention that one of the child's parents was always in the room, there is no doubt that pedophile behavior was occurring even behind a screen of scientific research. Kinsey also argued that early sexual activity in children, in analogy with animals, was a better preparation for successful activity in adults.[52]

We also noted that Kinsey's research techniques involved suggesting to, and even badgering, innocent and chaste college-age students with questions about when they began and how often continued all kinds of sexual activities. When the Kinsey reports on male and female behavior were published, what sort of harm may they have caused people who thought they should engage in these activities to be "healthy"? Did the Kinsey reports contribute to creating an environment conducive to the explosion of the seminarian and priest initiation of sexual activities with youths and children?

Michel Foucault, our other example of someone promoting a sex ideology, turns out to have participated in group sex in 1983 in the bathhouses of San Francisco, knowing he had AIDS and without informing others of his contagious fatal illness.[53] In his *History of Sexuality*, Fou-

---

52. See table 34 in Kinsey, Pomeroy, and Martin, *Sexual Behavior in the Human Male*, 180, and Reisman, *Kinsey*, 147n44.

53. See James Miller, *The Passion of Michel Foucault* (New York: Simon and Schuster, 1993), 27–29, 253, and Stanley Grenz, *A Primer on Postmodernism* (Grand Rapids, Mich.: Eerdmans, 1996), 125–26, who refers his reader to the more detailed account of these events in Miller's text.

cault "prophetically" predicted his own way of death: "The Faustian pact, whose temptation has been instilled in us by the deployment of sexuality, is now as follows: to exchange life in its entirety for sex itself, for the truth and the sovereignty of sex. Sex is worth dying for . . . ; the grumble of death [is] within it."[54] Sex ideology replaced the culture of life with the culture of death.

Returning to John Money's gender ideology, we discover that each member of the Reimer family was harmed by Money's use of them for his experiment to prove his theory of the gender gate between birth and two years of age. Dr. Paul McHugh stated unequivocally in his critique of Money's approach at John's Hopkins, "I have witnessed a great deal of damage from sex-reassignment. The children transformed from their male constitution into female roles suffered prolonged distress and misery as they sensed their natural attitudes. Their parents usually lived with guilt over their decisions—second guessing themselves and somewhat ashamed of the fabrication, both surgical and social, they had imposed on their sons."[55] The harsh reality of human suffering for the Reimer family was not only evident in the parents' struggles with alcoholism and depression, but it may have contributed significantly in 2002 when Brian Reimer died from an overdose of medicine for his mental disease of schizophrenia and again in 2004 when David Reimer died from shooting himself in the head after a time of despair.

In addition, John Money lectured on "Pornography in the Home: A Topic in Medical Education."[56] Dr. Money's approach to pornography is clearly stated in this professional essay. He explicitly showed pornographic images to audiences and argued forcefully for the so-called value of sharing of this kind of imagery in schools and homes "into the total context of sex education."[57] He argued that exposure to pornographic images, even at a young age, is valuable because they "lead to

---

54. Foucault, *History of Sexuality*, 156. Grenz, in *A Primer on Postmodernism*, summarizes the sex-acts that Foucault was choosing to undertake at the very same time he was writing his *History of Sexuality*, 253.
55. Paul McHugh, "Surgical Sex," 6.
56. Money, "Pornography in the Home," 409–40.
57. Money, "Pornography in the Home," 410.

the possibility of bettering one's own sex life, leading one to have less guilt and fewer 'hang-ups,' and more honesty and freedom about sex"; furthermore, he added that "one becomes better able to help others by achieving a position ... of non-judgmentalism."[58]

Money forged a solid connection between the more general theme of a woman or man's gender identity and erotic experience and sexual orientation, and he publicly promoted pedophilia.[59] In *Sexual Signatures* (1975) Money argued that it is good to encourage children to observe sexual intercourse of adults and that "the best time to introduce such pictures [*The Pictorial Guide to Sexual Intercourse*, by Schwenda and Leuchner, 1969] is before a child's biological clock has signaled the start of puberty."[60] He further argued against the "incest taboo."[61] Finally, in this same text, Money argued that it was possible that "all humans are capable of developing a bisexual gender identity/role ... and giving it an erotic expression."

Money's praise for pornography was also paired with a direct attack on the Catholic Church—a pattern that repeats itself over and over again. In his 1970 essay promoting pornography in the home and school, he draws an analogy called "an allegory of the Crucifixion." Money argues that even though millions of children for two thousand years have learned at church on Sundays about "how to commit a crucifixion," he adds that he has "not heard of children who come home and play crucifixion games with their dolls or playmates." Money concludes, "Pornography does not automatically have the power to incite behavior."[62]

Contemporary research proves otherwise, and it also demonstrates how pornography increases the culture of death against the civilization

---

58. Money, "Pornography in the Home," 418–19. For a more detailed description of his interactions with the Reimer twins about this theme, see Colapinto, *As Nature Made Him*, 86ff. Money also drew upon some hypotheses (which turned out later to be false) about the value of "sexual rehearsal play" among Australian aborigines, the Yolngu; 88ff.

59. Money, Interview in *Paidika: The Journal of Paedophilia* 2, no. 3 (Spring 1991): 5, as reported in Wikipedia, "On Pedophilia," available at http://wikipedia.org/wiki/John_Money (accessed 12/22/2011).

60. Money and Tucker, *Sexual Signatures*, 134.

61. Money and Tucker, *Sexual Signatures*, 182.

62. Money, "Pornography in the Home," 417.

of love. When working on research for gender ideology I was surprised to discover four of Dr. John Money's books in our seminary library, and again I thought about the innocent persons harmed by the behavior of some seminarians and priests because of the forcefulness of those promoting a gender ideology.

How Did Gender Ideology "Go Viral"?

As I pondered and researched the problem of gender ideology further I discovered that Money's works had soon after their publication become imbedded in secular feminist text books. An analogy with the way a virus spreads and the contemporary expression about an electronic photo or story "going viral" seemed to apply. A virus has to find a willing host cell to attach itself to, and it usually destroys the host cell or ends its normal activities before moving on to infect another cell.[63]

Adopted by Feminists

The original promoters of sex and gender ideologies were not educated in the academic field of perennial philosophy. Instead, they worked in areas of pseudo-science and social sciences such as anthropology. The next phase of gender ideology is formed by persons almost all of whom work in social sciences, literature, or politics. Again, these authors were really not engaged with traditional philosophers or theologians during this phase, when gender ideology mutated from a more isolated phenomenon into the broader culture of the women's movement.

Secular Feminists
In 1970, in chapter 2 of her book *Sexual Politics*, Kate Millett (1934–2017) introduced the term "gender" and its use with respect to establishing a core gender identity by the age of eighteen months.[64] She followed the

---

63. See Introduction to viruses: "Most virus infections eventually result in the death of the host cell ... (cell 'suicide') ... ; and often cell death is caused by cessation of its normal activity." Available from http://en.eikipedia.org/wiki/Introduction_to_viruses [accessed 2/6/12], 1 of 1.
64. Kate Millett, *Sexual Politics* (Garden City, N.Y.: Doubleday, 1970), 29.

line of thought of Robert Stoller, who had established a gender identity clinic in California.[65] Chapter 2 of this text was drawn from her Ph.D. dissertation in literature from Columbia University in 1970. Millett begins, "Indeed, so arbitrary is gender, that it may even be contrary to physiology."[66] Millet directly quotes Stoller, who in turn references John Money: "Although the external genitalia (penis, testes, scrotum) contribute to the sense of maleness, no one of them is essential for it, not even all of them together. In the absence of complete evidence, I agree in general with Money, and the Hampsons, who show in their large series of intersexed patients that gender role is determined by postnatal forces, regardless of the anatomy and physiology of the external genitalia.'"[67] Millett then directly quotes John Money, approving his view: "The condition existing at birth and for several months thereafter is one of psychosexual undifferentiation."[68] In 1966, Kate Millett became a member of the National Organization of Women (NOW) shortly after it was founded.

Another early feminist connection with Dr. Money occurred through *Dr. Alice Rossi* (1922–2009), who earned her doctorate in sociology at Columbia University—a sociologist who was a founding member of NOW in 1966.[69] Rossi was hired by Johns Hopkins University and Goucher College in Baltimore when Dr. Money was running his gender identity clinic. She participated with him in a 1970 symposium at Johns

---

65. Millett, *Sexual Politics*, 30, referring back to Robert J. Stoller, *Sex and Gender* (New York: Science House, 1968), 9.

66. Millett, *Sexual Politics*, 30.

67. Millett, *Sexual Politics*, 30, referring back to Stoller, *Sex and Gender*, 48, who in turn refers back to Money, Joan G. Hampson, and John L. Hampson, "An Examination of Some Basic Sexual Concepts: The Evidence of Human Hermaphroditism," *Bulletin of Johns Hopkins Hospital* 97, no. 4 (1955): 301–19, and Money, Hampson, and Hampson, "Imprinting and the Establishment of Gender Role," *Archives of Neurology and Psychiatry* 77, no. 3 (1957): 333–36.

68. Millett, *Sexual Politics*, 30, referring to John Money, "Psychosexual Differentiation," in *Sex Research, New Developments* (New York: Holt, 1965), 12.

69. A step in the rapid spread of gender ideology is found in the collaborative work of Dr. Money, with the previously well-established field of sexology as represented by the Kinsey reports (*Sexual Behavior in the Human Male* (1948) and *Sexual Behavior in the Human Female* (1953) and subsequent reports of Masters and Johnson (*Human Sexual Response* (1966) and *Human Sexual Inadequacy* (1970). All these elements were in place at the 61st Annual American Psychopathological Association Conference sponsored by Johns Hopkins University Medical School in Baltimore in 1970. Dr. Alice Rossi, a moderate feminist, was a participant in this same conference. In 1959, Rossi had been hired to teach full time in sociology at the University of Chicago.

Hopkins that also included Masters and Johnson. In addition, Alice Rossi's seminal work, *The Feminist Papers: From Adams to de Beauvoir*, was published in 1973, when many universities were beginning courses in women's studies and feminist studies. Alice Rossi also gave attention early on to abortion rights for women.[70]

Feminists also produced textbooks for academic courses using Money's descriptions about gender identity/role; this way, gender ideology spread throughout universities across America, Canada, England, Australia, and the English-speaking world. *Gender: An Ethnomethodological Approach* was published in 1978 in England, Australia, Canada, and the United States. In the preface, its two authors, Suzanne Kessler and Wendy McKenna, state, "Our theoretical position is that gender is a social construction, that a world of two 'sexes' is a result of the socially shared, taken-for-granted methods which members use to construct reality."[71] This textbook cites seven different sources authored by John Money, and it incorporates nearly verbatim many of Money's definitions. In just one example, "Gender identity refers to an individual's own feeling of whether she or he is a woman or a man, or a girl or a boy. In essence gender identity is self-attribution of gender."[72] The text repeats all the various arguments from cross-cultural studies and those that apply animal studies to humans.

A second example of a popular textbook is *The Question of Sex Differences: Psychological, Cultural, and Biological Issues*, authored by Katharine Hoyenga and Kermit Hoyenga. This book was published in the U.S. and Canada in 1979. Even though the title emphasizes the word "sex," the content completely adopts Money's use of terms and definitions for gender identity and gender role.[73] The Hoyengas changed

---

70. In the conference proceedings, Saul Rosenzweig supported early detection of fetal sex and simple abortion so that "parental choice of neonate sex would become fairly simple"; in Zubin and Money, *Contemporary Sexual Behavior*, 202. Rossi also wrote, "Feminists of all political stripes have been united in their insistence on the right of women to control their own bodies, have been sharply critical of masculine assumptions concerning female sexuality, and, hence, have demanded safe contraceptives and abortion repeal"; Zubin and Money, *Contemporary Sexual Behavior*, 155.

71. Suzanne J. Kessler and Wendy McKenna, *Gender: An Ethnomethodological Approach* (New York: John Wiley and Sons, 1978), vii.

72. Kessler and McKenna, *Gender*, 8.

73. Katharine Blick Hoyenga and Kermit T. Hoyenga, *The Question of Sex Differences: Psycholog-*

Dr. Money's list of sexes and genders to a list of genders in a chart entitled, "Eight Definitions of Gender: Chromosomal Gender, Gonadal Gender, Hormonal Gender, Gender of the Internal Sexual Accessory Organs, Gender of External Genitals, Gender of Rearing, Gender Identity, [and] Gender Role."[74] The academic secular feminists discussed in this section were moderate feminists who laid the groundwork for gender ideology to "go viral." In the next section, we will see how the word "gender" gets infused with a more radical meaning that adds to its virulence.

Marxist Feminists
Gayle Rubin (1949–), after completing her M.A. in anthropology at the University of Michigan, introduced the phrase "sex/gender system" in her 1975 article "The Traffic in Women: Notes on the 'Political Economy' of Sex." Following a Marxist approach, she stipulates, "The 'sex/gender system' is the set of arrangements by which a society transforms biological sexuality into products of human activity, and in which these transformed sexual needs are satisfied."[75] Arguing that men traffic in women to satisfy their sexual needs, Rubin argued, "Gender is a socially imposed division of the sexes [into men and women]. It is a product of the social relations of sexuality."[76]

Rubin's solution to the so-called division of sexes is to reorganize the sex/gender system, in her words, by "the elimination of obligatory sexualities and sex roles. The dream I find most compelling is one of an androgynous and genderless (though not sexless) society, in which one's sexual anatomy is irrelevant to who one is, what one does, and with whom one makes love."[77]

Rubin leaned toward a Marxist political interpretation of gender. By 1978 she was doing research toward completing her doctorate in

---

ical, Cultural, and Biological Issues (Boston and Toronto: Little, Brown, 1979), 4, referring back to Money and Ehrhardt, *Man and Woman*.

74. Hoyenga and Hoyenga, *Question of Sex Differences*, 5.
75. Gayle Rubin, "The Traffic in Women: Notes on the 'Political Economy' of Sex," in *Toward an Anthropology of Women*, ed. Rayna R. Reiter (New York: Monthly Review, 1975), 159.
76. Rubin, "Traffic in Women," 179.
77. Rubin, "Traffic in Women," 204.

anthropology for the University of Michigan on sadomasochism in gay men and lesbian women from San Francisco.[78] Dr. Rubin is presently teaching a course on Foucault in her position as associate professor of comparative literature and assistant professor of anthropology and women's studies at the University of Michigan.

Rubin's phrase "the sex/gender system" became popular among many feminists, including many who did not realize its Marxist roots. More popularly the phrase "sex/gender system" was used to emphasize that sex is a biological category totally separated from gender as a psychosocial category. Following a Cartesian mind/body dualism, sex is limited to bodily characteristics and gender is limited to social psychological characteristics felt in the mind.

Over time, however, the "category" of gender broadened to include various kinds of sexual activity and medically transgendered human beings. Once this happened, the body entered into gender through the back door, and we began to get the original two genders of man and woman expanded to five, ten, or fifteen, including, variously, examples as intersex bisexuals (male or female), homosexuals (male or female), heterosexuals (male or female), transgendered males, transgendered females, and so on. So the original sex/gender system, the separation of gender from sex, collapses in on itself.

Postmodern Feminists

Another pathway to the new sexual ideology mentioned by Rubin follows a postmodern or nominalist approach to words and categories. In this understanding both sex and gender differentiation disappears into a sexless and genderless human being that, as we saw in Michel Foucault, in turn itself disappears. The identity of the person evaporates.

Some intellectual radical feminists began to follow this pathway of collapse. Monica Wittig argues in 1980 that since gender is a socially constructed political concept, it ought to be reconstructed:

"Man" and "woman" are political concepts of opposition, and the copula which dialectically unites them is, at the same time, the one which abolishes them.

---

78. Rubin, "The Valley of the Kings: Leathermen in San Francisco 1960–1990," Ph.D. diss. (University of Michigan, 1994).

It is the class struggle between women and men which will abolish men and women. The concept of difference has nothing ontological about it. It is only the way that the masters interpret a historical situation of domination. The function of difference is to mask at every level the conflicts of interest, including the ideological ones.

In other words, for us, this means there cannot any longer be women and men, and that as classes and categories of thought or language they have to disappear, politically, economically, ideologically.[79]

Wittig concludes that since sex and gender are socially constructed, they ought to be abolished.

Teresa de Laureates, in her 1987 text *Technologies of Gender*, claims that gender is the effect produced in bodies by complex political technology that produces technologies of sex, technologies of gender, and socially constructed engendered beings. She describes the partial deconstruction of the human being in *Technologies of Gender*: "We cannot resolve or dispel the uncomfortable condition of being at once inside and outside gender either by desexualizing it (making gender merely a metaphor, a question of *difference*, of purely discursive effects) or by androgynizing it (claiming the same experience of material conditions for both genders in a given class, race, or culture).[80]

In 1988, Biddy Martin takes a further step in developing contemporary consequences of Foucault's social construct argument when she states that:

For Foucault, the question of the truth of one's sex, of one's self is not a self-evident question, and the answers which literature, medicine, psychiatry and religion provide are, in fact, a matter of rendering our bodies and psyches subject to control. Having created sex and gender as problems of a particular kind, the experts must necessarily intervene in our lives to provide solutions and to bind us within a particular identity, a subjectivity.[81]

---

79. Monique Wittig, "The Straight Mind," *Feminist Issues* 1 (Summer 1980): 108.

80. Teresa de Laureates, *Technologies of Gender* (Bloomington: Indiana University Press, 1987), 11.

81. Biddy Martin, "Feminism, Criticism, and Foucault," *Feminism and Foucault: Reflections on Resistance*, ed. Irene Diamond and Lee Quinby (Boston: Northeastern University Press, 1988), 14.

Martin considers what she perceives as a difficulty of modern feminists, or how to "desexualize the category of woman" at the same time as woman is kept as a starting point for critical reflection on oppressive structures of society. She sees this as the paradox of desexualization and cultural criticism.

By 1990, Judith Butler entered the dialogue about the deconstruction of gender with her book *Gender Trouble: Feminism and the Subversion of Identity*. She recognizes the contradictions that catch postmodern feminists: "Wittig calls for the destruction of 'sex' so that women can assume the status of a universal subject."[82] In this paradoxical move, Wittig seeks to keep some semblance of gender identity at the same time as she is abolishing the ontological grounds for its stability. In Butler's words, "Wittig appears to dispute the metaphysics of substance, but on the other hand, she retains the human subject, the individual, as the metaphysical locus of agency."[83] Butler recognizes the serious implications of the deconstructive approach that flows from a theory that gender and sex are only socially constructed:

> But once we dispense with the priority of "man" and "woman" as abiding substances, then it is no longer possible to subordinate dissonant gendered features as so many secondary and accidental characteristics of a gender ontology that is fundamentally intact. If the notion of an abiding substance is a fictive construction produced through the compulsory ordering of attributes into coherent gender sequences, then it seems that gender as substance, the viability of *man* and *woman* as nouns, is called into question by the dissonant play of attributes that fail to conform to sequential or causal models of intelligibility.[84]

More recently, in her 2004 text *Undoing Gender*, Judith Butler continues her philosophical critique of postmodern feminist and political approaches to the question of sex and gender identity. Her questions raise fundamental issues, while her solutions at times get caught in the crossfire of the social sciences, politics, and philosophy.[85]

---

82. Judith Butler, *Gender Trouble: Feminism and the Subversion of Identity* (New York: Routledge, 1990), 20.
83. Butler, *Gender Trouble*, 25.
84. Butler, *Gender Trouble*, 24.
85. Butler, *Undoing Gender* (Routledge: New York, 2004). See especially chapter 9, "The End of Sexual Difference?," 174–273.

How did the Gender Ideology Virus "Get Mapped"?

When a new virus gets noticed, medical experts begin immediately to map its movement from one location to another. By analogy, Catholic journalists and attorneys began to map the gender ideology virus. Their persistent sounding of alarm was remarkable, and we have to be very grateful for their work.

Catholic Journalists and Attorneys

The American writer *Dale O'Leary* described in her book *The Gender Agenda* how preparations were being made in different regional meetings of nongovernmental organizations (NGOs) for the United Nations world conference in Mexico City in 1975 for the UN Year of the Woman and to prepare for the Decade of Women proclaimed by the United Nations (1976–85). At one regional conference for Latin America in 1977 that met in Mar del Plato, Argentina, Marta Llamas, a Mexican feminist, proposed a theory of five sexes. Her words sound like a carbon copy of Dr. John Money's theory:

> Biology shows that, outwardly, human beings can be divided into two sexes; nevertheless, there are more combinations that result from the five physiological areas which, in general and very simple terms, determine what is called the biological sex of a person: genes, hormones, gonads, internal reproductive organs and external reproductive organs (genitals). These areas control the five types of biological processes in a continuum.... A quick but somewhat insufficient classification of these combinations obliges one to recognize at least five biological sexes: men (persons who have two testicles); women (persons who have two ovaries); hermaphrodites or herms (in which there are at the same time one testicle and one ovary); masculine hermaphrodites or merms (persons who have testicles, but present other feminine sexual characteristics); [and] feminine hermaphrodites or ferms (persons with ovaries, but with masculine sexual characteristics).[86]

---

86. Marta Llamas, "Cuerpo: Diferencia sexual y género," in Dale O'Leary, *The Gender Agenda: Redefining Equality* (Lafayette, La.: Vital Issues, 1997), 69–70.

In addition to this proposal for five equal sexes, Marta Llamas also argued that a person's identity as a man or woman is simply socially constructed. She often spoke of gender and defined it as "the symbolization that each culture establishes over sexual difference."[87]

During September 1–4, 1994, representatives from 179 governments around the world met in Cairo for a United Nations Program of Action on a variety of global issues. A large group of NGOs met just before the United Nations Conference on Population and Development in Cairo. At this conference a rather intense argument erupted over the meaning of the word "gender," which was frequently used in a draft text.

American secular feminist and National Organization for Women leader, Congresswoman Bella Abzug tried to redefine gender, or blur distinctions when others tried to stop her.[88] In her words, "The current attempt by several Member States to expunge the word *gender* from the Platform for Action and to replace it with the word *sex* is an insulting and demeaning attempt to reverse the gains made by women, to intimidate us, and to block further progress."[89] Politicizing the discussion of the meaning of the words "sex and gender," Abzug continued, "We urge the small number of male and female delegates seeking to sidetrack and sabotage the empowerment of women to cease this diversionary tactic. They will not succeed. They will only waste precious time. We will not go back to subordinate inferior roles."[90] Her political position was based on a kind of Cartesian unisex equality that promoted abortion rights and the social construction of several sexes and genders. After considerable discussion, in the end, the word "gender" was left vague in the documents to mean "as it has been commonly used and understood."[91]

This common usage of the word "gender," which had been generally understood as referring to the two basic divisions into male and female

---

87. Llamas, "Cuerpo," 71.
88. For a thorough description of the arguments and tactics, see O'Leary, *Gender Agenda*, 86ff.
89. O'Leary, *Gender Agenda*, 87.
90. O'Leary, *Gender Agenda*, 87.
91. O'Leary, *Gender Agenda*, 159.

human beings, now became the target of the gender ideology virus. It is at this point that gender ideology proponents sought to dominate the discussion and resolutions at the United Nations Fourth Conference on Women in Beijing, China, in 1995, by redefining equality of men and women to mean statistical equality in every kind of work or political situation. Dale O'Leary summarized it: "The Gender Agenda begins with a false premise—the differences between men and women are social constructs—and then goes on to demand that this premise be 'mainstreamed' in every program and policy."[92] As a result of her research on gender ideology, Dale O'Leary concluded that the word "gender" itself was toxic. She recommended abandoning the use of the word "gender" in "Don't Say Gender When You Mean Sex."[93]

Mary Ann Glendon, Harvard law professor, was appointed head of the Vatican Delegation to the UN Beijing World Conference on Women in 1995. Glendon provides a welcome insight into the mind of John Paul II toward the actual work of that conference in her written summary: "Our assessment of [documents of the conference] their pros and cons was communicated to the Vatican Secretariat of State. On Thursday morning, we received the Holy Father's decision: Accept what is positive, but vigorously reject what cannot be accepted."[94]

Details about the fight over the use and meaning of the word "gender" in the preliminary conferences leading up to the UN international conference were reviewed. Mary Ann Glendon states, "Accordingly, the Holy See delegation associated itself in part, with several reservations, with the conference documents.... A controversy over the word 'gender' that loomed before the conference had been largely defused with a consensus that gender was to be understood according to ordinary usage in the United Nations context."[95] Consequently, Pope John Paul recognized the need to clearly set boundaries for the conflict between those who wanted to take over the word "gender" for political purposes

---

92. O'Leary, *Gender Agenda*, 161.

93. O'Leary, "Don't Say Gender When You Mean Sex," *Pontifical Council on the Laity: Women's Section* (January–February 2012), 2.

94. Mary Ann Glendon, chapter 37, "What Happened at Beijing," in *Traditions in Turmoil* (Ann Arbor, Mich.: Sapientia Press of Ave Maria, 2006), 310.

95. Glendon, "What Happened at Beijing," 310.

and those who desired to keep its meaning within the usual range referring to women and men. In her words:

> The Holy See, however, deemed it prudent to attach to its reservations a further, more nuanced, statement of interpretation, in which it disassociated itself from rigid biological determinism as well as from the notion that sexual identity is indefinitely malleable. In keeping with the Holy Father's instruction to vigorously reject what was unacceptable, my concluding statement was sharply critical of the conference documents for the remaining deficiencies that our delegation had tried from the beginning to publicize and remedy."[96]

In addition, Mary Ann Glendon's fight in Beijing against the expanding reach of gender ideology led her to realize that the gender ideology virus had mutated far from the textbooks of academics into a worldwide epidemic that was poised to redound back onto individual nations with a new virulence. In her words:

> The most important political lesson to be taken from the Beijing conference is that huge international conferences are not suitable settings for addressing complex questions of social and economic justice or grave issues of human rights. Unfortunately, there is an increasing tendency for advocates of causes that have failed to win acceptance through ordinary democratic processes to resort to the international arena, far removed (they hope) from scrutiny and accountability.... They can be expected to keep on trying to insert their least popular ideas into U.N. documents for unveiling at home as "international norms."[97]

---

96. Glendon, "What Happened at Beijing," 310.

97. Glendon, "What Happened at Beijing," 310. Congressman Chris Smith corroborated Glendon's conclusion in his keynote address to the Fellowship of Catholic Scholars in Pittsburgh (2004). He stated that he had received anonymously a package that listed the ten or so steps that U.S. feminists had decided to take to circumvent the difficulty at that time of changing U.S. law. Among these steps was the plan to go first to the United Nations and get certain rights approved there (as it was easier to accomplish) and then return to the United States to argue that this country should conform itself to the international precedent established at the UN. Another step in the plan was to insert their own members into the middle tier of administrators, who took the UN policies and its finances out to the world, and country-by-country to make sure they could be put in place. See Representative Christopher H. Smith (R.-N.J.), Keynote Address "Pro-Family Prospects in the Congress," chapter 1 in *The Church, Marriage and the Family*, ed. Kenneth D. Whitehead (Notre Dame, Ind.: St. Augustine's Press, 2007), 1–10. Unfortunately, these informal remarks in the context of his lecture are not included in the published written text.

Glendon's summary also included a warning about the European Union (EU)'s radical promotion of abortion rights, contestation of every place the word "motherhood" positively appeared in documents, and removal of all references to religion, morals, ethics, spirituality, and even human dignity.[98] The virus had spread its infection not only through the United States, but also through Europe.

*

Dr. Marguerite A. Peeters, journalist and director of the Institute of Intercultural Dialogue Dynamics in Brussels and faculty member of the Pontifical Urbaniana University, has written extensively on the ideology of gender and is at the forefront of mapping its intellectual and political expansions. Her article maps very well the strategy of "gender mainstreaming, from 1968 Teheran, 1974 Bucharest, 1975 Mexico City, 1980 Copenhagen, 1985 Nairobi, and 1995 Beijing."[99] Her work is an invaluable reference for the viral spread of gender ideology. Peeters correctly identifies that "in the gender revolution, the real power is wielded by experts ... [who] are given direct access to senior civil servants and all the real decision-makers in every country, in order to be able to exert their influence without hindrance."[100] And she prophesies correctly that "the gender revolution is spreading like wildfire, albeit silently, without any form of public debate, and without anyone feeling the need to give it any democratic legitimacy."[101]

In her book *The Globalization of the Western Cultural Revolution: Key Concepts, Operational Mechanisms*, Dr. Peeters analyzes the rights-based approach strategy of gender [ideology]: "The first is the integration into human rights of the objectives of the erotic revolution.... The second is the integration of socioeconomic development into human rights; ... and the post-modern right to choose."[102] She traces the gender main-

---

98. Glendon, "What Happened at Beijing," 304–6.

99. Marguerite A. Peeters, "Current Proposals and the State of the Debate," in *Men and Women: Diversity and Mutual Complementarity*, by the Pontifical Counsel for the Laity (Vatican City: Libreria Editrice Vaticana, 2006), 85.

100. Peeters, "Current Proposals," 95.

101. Peeters, "Current Proposals," 96.

102. Peeters, *The Globalization of the Western Cultural Revolution: Key Concepts, Operational Mechanisms*, trans. Benedict Kobus (Brussels: Institute for Intercultural Dialogue Dynamics [ASBL], 2007), 88–89.

streaming at the UN and its use of "global gender specialists through the UN's Office of the Special Adviser on Gender Issues and Advancement of Women, or OSAGI."[103] In addition, Marguerite Peeters correctly describes a new battleground for gender ideology vs. gender reality in the field of education through a clear agenda from UNICEF for transforming schools in five stages: gender sensitive; gender healthy; gender priority to girl's education; gender rights of children to express their opinions and to have access to sexual and reproductive health; and evaluation on the children's positive participation in society.[104]

Dr. Peeters's mapping of the globalization of gender ideology is excellent. She identifies a "gender paradigm" supported by "gender feminists" who "have established a dialectical distinction between the concept of sex, feminine or masculine, whose differences are written in biology and are therefore unchangeable, and gender, feminine or masculine, whose differences, according to them, are socially constructed, unstable, and changeable."[105] There is, however, one aspect of her argument that I strongly disagree with—namely, that she suggests that we not use the word "gender" at all because it is so contaminated by the ideology of gender. My position, which will be articulated in the final section of this essay, is that we should fight to reclaim the word "gender" for its true meaning in gender reality.

Pontifical Council for the Laity—Women's Section

In 2008, at a conference sponsored by the Pontifical Council for the Laity in Rome on the occasion of the twentieth anniversary of *Mulieris Dignitatem*, Marguerite Peeters gave a lecture entitled, "Gender: An Anthropological Deconstruction and a Challenge for Faith." This lecture began with the strong claim that "gender is one of the most harmful categories in the feminist, sexual and cultural revolution that we are experiencing in the West."[106] Peeters generally used the word "gender"

---

103. Peeters, *Globalization*, 131–33.
104. Peeters, *Globalization*, 161–62.
105. Peeters, *Globalization*, 71.
106. Peeters, "Gender: An Anthropological Deconstruction and a Challenge for Faith," in *Woman and Man the "Humanum" in Its Entirety*, ed. Pontifical Council for the Laity (Vatican City:

without the qualifier "ideology." She concluded that "the concept of gender has the revolutionary objective of restructuring society according to a new model of gender equality."[107]

At times in her presentation Peeters brought up the concept of the ideology of gender. She argued that "gender is not an ideology in the proper sense of the term," because it did not flow from a master who created it like Marx or from a systematic great theory.[108] Later on in her presentation, Peeters correctly referred to gender ideology's attack on mothers and on man-woman complementarity. I was present at this conference, and in a public discussion I raised the question about whether we could ransom "gender" because it was our word from the beginning. Her clear response was that the meaning of gender could not be retrieved from its associations with an ideology of gender.

The Council for the Laity—Women's Section has *left the debate about gender open* by being willing to post articles written against the use of the word "gender" by Dale O'Leary and Marguerite Peeters alongside articles written by me in which I use the word "gender" in the sense of gender reality.[109] With the increasing urgency with which Peeters and O'Leary are expressing concern about using the word "gender," I felt that it was time to make a direct case for ransoming gender as part as an effort of new evangelization.

In 2006, the Pontifical Council for the Family produced a *Lexicon: Ambiguous and Debatable Terms Regarding Family Life and Ethical Questions*. In this lexicon, there are two essays on the meaning of "gender." In the article called "Gender," by Jutta Burggraf, after tracing the his-

---

Libreria Editrice Vaticana, 2010), 289–99, on the twentieth anniversary of John Paul II's Apostolic Letter *Mulieris Dignitatem*, 1998–2008.

107. Peeters, "Gender," 297.

108. Peeters, "Gender," 290. She stated correctly that "gender carries in its wake residue from feminism and Marxism."

109. For example, the Council for the Laity posted an article by Peeters entitled, "A New Global Ethics: Challenges for the Church, and an Interview with Marguerite A. Peeters on the Gender Theory." It also posted articles by Dale O'Leary on "A Woman's Perspective on Mainstreaming a Gender Perspective" and "Don't Say Gender When You Mean Sex." And during the same timeframes it posted articles by me that use gender basically to mean woman and man as the two ways of being human, in "*Mulieris Dignitatem* Twenty Years Later: An Overview of the Document and Challenges" and "Man-Woman Complementarity: The Catholic Inspiration," all available at www.laici.va/content/laici/en/sezioni/donna/articoli.html.

tory of the word, the question is left open about whether nor not to use the word "gender." While not accepting "the ideology of gender," Jutta Burggraf proposes a "gender perspective" that defends the right to differences between men and women and promotes co-responsibility in work and family.[110]

In the same *Lexicon*, Oscar Alzamore Revoredo defines gender in "An Ideology of Gender: Dangers and Scope." Drawing from the UN conference in Beijing, he states, "Gender refers to the relations between men and women based on the socially defined roles assigned to one sex or the other."[111] Then, drawing from his experience of the regional conference at Mar de Plato, Argentina, Revoredo cautions, "It becomes clear that the supporters of the gender perspective were advancing something more reckless, like, for example, 'a natural man or woman does not exist.'"[112] These two conflicting positions in the *Lexicon* of ambiguous terms leave the question of gender open for further study and clarification.

I am very grateful to the Women's Section of the Pontifical Council for the Laity for the decision to leave the question of the use of the word "gender" open at this time. In its posting for September–October 2013, *A Synthesis by the Women's Section—Pontifical Council for the Laity*, subtitled "Safeguarding the Human Being, Created as Man and Woman," summarizes the conflicting approaches to the use of the word and concept of "gender." In this document, written "fifteen years on from John Paul II's Letter to Women and from the 4th UN Conference on Women (1995–2010)," we read the following summary: "There was some doubt as to whether or not the term 'gender' ought to be used in the present context. Although the term is in itself neutral, it has become highly charged with ideology nowadays and using it can be confusing. However, other experts were in favour of its use as long as it is placed within the rich categories of a Christian anthropology."[113]

---

110. Jutta Burggraf, "Gender," in *Lexicon: Ambiguous and Debatable Terms Regarding Family Life and Ethical Questions*, ed. Pontifical Council for the Family (Front Royal, Va.; Human Life International, 2006), 408.

111. Oscar Alzamore Revoredo defines gender in "An Ideology of Gender: Dangers and Scope," in *Lexicon: Ambiguous and Debatable Terms regarding Family Life and Ethical Questions*, ed. Pontifical Council for the Family (Front Royal, Va.: Human Life International, 2006), 466.

112. Revoredo, "Ideology of Gender," 467.

113. A Synthesis by the Women's Section, "Safeguarding the Human Being, Created as Man

The document continued with a contribution by Maria Eugenia Cárdenas, who said that "if Catholics abide by the recommendation (to avoid using the term gender) they will leave the field open to radical feminists, who would eliminate the counter-balance achieved by the laity in many countries. If we refuse to use the term, radical groups will infiltrate with their own agenda faster."[114] The rest of my presentation is focused on providing a number of arguments to defend the continued use of the word "gender" and to distinguish gender reality from gender ideology in each context it is used.

Abandon Gender or Ransom Gender?

In this final section I offer several arguments to defend the claim that we should ransom the word and concept of "gender." In particular, my arguments discuss *why* we should ransom gender, *how* we could ransom gender, and some fruits of ransoming gender. The root of the concept of gender belongs to the beginning of Western history. It is for Catholics to have, to keep, and to foster if we accept the gift of the meaning that has been entrusted to us.

Ransoming Gender through Scripture and Philosophy
The Root of Gender in the Old Testament

A first step in ransoming gender reality is *to reclaim the meaning of the root "gen" in the word "generation"* as articulated in the Old Testament. The meaning of the root *"gen"* in its verb form is "to produce" or "to beget"; in its noun form it refers to offspring or kin. This meaning is explicit in early Jewish history. A clear example, dated variously between 1400 B.C. and 900 B.C., is found in book 5:1 of *Genesis*, which begins, "This is the book of the generations of Adam"; it continues through verse 32 marking off different periods of history in record-

---

and Woman," *Pontifical Council for the Laity* (September–October 2013): 44. Available at http://www.laici.va/content/laici/en/sezioni/donna.html (accessed October 4, 2013).

114. "Safeguarding the Human Being, Created as Man and Woman," 44–45.

ing the generations from Adam to Noah and his sons.[115] The root *"gen"* from the beginning of Judaism establishes the significance of the history of a people living in continuity generation after generation. It incorporates the act of sexual intercourse of a male and a female, of a man and a woman who become father and mother through their synergetic union. Thus we can also say that the concept of sex is inherently included within the concept of the root of generation, or *"gen."*

The Root of Gender in Ancient Greek Philosophy

A second example is found in ancient Western philosophy, more specifically in Aristotle's *Generation of Animals*, generally dated 350 B.C.. Aristotle examined in this philosophical text *how* animals generate. Higher animals are divided into male and female distinguished by the functions of their respective sexual parts or genitals: "They differ in their *logos*, because the male is that which has the power to generate in another..., while the female is that which can generate in itself, i.e., it is that out of which the generated offspring, which is present in the generator, comes into being."[116] Aristotle's erroneous hypotheses about how this generative activity is accomplished, with the male providing a single seed and the female providing only matter, was corrected over time. However, the concept of union of the male and female sexes is inherent within the concept contained in the root of generation or *"gen."*

The Root of Gender in the New Testament

A third example, some four centuries later, is seen in the beginning of the first book of the Gospel of *Matthew*: "The book of the genealogy of Jesus Christ, the Son of David, the son of Abraham." In verses 1:1–16 the Latin word *"genuit,"* with the root *"gen"* (meaning "to beget," "to generate," "to father"), is repeated thirty-nine times. In verse 17, the root *"gen"* is repeated in the word *"generationes"* (meaning "generations")

---

115. *Genesis: The Ignatius Catholic Study Bible*, introduction, commentary, and notes by Scott Hahn and Curtis Mitch (San Francisco: Ignatius Press, 2010); RSV Bible text, 2nd Catholic ed., introduction, 13–14, and Gn 5:1–10.

116. Aristotle, *Generation of Animals* I.ii.716a, trans. and ed. A. L. Peck (Cambridge, Mass.: Harvard University Press, 1943), 19–24.

four times. Christianity follows Jewish tradition in recording history through counting births following specific acts of sexual intercourse of a particular man and a particular woman. The Incarnation of Jesus Christ, a focal point of Christian history, transforms this history through the action of the Holy Spirit at the same time as it enters into it and depends upon it. Thus, as in the previous two examples, here the root "gen" in "generation" or "generate" incorporates within it the meaning of sex.

These three historical examples from the Old Testament, ancient Greek philosophy, and the New Testament reveal that for over one thousand years the concept of the root of gender, *"gen,"* was commonly used in both philosophy in Athens and theology in Jerusalem. *The Oxford Dictionary of English Etymology* records the growth of these theological and philosophical concepts in the development of the English language. It includes the following rich ever-expanding language family related to the root "gen": gender, genealogy, generate, generous (nobly born), genesis, genetic, gene, genial (nuptial, productive, joyous), genital (external generative organs), genitive (grammatical possessor or source), genius (innate capacity, of a person), genocide, gens, gentleman, gentlewoman, genuine, and the suffix -geny (for instance, progeny).[117] From this evidence alone, it would appear that the radical separation of the concept and word "sex" from the concept and word "gender" suggested by some twentieth-century authors is artificial indeed.

Ransoming Gender in Ordinary Language

Another approach is to ransom the *ordinary use* of the word "gender." John Paul II in *Fides et Ratio* encourages philosophers to test out the truth of their theories by the anchor of revelation. In the controversial sets of arguments about gender, we are very fortunate to have a clear and unambiguous revelation in Genesis that God created a human being as one of two and only two genders, as male and female; and he mandated them into a fertile union: "Go forth and multiply and fill the

---

117. *The Oxford Dictionary of English Etymology*, ed. Charles Talbut Onions (Oxford: Clarendon, 1966).

earth." This revelation sets the boundaries for philosophers' thought in a rich way.

Aristotle, as a natural philosopher, recognized that claims about nature or science are directed toward what is "always or for the most part" the case.[118] He realized that in natural beings there is always some "gray" area that allows for exceptions to be explained within the wider brackets of what is always or for the most part the case. In ordinary use of the word "gender," the human being is identified as male or female, man or woman. I would argue that the more the word "gender" is used by men and women within a Catholic understanding of the way in which a man and a woman are equally human persons and simultaneously two significantly different ways of being a human person, this will help ransom gender from its present ideological distortions.

This public defense of gender reality by using the word "gender" in its ordinary meaning is a method of new evangelization that will help to defend the integral gender complementarity that Saint John Paul II worked so hard to articulate. At the same time, several philosophers in the last century through the present have each one, individually and together, collaboratively provided a remarkably rich intellectual treasury of solid arguments to defend gender reality in the more technical sense against fallacious and distorted ideologies.

Ransoming Gender through
Catholic Philosophy

The twentieth century experienced an extraordinary dynamic within the intellectual community of Christian philosophers who were writing about the human person. In the first place, many who had received baptism later publicly rejected their faith. Among those are included the prominent philosophers Jean-Paul Sartre, Simone de Beauvoir, Michel Foucault, and Mary Daly and the social scientists Alfred Kinsey, Margaret Mead, and John Money. Second, during the same historical timeframe, many other philosophers converted to the Catholic faith. Among those

---

118. Aristotle, *Metaphysics* 1065a, ed. W. D. Ross (Oxford: Clarendon, 1924), 2–6.

are included Dietrich von Hildebrand, Edith Stein, Jacques and Raissa Maritain, and Gabriel Marcel. These Catholic philosophers formed a new intellectual community dedicated to defending the truth about the human person and about the integral complementarity of woman and man. In this endeavor they were joined by other Catholic philosophers such as Bernard Lonergan, Emmanuel Mounier, and Karol Wojtyla/John Paul II to provide a rich patrimony of deep philosophical thought that we can draw upon to ransom gender today.

The Thomistic Foundation for Ransoming Gender

Two crucial innovations by St. Thomas Aquinas of Aristotle's *hylomorphism* are the essential foundation of this patrimony. First, Thomas developed Aristotle's notion of the human soul as the form of the body by demonstrating that the *same* human soul operates both as form organizing a living material body and as spirit in communication with other spirits. Msgr. John Wippel summarizes Thomas' innovation: "*Hence it is through its essence that the human soul is a spirit and through that same essence that it is the form of the body.*"[119]

Second, Thomas's principle of the metaphysical unity of a human being whose soul is both spirit and form of the body provides a foundation for the development of the integral complementarity of woman and man. A *commensuration* of each soul to a particular body solves the problematic legacy that Aristotelian metaphysics of contrariety (that is, the female is a privative contrary of the male) left for the history of generation of females and males. In the *Summa contra Gentiles*, Thomas describes it this way:

Diversity, nevertheless, does not result from a diversity in the essential principles of the soul itself, nor from otherness in respect of the intelligible essence of the soul, but from diversity in the *commensuration of souls to bodies*, since this soul is adapted to this and not to that body, and that soul to another

---

119. John F. Wippel, *The Metaphysical Thought of Thomas Aquinas: From Finite Being to Uncreated Being* (Washington, D.C.: The Catholic University of America Press, 2000). Wippel continues, "[Thomas] argued that there are not two forms in the human soul but only one, which is its essence" (337).

body, and so in all other instances.... Now it is as forms that souls have to be adapted to bodies.[120]

This Thomistic development of the Aristotelian form/matter structure of reality has important implications for the concept of woman and of man as soul/body composite beings. The composite structure of real things is both *ontological*—that is, about how a real woman or a real man is in the world—and *epistemological*—that is, about how we come to know analogically what it is to be a woman or a man.

The Gift of German Phenomenology to Gender Identity

Phenomenology added a systematic account of different kinds of human experiences to the study of philosophical anthropology.[121] In 1923, Dietrich von Hildebrand, a convert to Catholicism in 1914, gave a public lecture, *On Marriage* [Die Ehe], in which he introduced the concept that in marriage a man and a woman are "metaphysically" complementary persons.[122] By this he means that each woman and each man is understood individually as a composite human soul/body unity with equal dignity, significant differentiation, and together with synergetic relations. Von Hildebrand continued to explore the nature of this complementary relation in 1966 in *Man and Woman: Love and the Meaning of Intimacy*, in which he characterized the relationship as "more in a face-to face position than side-by side" so that "it is precisely the general dissimilarity in the nature of both which enables this deeper penetration into the soul of the other ... a real complementary relationship."[123] Dietrich von Hildebrand also elaborated extensively on

---

120. Thomas Aquinas, *Summa contra Gentiles* II, ch. 81, para. 8, trans. J. F. Anderson (New York: Doubleday, 1956). See also W. Norris Clarke, SJ, *The One and the Many: A Contemporary Thomistic Metaphysics* (Notre Dame, Ind.: University of Notre Dame Press, 2001), 103.

121. See Robert Sokolowski, "What Is Phenomenology? An Introduction for the Uninitiated," *Crisis* 12, no. 4 (April 1994): 26–29; *Introduction to Phenomenology* (Cambridge: Cambridge University Press, 2000); and *Phenomenology of the Human Person* (Cambridge: Cambridge University Press, 2008).

122. Dietrich von Hildebrand, *Marriage: The Mystery of Faithful Love* (Manchester, N.H.: Sophia Institute Press, 1991), 14, 21, and 53–55.

123. Dietrich von Hildebrand, *Man and Woman: Love and the Meaning of Intimacy* (1966; repr. Manchester, N.H.: Sophia Press, 1992), 91.

different values in a personal gift of love in human relations.[124] In collaborating with his wife, Alice von Hildebrand, who wrote *The Privilege of Being a Woman*,[125] the couple brought their considerable philosophical talents to bear on the truth about woman's and man's respective identities.

Reacting against the unisex model of gender identity, in 1928 Edith Stein, a convert to Catholicism in 1922, concluded that "the Suffragettes erred so far as to deny the *singularity* of woman altogether."[126] Using the phenomenological method to analyze experiences of women and men, Stein suggested some unique ways a woman approaches human relations:

Her *point of view embraces the living and personal* rather than the objective; ... she tends towards *wholeness and self-containment* in contrast to one-sided specialization; ... [with an ability] to become a *complete person* oneself ... whose faculties are developed and coexist in harmony; ... [who] helps others to become *complete human beings*; and in all contact with other persons, [who] *respects the complete human being*.[127]

Stein joined to her phenomenological analysis a Thomistic metaphysical foundation for the ontological unity of the human person to uncover essential characteristics of the "lived experience of the body" in both women and in men.

In her *Essays on Women*, Stein articulated complementary hierarchical structures of female, feminine/masculine within a woman and of male, masculine/feminine within a man. In female/male complementarity, the female corporeal structure is oriented toward supporting new life within the mother while the male corporeal structure is oriented toward reproducing by detachment of seed as father. This difference leads to a different lived experience in which a feminine

---

124. Dietrich von Hildebrand, *The Nature of Love* (South Bend, Ind.: St. Augustine's Press, 2009).

125. Alice von Hildebrand, *The Privilege of Being a Woman* (Ann Arbor, Mich.: Sapientia Press of Ave Maria, 2002).

126. Edith Stein, *Essays on Women*, 2nd rev. ed. (Washington, D.C.: ICS, 1996), "Outline of Lecture given to Bavarian Catholic Women Teachers in Ludwifshafen on the Rhine, April 12, 1928," 27–28. Her italics.

127. Stein, *Essays*, introduction, 38–39. Her italics.

psychic structure receives the world inwardly more through the passions and a masculine psychic structure, because it is less affected by the body, receives the world more through the intellect. She proposes that a woman's intellect tends to comprehend the value of an existent in its totality while a man's intellect tends to judge in a compartmentalized manner. Further, she suggested that a woman's will tends to emphasize personal and holistic choices, while a man's will tends to emphasize exterior specialized choices. While Stein's contribution to gender complementarity tends at times to accept stereotyped generalizations about femininity and masculinity, she nonetheless discovered important psychic effects of the lived experience of a woman's cycles of ovulation and pregnancy and of a man's generation outside of his body.

In her later work on *Finite and Eternal Being*, after entering a Carmelite monastery and receiving the name "Sr. Benedicta of the Cross," she elaborated a rich analysis of four different kinds of forms that a woman has in her identity as a soul/body composite unity: her essential human form, her unique individual form given at her conception, her pure form or who she is created to be in the mind of God, and her empty form when others describe her characteristics. Stein's analysis opened up a dynamic understanding of the relation of actuality and potentiality beginning the moment a person "steps into existence" and continuing, as the person discovers his or her vocation, until death and beyond. Sr. Benedicta of the Cross followed von Hildebrand in giving an extensive analysis of love as the "mutual self-giving of persons."[128]

The Gift of French Personalism to Gender Reality
A striking aspect of the emergence of neo-Thomist philosophers in the early twentieth century is that in addition to their attempts to offer rigorous philosophical arguments to describe woman and man's identity and integral relations, they also began to foster dialogue with one another and to form new communities of philosophers. Edith Stein corresponded with Dietrich von Hildebrand, Hedwig Conrad-Martius, Roman Ingarden, and Jacques Maritain.

---

128. Edith Stein, *Finite and Eternal Being* (Washington, D.C.: ICS, 2002), 453–59.

Jacques and Raissa Maritain organized Thomistic study retreats in Meudon, one of which Edith Stein attended.[129] In 1932 Emmanuel Mounier organized a personalism study group in Paris with Jacques Maritain, and the group began publishing *Esprit*, a personalist review. Within two years Gabriel Marcel and Nicholai Berdjaev joined them. The goals of these communities of philosophers were not only to study the works of Thomas Aquinas but also to consider how some of his principles could be applied in ethical, educational, and political areas of common life in the world. In 1934 Mounier published an article in a Polish review (*Wiadomosci Literackie*) describing the personalist movement in France.

In the context of these dynamic series of conversations about the human person, the French personalists began to articulate and defend the fundamental principles of gender reality—namely, the equal dignity of women and men, the significant differences between women and men, and the synergetic effect of their integral relations. In 1936 Mounier published in *Esprit* an important article on the relation between personalism and woman's identity entitled, "La femme aussi est une personne" (Woman Is Also a Person).[130] Mounier critiqued cultural patterns that inhibited women's full development toward actualizing her personal dignity.

As lay men, many of the writings of the French personalists focused on dynamics of integral complementarity in the relationship in marriage. In one essay, Mounier argued against utilitarian and secular feminist critiques of marriage: "Man and woman can only find fulfillment in one another, and their union only finds its fulfillment in the child; such is their inherent orientation towards a kind of abundance and overflow, not to an intrinsic and utilitarian end."[131] Gabriel Marcel, a convert to Catholicism in 1929, added important dimensions to the analysis of synergetic relations among women and men. The first was a

---

129. See Jacques Maritain, chapter 5, "Thomist Study Circles and Their Annual Retreats (1919–1939)," in *Notebooks*, trans. Joseph W. Evans (Albany, N.Y.: Magi, 1984), 134–35.

130. Emmanuel Mounier, "La femme aussi est une personne" [Woman Is Also a Person], *Esprit* (June 1936): 292–97.

131. Mounier, *Personalism*, trans. Monks of St. John's Abbey (Notre Dame, Ind.: University of Notre Dame Press, 1952), 108.

rich insight into fatherhood: "I am a father!"... "It is impossible to reduce fatherhood to a biological category, and yet it belongs to the flesh. Adoption is a grafting."[132] Marcel's second insight was his description of the importance of the will in creative fidelity to one's spouse or child in lifelong, loving commitment.[133]

In 1936 Emmanuel Mounier published a nearly three-hundred-page manuscript entitled, *A Personalist Manifesto*. By 1938 it was translated from French into English and published in London, New York, and Toronto.[134] *The Personalist Manifesto* was translated into Polish and distributed underground in Poland during World War II. Underground copies of this work circulated in Poland radiating from philosophers associated with the Krakow Jagellonian University.

The Gift of Science to Gender Reality

Although Aristotle's original attempt at a scientific explanation of generation led to two thousand years of a kind of "sex ideology," identifying the human female with incapacity for contributing fertile seed to generation, his philosophy of science also advanced empirical observation that eventually led to science's great capacity for self-correction. Thus, by the eighteenth century, woman's active fertile contribution of egg to man's active fertile contribution of sperm opened the door to the discovery of the biological complementarity (equal dignity, significant differentiation, and synergetic union) of men and women.

The renewal of twentieth-century philosophy through neo-Thomism included attention to new developments in science. In 1927, at Lake Como, Niels Bohr first used the word "complementarity" to describe the wave-particle theory of light. Dietrich von Hildebrand applied the word "complementarity" two years later to the metaphysical relation of

---

132. Gabriel Marcel, *Metaphysical Journal 1943*, in *Presence and Immortality* (Pittsburgh, Pa.: Duquesne University Press, 1967), 91.

133. Marcel, *Homo Viator: Introduction to a Metaphysic of Hope*, trans Emma Craufurd (New York: Harper Torchbooks, 1962): "The Mystery of the Family," 68–97; "The Creative Vow as Essence of Fatherhood," 98–124; and "Obedience and Fidelity, 125–34"; see also Marcel, chapter 8, "Creative Fidelity," in *Creative Fidelity*, trans. Robert Rosthal (New York: Fordham University Press, 2002), 147–74.

134. Mounier, *A Personalist Manifesto* (London: Longmans, Green, 1938).

a woman and man in marriage. When Edith Stein entered the Carmelite convent she wrote a letter to her friend Hedwig Conrad-Martius asking her to send her information about the latest developments in the sciences of physics and of biology: "I would like very much to have an introductory presentation on the latest on atomic theory, if you have anything on that."[135] Stein herself had studied psychology in her undergraduate years and seriously integrated aspects of the psychology of woman and man's identities in her work in phenomenology.

The Thomistic renewal in Canada and the United States began through the work of Étienne Gilson (1927), Jacques Maritain (1933), and Bernard Lonergan, SJ (1940); it spread through universities in Toronto, Ottawa, Boston, Montreal, and Halifax. In 1942 Dietrich von Hildebrand's book on marriage was translated into English with its description of the metaphysical complementarity of husband and wife.[136] Bernard Lonergan wrote a review of it for the *Canadian Register* (Quebec edition), and he soon adopted the word "complementarity" to describe man-woman relations in his 1943 essay "Finality, Love, Marriage."[137] In his seminal work, *Insight*, Lonergan expanded the metaphysical principle of the *hylomorphic or form/matter* structure of a human person to include a woman or man's central form (traditional substantial form) organizing a hierarchical series of conjugate forms. These conjugate forms explain the complementary differentiation of the sexes at the level of "semi-fecundities" (referring to chromosomes, endocrine glands, anatomical structure, and physiological functions) and other levels of vital, psychic, sensitive, emotional, and higher nonorganic activities of reason and rational appetite. By 1957, Lonergan had combined the notion of complementarity in *Insight* to emergent probability to explain how conjugate forms organized by a central form in the human person moved through the sciences of physics, chemistry, biology, and psychology to philosophy and theology.

---

135. Stein, *Self-Portrait in Letters: 1916–1942* (Washington D.C.: ICS, 1993), nos. 228, 240.

136. See Allen, "Metaphysics of Form, Matter, and Gender," in *Lonergan Workshop* 12 (1996): 1–26.

137. Bernard Lonergan, "Finality, Love, Marriage," *Theological Studies* 4, no. 4 (1943): 477–510. Reprinted in *Collected Works of Bernard Lonergan*, ed. Frederick E. Crowe and Robert M. Doran (1967; repr. Toronto: University of Toronto Press, 1988), 17–52.

For Lonergan, sex and gender identity were not just a matter of division, but also of union. Sexual activity unites not only the semifecundities of spermatozoon and ovum but also their bearers: male and female complementary beings. A man and woman united in marriage may enter the spiritual realms of friendship and grace. In Poland, at the Catholic University of Lublin, M. A. Krapiec also integrated the advanced discoveries of science into a renewed Thomistic metaphysics. More recently, Msgr. Robert Sokolowski at the Catholic University of America has begun to explore the similarities and differences of forms and DNA. An important dimension of the gift of science is that the unity of the individual woman or man ontologically precedes any particular level of analysis.

The Gift of Polish Existential Personalism to Gender Reality

After World War II, in May 1946, Emmanuel Mounier was invited to lecture on personalism at the Jagallonian University in Krakow when Karol Wojtyla was a seminarian studying there. John Paul II tells us directly in *Gift and Mystery* that "my formation within the cultural horizon of personalism also gave me a deeper awareness of how each individual is a unique person."[138]

In 1954, M. A. Krapiec, chair of the department and professor of metaphysics, hired Karol Wojtyla to teach ethics at the Catholic University in Lublin. By 1960, Wojtyla published a book in Polish, which was later translated into English as *Love and Responsibility*. This text described some significant differences between a woman and a man and invited them to become aware and responsible for their engendered actions in relations with one another. Also, Wojtyla conveyed with respect to gender reality not only differences in one's male or female psyches but also the important challenge through acts of will to become virtuous men and women in their mutual relations.

Roman Ingarden, who had been a classmate of and frequent correspondent with Edith Stein in Germany, introduced her work to Karol

---

138. John Paul II, *Gift and Mystery: On the Fiftieth Anniversary of My Priestly Ordination* (New York: Doubleday, 1996), 94.

Wojtyla in Krakow. In *Rise, Let Us Be on Our Way*, Saint John Paul had this insightful thought to share: "In Krakow I also tried to maintain a good rapport with the philosophers: Roman Ingarden.... My personal philosophical outlook moves, so to speak, between two poles: Aristotelian Thomism and phenomenology. I was particularly interested in Edith Stein, an extraordinary figure, for her life story as well as her philosophy."[139]

In addition, in the 1950s, Karol Wojtyla had developed a collaborative friendship with Dr. Wanda Półtawska, a medical doctor and psychiatrist who specialized in the care of women.[140] Following these two different sources, Wojtyla noted that the monthly cycles of ovulation from puberty through menopause dispose a woman to receive new life and foster its growth.[141] This disposition is not a biological determinism because of a woman's free will; she can act against it through abortion or contraception, or she can act with it. In his later works as Pope John Paul II, he suggested that when a woman follows this disposition, her genius flourishes through the particular ways that she receives and fosters the growth of persons in her own sphere of activity. This feminine genius will flourish in spiritual maternity and intellectual maternity, as well as in physical maternity.[142]

In *Love and Responsibility*, Karol Wojtyla suggested that the inheritance of original sin tends to affect women differently in some respects than men; a woman tends to want to possess others (husband and children), while a man tends to want to dominate others (wife and children). A woman also tends to desire a man through sentimentality, while a man tends to desire a woman through sensuality. Wojtyla's text elaborates ways that men and women can take this "raw material of

---

139. John Paul II, *Rise, Let Us Be on Our Way* (New York: Warner, 2004), 90.

140. Ted Lipien, *Wojtyla's Women: How They Shaped the Life of Pope John Paul II and Changed the Catholic Church* (Winchester, UK: O Books, 2008), 285–309.

141. Karol Wojtyla, *Love and Responsibility* (San Francisco: Ignatius Press, 1981), 280: "Every woman can observe in herself the changes which occur in the relevant phase of the cycle. Apart from this there exist objective scientific methods known of biology and medicine, which help us to determine the moment of ovulation, i.e., the beginning of the fertile period."

142. See John Paul II, *Mulieris Dignitatem* (Apostolic Letter, August 15, 1988) (Boston: St. Paul Books and Media, 1988), nos. 30–31, and NCCB/USCC, *John Paul II on the Genius of Women* (Washington, D.C.: United States Catholic Conference, 1997), nos. 27 and 28.

love" and transform it into mature married love. Spiritual, intellectual, or physical paternity has some significantly different dispositions. Because a man generates outside of himself, John Paul II observes that he needs to make an act of will to "adopt" a child or wife as his own. Once this is done, he tends then to protect and to provide for them. In a later text, St. Joseph is described as manifesting these characteristics.[143] A man's genius is how he does this for members of his family or for his work projects and other significant attachments.

Attending the Second Vatican Council in the 1960s, then Bishop Wojtyla helped elaborate some important principles in *Dignitatis Humanis* and *Gaudium et Spes*. In sum: (1) Truth persuades by its own gentle power; (2) Human dignity and Christian solidarity for the common good are the two principles for guiding the interaction of the church with the world; and (3) Marriage and family are one of five urgent problems that need to be addressed by the church.

By 1969, Karol Wojtyla published the Polish version of his book entitled *The Acting Person*. This text integrated a Thomistic metaphysical foundation for the human person with a phenomenological elaboration of the dynamic experience of being a person with self-possession, self-determination, and self-government, called into authentic interpersonal relations.[144] It did not differentiate between men and women, but rather assumed their equal dignity as persons called to recognize the personalistic value of their actions (how each one redounds back on the person) and how to authentically participate in living the commandment of love.

At Lublin, M. A. Krapiec and Karol Wojtyla together supported higher education for Ursuline sister Zofia J. Zdybicka, and they also convinced her to join the philosophy department at KUL; eventually she became the chair and dean of philosophy. Father Krapiec also introduced a theory of existential analogies among human beings. This theory opened research into how women are existentially analogous to

---

143. John Paul II, *Guardian of the Redeemer* (*Redemptoris Custos*: Apostolic Exhortation, August 15, 1989) (Boston: St. Paul Books and Media, 1989), nos. 1–2, 7–8, 17, and 22.

144. Wojtyla, *The Acting Person*, trans. Andrzej Potocki (Dordrecht: D. Reidel, 1979).

one another in one way and how a woman and a man are existentially analogous to one another in a different way.[145] I can attest personally to the openness of Lublin existential personalism to the serious study of sex and gender identity with gender complementarity, as Sr. Zdybicka invited me in to give a series of four lectures to the students and faculty on this topic; two of these lectures were given in Fr. Krapiec's metaphysics class.

In 1974–75, Cardinal Wojtyla also elaborated his approach to building a community of persons in the family and through parenthood.[146] Later on he elaborated a theological foundation for complementary human vocations in the context of being called in likeness to the Divine Communion of Persons, as communions of knowledge and love. These themes are important for ransoming gender reality because they provide both the intellectual principles for the ransoming and practical applications of these principles in daily life.

The New Evangelization of the Meaning of "Gender"

After Karol Wojtyla became Pope John Paul II in October 1978, for the next twenty-five years he shared his great insights into the integral and complementary identities of woman and man from their creation through the fall and their redemption in Jesus Christ, True God and True Man. To summarize some key points he made: that God has created us male and female is revealed particularly in Genesis 2:23, and that our knowledge of man, what it is to be human, "passes through masculinity and femininity ... two reciprocally completing ways of 'being a body' and at the same time of being human—as two complementary dimensions of self-knowledge and self-determination and, at the same

---

145. See Allen, "A Woman and a Man as Prime Analogical Beings," *American Catholic Philosophical Quarterly* 66, no 4 (1992): 456–82.

146. See Wojtyla, chapter, 20, "The Family as a Community of Persons" (1974), and chapter 21, "Parenthood as a Community of Persons" (1975), in *Person and Community: Selected Essays*, ed. Andrew Woznicki, trans. Theresa Sandok, OSM (New York: Peter Lang, 1993), 315–42.

time two complementary ways of being conscious of the meaning of the body."[147]

An innovation of John Paul II, yet unrealized by most people, is that he uses the word "masculinity" *only* for men and "femininity" *only* for women. This is a change from preceding practices of many authors, including Edith Stein, who attributed both masculinity and femininity to each man or woman. John Paul II argued that our sex identity as male or female is "not only an attribute of our individual identity," it is "constitutive for the person" . . . "who is constituted by the body as 'he' or 'she.'"[148] The meaning of our gender identity essentially includes our sex, and it is not reducible to a style or to a role. It is a core of who we are at the most profound metaphysical level of our being. Exceptions in nature that do occur are embraced with love and compassion for their suffering and are welcomed into the communion of persons created by God and redeemed by Jesus Christ. But they do not change gender reality.

A further important innovation of St. John Paul II was to state that the meaning of masculinity is revealed to a man through his fatherhood, in biological and/or spirituality paternity, and the meaning of femininity is revealed to a woman through her motherhood, in biological and/or spiritual maternity.[149] This new insight is elaborated in depth in his analysis of the vocation to marriage and the conception, birth, and education of children. It also opens up to his wonderful analysis of the complementarity of vocations through the mystery of being living signs to one another of the love of the Bridegroom and the love in response of the Bride. The ordained priesthood participates in a particular way in being the living sign of Jesus Christ, the Bridegroom; a married couple together are a living sign of the love between the Bridegroom and the Bride, his church; and consecrated persons are the living eschatological sign of the love of the Bride for the Bridegroom.[150]

---

147. John Paul II, *Man and Woman He Created Them: A Theology of the Body*, trans Michael Waldstein (Boston: Pauline Books and Media, 2006) (General Audience of November 21, 1979), sect. 10, para. 1. Emphasis from the original text deleted.

148. John Paul II, *Man and Woman He Created Them*, sect. 10, para. 1.

149. John Paul II, *Man and Woman He Created Them*, sect. 21, para. 2.

150. See Allen, "*Mulieris Dignitatem* Twenty Years Later: An Overview of the Document and Challenges," *Ave Maria Law Review* 8, no. 8 (Fall 2009), and "Catholic Marriage and Feminism,"

Within all his many elaborations of this deep mystery of the relation of vocation to sex and gender identity, St. John Paul reveals the new evangelization of relations and gifts of self to others, in equal dignity, significant difference, and chaste love filled by the Holy Spirit in communion of persons for the redemption of the world. He has provided a rich treasury of philosophical, scriptural, and theological foundations for us to draw upon in the new evangelization of gender.

Many women philosophers and theologians have built upon John Paul II's invitation to develop a new feminism that is based on a sex and gender reality. In *Evangelium Vitae* no. 99, he called for this new evangelization: "In transforming culture so that it supports life, women occupy a place, in thought and action, which is unique and decisive. It depends on them to promote a 'new feminism.'"[151] Many contemporary Catholic authors have contributed in many different ways to the New Feminism.[152] John Paul added an urgency to this mission as an essential aspect of the new evangelization: "I address to women this urgent appeal: 'Reconcile people with Life.' You are called to bear witness to the meaning of genuine love, or that gift of self and of that acceptance of others which are present in a special way in the relationship of husband and wife, but which ought to be at the heart of every other interpersonal relationship."[153]

If the present virus of gender ideology is allowed to run wild, then many women and men will miss discovering their true vocations. They will be confused about what it means to be a human person, and they will be confused about what it means to be a woman or a man. They will be confused about the chaste ways to relate to one another in marriage and in celibate life.

---

in *The Church, Marriage, and the Family: Proceedings of the 27th Annual Fellowship of Catholic Scholars Convention*, ed. Kenneth D. Whitehead (South Bend, Ind.: St. Augustine's Press, 2007), 95–144.

151. John Paul II, *Evangelium Vitae: The Gospel of Life* (Boston: Pauline Books and Media, 1995), no. 99.

152. See, for example, Michelle M. Schumacher, ed., *Women in Christ: Towards a New Feminism* (Grand Rapids, Mich.: Eerdmans, 2004); Jo Garcia-Cobb, "In Focus: New Feminism," *Our Sunday Visitor* (August 16, 2009); and Francis Martin, *The Feminist Question: Feminist Theology in the Light of Christian Tradition* (Grand Rapids, Mich.: Eerdmans, 1994).

153. John Paul II, *Evangelium Vitae*, no. 99.

When we reflect on the incredible courage of those who began the Thomistic renewal in the context of the two world wars, we discover men and women who risked everything to defend the truth of the human person, the truth about woman and man as "always or for the most part" the two ways of being a human person. They followed the call of their specific vocations by offering their work, their suffering, and even their lives to defend this truth. Can we today do the same, standing on their shoulders, and fighting for the truth that persuades by its own gentle power?

CHAPTER 3

Woman and Man

Identity, Genius, and Mission

Deborah Savage

Since its initial publication as *The Original Unity of Man and Woman* in 1981, Pope St. John Paul II's widely studied work *A Theology of the Body* has generated widespread interest, debate, and scholarship.[1] His investigation into the sacramental meaning of the human body and its implications for our understanding of human sexuality and the complementarity of man and woman constitute an irreplaceable contribution, not only to the Magisterium but, indeed, to all of humankind. It is a beautiful teaching, a gift to the world at a time when human relationships have undergone a truly dramatic upheaval, leaving many confused and uncertain—and complicating our public and private lives in unexpected and often tragic ways.

It seems clear that the late Holy Father entered into his papacy in 1978 fully prepared to turn the church's attention toward the questions he explores in the theology of the body. The series of Wednesday audiences at which the teaching was given began almost immediately upon his elevation to pope and, significantly, practically simultaneously with

---

1. John Paul II, *The Original Unity of Man and Woman* (Boston: Daughters of St. Paul, 1981). John Paul's original text was revisited, retranslated, and reordered according to the late Holy Father's own schema by Dr. Michael Waldstein and republished under the title *Man and Woman He Created Them: The Theology of the Body* (Boston: St. Paul Media, 2006). All references in this chapter are to the Waldstein edition, cited hereafter as *TOB*.

the preparations that led up to the Synod on the Marriage and the Family in 1980. They ended four years later, not long after the publication of his Apostolic Exhortation *Familiaris Consortio* (On the Role of the Christian Family in the Modern World, 1981). John Paul himself states clearly that the purpose behind both of these initiatives was to provide a richer framework for grasping the truths at the heart of *Humanae Vitae*.[2] The two documents that resulted encouraged theologians in particular to "work out more completely *the biblical and personalistic aspects of the doctrine*" contained in Paul VI's controversial encyclical, launching decades of investigation into these questions on the part of the Magisterium and scholars.[3] By 1987, these efforts prompted the church fathers to call more specifically for a rigorous investigation of two fundamental questions: How are we to understand the Creator's *purpose* in determining that human beings would always exist as only either a man or a woman? And what are the consequences of that decision?[4]

These two questions can be said to frame the purpose of this chapter. It is an investigation of what scripture reveals and what reason can conclude concerning "the meaning and dignity of being a woman and of being a man."[5]

Now, without question, this entire body of work has been amplified in particular by John Paul's profound reflections on women. Indeed, they constitute a seismic shift in the church's understanding of the dignity and vocation of woman. But the late Holy Father's examination should be seen as part of a longer papal tradition; the changing roles of women that marked the last 150 years sparked a real concern and a genuine interest on the part of the *Magisterium*. Papal reflections on the "woman question" actually began with Pope Pius XII and has found

---

2. *TOB*, sect. 133, para. 1–4.
3. *TOB*, sect. 133, para. 2.
4. In October 1987, the Synod of Bishops on the Vocation and Mission of the Lay Faithful resulted in thirty-four propositions, one of which was the recommendation that further study be devoted to the anthropological and theological bases of the "dignity of being a woman and being a man"; *Enchiridion* I.xxx. John Paul's August 1988 Apostolic Letter *Mulieris Dignitatem* was one response to this recommendation. The synod's propositions also provided the basis of his December 1988 Post-Synodal Apostolic Exhortation *Christifideles Laici*.
5. Pope St. John Paul II, *Mulieris Dignitatem*, no. 1.

expression in the thought of every pope since 1945.⁶ The Second Vatican Council's "Closing Address to Women" is singularly eloquent in its affirmation of women's vocation; its plea for them to "keep humanity from not falling" is both heartfelt and urgent.⁷ Thus, Pope Francis's recent call for the development of a "theology of women" is but a possible next step in a trajectory that the church has been following throughout the latter half of the twentieth century.⁸

Still, it must be acknowledged that John Paul's teachings in this regard are clearly unprecedented in their scope and significance. Perhaps more than any other pope in history, his entire legacy is marked by his tireless pursuit of an authentic understanding of womanhood. It is no accident that he has been referred to as the "feminist Pope."⁹ But it also seems clear that, perhaps out of a recognition of the need for an unequivocal affirmation of women and their place in life and culture, arguably quite timely at this point in history, John Paul made it his special mission to focus primarily on the dignity of woman, leaving out any extended treatment of what it might mean to be man.¹⁰

His teachings on women are remarkable for many reasons, but

---

6. See Pius XII, *Women's Duties in Social and Political Life: Address of His Holiness Pope Pius XII to Members of Various Catholic Women's Associations* [Questa Grande Vostra Aduntana], October 21, 1945 (London: Catholic Truth Society, 1955); Pope St. John XXIII, Encyclical Letter *Pacem in Terris*, April 11, 1963, 41; Second Vatican Council, Closing Address to Women, 1965, 1; Pope St. Paul VI, "Discourse à La Commission d'etude sur la Femme dans las Societe et dans l'Eglise" (January 1976), 4; "Discorso Alle Partecipanti al Congresso Nazionale Del Centro Italiano Femminile" (December 1976); Pope St. John Paul II, Apostolic Letter, *Mulieris Dignitatem* (August 15, 1988); Encyclical Letter *Evangelium Vitae* (March 25, 1995), especially no. 99; Pope Benedict XVI, Easter Monday Message, 2012. Read an account of the message at http://vaticaninsider.lastampa.it/en/the-vatican/detail/articolo/settimana-santa-holy-week-semana-santa-14170/; Pope Francis, "Address to the Participants in the National Congress Sponsored by the Italian Women's Center," January 2014.

7. Vatican Council II, "Closing Address to Women," December 8, 1965, https://w2.vatican.va/content/paul-vi/en/speeches/1965/documents/hf_p-vi_spe_19651208_epilogo-concilio-donne.html.

8. In 1971, Pope Paul VI set up a special commission to study the problems surrounding the effective promotion of the dignity and responsibility of women.

9. There are many resources that document the "feminism" of Pope John Paul II. For one particular example, please refer to Mary Ann Glendon's fine essay "The Pope's New Feminism," *Crisis* 15, no. 3 (March 1997): 28–31.

10. The one exception to this is his wonderful Apostolic Letter on Joseph, *Redemptoris Custos*, promulgated in August 1989, exactly one year after the publication of *Mulieris Dignitatem*. We will come to this later in the chapter.

perhaps, above all, because they have introduced into the Catholic tradition an entirely new category in the church's understanding of the human person: the so-called feminine genius.[11] This quality or characteristic, ascribed universally to all women and epitomized most perfectly by the person of Mary the Mother of God, has become an integral part of the church's magisterial teaching.[12] The genius of women, as well as the complementarity that characterizes the relationship of man and woman, are now tenets of Catholic doctrine.[13]

Certainly, these are important developments, especially in light of our contemporary context. The church's profoundly affirming teaching on women has been a surprise to many and a rich resource in our efforts to evangelize the culture. But the account that follows is grounded in the conviction that any further exploration of the "genius" of woman cannot properly take place without a concomitant investigation into the "genius" of man. In fact, it can be argued that if, as St. John Paul demonstrates and human experience confirms, man and woman are complementary creatures, reflecting two "equal" but different ways of being in the world, then we must also conclude that the nature and genius of woman actually cannot be understood apart from that of man.[14] This point seems to be confirmed by John Paul himself in his Apostolic Exhortation *Christifideles Laici* ("On the Vocation and the Mission of the

---

11. I would argue that Saint John Paul II uses this phrase as primarily a rhetorical device to describe what is certainly a phenomenologically accessible reality but that it was not his intention to argue that this represents a newly discovered power of the soul or supplant more ancient terms such as "charism."

12. Pope John Paul II, "On the Dignity and Vocation of Women," *Mulieris Dignitatem*, 1988; *Letter to Women*, June 29, 1995.

13. The *Compendium of the Social Doctrine of the Church* makes frequent mention of both complementarity and the feminine genius. See, for example, *Compendium of the Social Doctrine of the Church* (Vatican City: Libreria Ed. Vaticana, 2004), nos. 146, 147, 295, just to name a few.

14. I am grateful to Dr. Joseph Atkinson for pointing out to me that an undifferentiated reliance on the word "equal" is problematic since, in mathematics, "equal" means "interchangeable," a notion that simply cannot be meaningful in an investigation into the question of the nature of woman and man. Indeed, it is this precise issue that must be clearly understood and disputed. It may have legitimate uses in a political context, for certainly men and women are "equal" under the law, though even there it can lead to social policies that refuse to recognize the differences that exist between men and women (in the area of family law, for example). Any reference to the "equality" of man and woman in this essay is an allusion to their fundamental dignity that both possess in equal measure, since both are created by God and both are instantiations of the same substantial form, the rational soul.

Lay Faithful in the Church and in the World"), where he declares unequivocally that:

> the only condition that will assure the rightful presence of woman in the Church and in society is a more penetrating and accurate consideration of the *anthropological foundation for masculinity and femininity* with the intent of clarifying woman's personal identity in relation to man, that is, a diversity yet mutual complementarity, not only as it concerns roles to be held and functions to be performed, but also, and more deeply as it concerns her make-up and meaning as a person.[15]

If we are to take the next step in this trajectory, it must be with the full realization that a one-sided emphasis on the *feminine* genius would reflect its own kind of gender polarity (where one sex is considered superior to the other) and would almost certainly risk distorting our vision of the integral complementarity that characterizes the reciprocal relationship of man and woman.[16] Given the current crisis of understanding of masculinity, femininity, and gender in Western culture, it is urgent that we affirm and communicate to the world at large that it is this very "uni-duality" that gives man and woman their *mission*, for "to this unity of the two God has entrusted not only the work of procreation and family life, but the creation of history itself."[17] For this reason, our task in this chapter is to explore what might constitute a "theology of *complementarity*" and not of *women*. We simply must seek the devel-

---

15. Pope St. John Paul II, Apostolic Exhortation *Christifidelis Laici*, December 30, 1998, 50; italics in original.

16. Sister Prudence Allen, "Man-Woman Complementarity: The Catholic Inspiration," *Logos: A Journal of Catholic Thought and Culture* 9, no. 3 (Summer 2006). Sr. Allen does not make this particular argument in her essay, but her explanation of the various forms of gender polarity and her criteria for evaluating theories of complementarity are normative for this investigation. As evidence of the urgent nature of these questions, I would point the reader toward two particular texts. The first, *Women After All: Sex, Evolution, and the End of Male Supremacy* (New York: W. W. Norton, 2015), by Melvin Konner, M.D., argues that women are in fact superior to men and always have been. The nature of the crisis can be understood by considering Konner's arguments in light of the careful analysis found in Nicholas Eberstadt's recent book *America's Invisible Crisis: Men without Work* (West Conshohocken, Pa.: Templeton, 2016). Men in our culture are indeed in crisis. Just one example: there are more men unemployed *and no longer seeking work* in 2016 than there were during the Great Depression.

17. *Compendium of the Social Teaching of the Church*, no. 147, quoting John Paul II, *Letter to Women*, 8.

opment of a comprehensive theological anthropology that can account for the full meaning of both man and woman. Only this will ground an informed response to the confusion about it that has captured our culture.

The theological framework I propose takes its point of departure from St. John Paul's own starting place in the *Theology of the Body*, the two creation accounts found in Genesis 1 and 2, but viewed here through a more thorough exploration of the lens provided by the metaphysical anthropology of St. Thomas Aquinas, itself refracted through a more properly Hebraic anthropology.[18] This investigation has led to some additional insights into the texts. And so, in what follows, though I rely on John Paul's account to some extent, I also offer my own exegesis of Genesis 1 and 2. Since our purposes here are more limited, I only provide a summary of what I have demonstrated more fully elsewhere.[19] It provides the backdrop within which both the equal dignity of man and woman and what distinguishes them from each other can be understood.[20] It permits me to demonstrate that an account of *both the masculine and feminine "genius"* can be derived from the opening chapters of Genesis.

We then turn to our main purpose in this chapter: to fill an indisputable lacuna in the tradition by offering a fuller investigation of the particular genius of man, focusing on the specific gifts brought by men to the tasks of human living.[21] This culminates in an examination of the consequences of the fall and the differing ways in which original sin manifests in man and woman. Last, we consider the possibility that Jo-

---

18. For a fuller account, see Deborah Savage, "The Nature of Woman in Relation to Man: Genesis 1 and 2 through the Lens of the Metaphysical Anthropology of Thomas Aquinas," *Logos: A Journal of Catholic Thought and Culture* 18, no.1 (Winter 2015): 71–93.

19. I believe this exploration constitutes a legitimate development of John Paul's own project.

20. The research presented here into the masculine genius was originally published in Savage, "The Genius of Man," in *Promise and Challenge: Catholic Women Reflect on Feminism, Complementarity, and the Church*, ed. Mary Hasson (Huntington, Ind.: Our Sunday Visitor, 2015). That essay was informed by my original research into the complementarity of man and woman published in *Logos* and mentioned earlier. The account I offer here reflects some important refinements of the general theory found in both essays.

21. Since the main contribution of this chapter is to broaden our understanding of what might constitute the "masculine genius," I will provide a more detailed account of that aspect of the theory.

seph, Mary's spouse, is an icon of this masculine genius in a manner analogous to Mary's embodiment of the feminine. We close with a reflection on the possibility that both masculine and feminine genius are in fact both natural *and supernatural* realities that only arrive at their fullest expression through the action of grace.

Genesis 1 and 2 Revisited

Our starting place is found in the opening pages of *The Theology of the Body*. In these pages, the late Holy Father argues that we can derive the meaning of man from the two distinct creation accounts found in Genesis 1 and 2, first as an objective reality created in the image of God and, second, in the aspect of his subjectivity.

St. John Paul states that the "powerful metaphysical content" hidden in Genesis 1 has provided "an incontrovertible point of reference and a solid basis" for metaphysics, anthropology, and ethics and has been a source of reflection throughout the ages for those "who have sought to understand 'being' and 'existing.'"[22] But in Genesis 2, he goes on to say, the depth to be uncovered in this second (though said to be historically earlier) creation account has a different character; it "is above all subjective in nature and thus in some way psychological." Here we find man in the concrete, as a subject of self-understanding and consciousness; here the account of the creation of man refers to him "especially in the aspect of his subjectivity."[23]

Those familiar with the late Holy Father's extensive body of work will recognize these two categories, being and existence and personal subjectivity, as foundational to the thought of Karol Wojtyła/John Paul II. Indeed, throughout his writings, this philosopher pope frequently contrasts the philosophy of being and the philosophy of consciousness and seeks ways to reconcile and synthesize their claims. His own anthropology is a creative development of the Aristotelian-Thomistic account of man, which, he argues, though it provides the necessary

---

22. *TOB*, sect. 2, para. 4.5, pp.136–37.
23. *TOB*, sect. 3, para. 2.1, pp. 138–39.

"metaphysical terrain" in the dimension of being and paves the way for the realization of personal human subjectivity, leaves out an adequate investigation of lived human experience and thus lacks an essential component of what it means to be an actual living person.[24] The thrust of his effort is to capture the meaning of human personhood in light of both the objective nature of the person and his lived experience as the subject of his own acts.[25]

This is the subtext of John Paul's claim that the two creation accounts provide the scriptural basis of an account of man qua man and man in his subjectivity. However, John Paul does not fully exploit it, stating that his intent is not to pursue this more metaphysical account of the soul in union with the body but to focus instead on the "meaning of one's own body."[26] But it is precisely this claim that informs our investigation here.

I have shown elsewhere that a careful analysis of these two creation accounts, when considered in light of Aquinas's metaphysical account of the soul in union with the body, does support John Paul II's proposal: they reveal the meaning of both man in the abstract—that is, man qua man—and man in the concrete, created as male and female.[27] Here we will take an additional, preliminary step and look at John Paul's claim through the lens of two central principles of Hebraic anthropology: the notion of "corporate personality" and the Hebraic theory of the soul. We will see that a closer read of the creation accounts through a more properly Hebraic anthropology also supports the more philosophical

---

24. Karol Wojtyła, "Subjectivity and the Irreducible in the Human Being," in *Person and Community* (New York: Peter Lang, 1993), 212. See also Savage, "The Centrality of Lived Experience in Wojtyła's Account of the Person," *Roczniki Filozoficzne* [Philosophical Annals] 61, no. 4 (January 2014): 19–51.

25. See, in particular, John Paul II, *Love and Responsibility* and *The Acting Person*, as well as *Fides et Ratio* and several essays in *Person and Community*.

26. Pope St. John Paul II, *TOB*, sect. 7, para. 1–2. He certainly does explore the meaning of Genesis 1 and 2 in light of this proposal. But he does not explicitly extend his philosophical investigation to account fully for the claim that Genesis 1 concerns the nature of man in the abstract, while Genesis 2 is a description of man in the subjective sense. To do so would have required what we are investigating here: an attempt to look at Genesis 1 and 2 through the lens of the Thomist account of man, both in the abstract and in the concrete.

27. Savage, "Nature of Woman in Relation to Man." See note 8. I have, however, made rather significant corrections and refinements in the version offered here.

analysis proposed by John Paul II.[28] The summary of that analysis that follows will illuminate the essential "equality" of man and woman, while providing the necessary foundation for an exploration of the genius of man and of woman. A few general comments about these two accounts as stand-alone texts are in order before we look at them together.

Genesis 1

The specific pericope of interest to us first is Genesis 1:26–27. At 1:26, God says, "Let us make man (*adam*) in our image"; at 1:27 we read, "So God created man (*ha'adam*) in his own image, in the image of God he created him (*otho*); male and female (*zâchâr* and *nikevah*) he created them (*otham*)."[29]

The starting place for my hypothesis is the use of the terms *adam* in the first passage and *ha'adam* in the second. These will provide us with our point of departure and allow us to claim that the first cre-

---

28. This constitutes a major refinement to the theory I have proposed in previous iterations. Those earlier attempts were limited to a strictly philosophical analysis of the texts in question. I have had to conclude that interpreting Genesis 1 and 2 through the lens of scholastic philosophical categories bears the risk of ascribing meaning to the text that it really doesn't have. For example, the Semitic worldview does not contain the notion of "substantial form" or the distinction between "substance and accident." These terms were introduced into the tradition by Aristotle, in particular, and subsequently leveraged by Aquinas. They are categories essential to the metaphysical lens employed here. But before we can employ that lens, we must account for the more properly Hebraic anthropology at work in Genesis 1 and 2. However, we will see that the validity of John Paul's claim actually is even more apparent once we take that step. I am forever in debt to Dr. Joseph Atkinson for pointing this out to me and for his help in identifying the key principles at work. A more integrated version of this analysis can be found in "Redeeming Woman: A Response to the 'Second Sex' Issue from within the Tradition of Catholic Scriptural Exegesis," *Religions* (Fall 2020).

29. As I am not a scripture scholar, I am indebted to several scholars who translate and interpret these passages: first, Monsignor Michael Magee, chair of the Systematic Theology Department and professor of sacred scripture at St. Charles Borromeo Seminary in Philadelphia, who helped with the meaning of the original Hebrew texts and affirmed my hypothesis. Dr. Joseph Atkinson, associate professor of scripture at the John Paul II Institute in Washington, D.C., has also confirmed aspects of my interpretation and helped me to extend it. Further research is underway to investigate his suggestion that I consider my theory through the lens provided by a more properly biblical anthropology. Dr. Michael Waldstein, editor of the definitive text of John Paul II's *Theology of the Body* and professor of theology at the University of Steubenville, has been extremely helpful in assisting me to refine my interpretation.

ation account reveals that man and woman are both instantiations of the same human nature, with all that this implies. My argument begins with a consideration of the meaning of the word *adam*, traditionally translated as "man." It is the full meaning of this term that we need to investigate first. We will start with a consideration of the two principles central to Hebraic anthropology mentioned earlier: the meaning of "corporate personality" and its relationship to the theory of the soul.

It can be difficult for those invested in modern notions of the person as an autonomous, self-determining individual to grasp how profoundly different is the point of departure for the Hebraic account of the person. Its starting place is the principle of the "corporate personality."[30] It is this concept that provides the first hermeneutical key to interpreting the biblical texts under investigation. It will allow us to unpack the intended meaning of *adam* and *ha'adam*.

In the Semitic account of the person, itself derived from scripture, the individual is never, even in his concrete existence, an atomistic self, isolated from the community in which he is imbedded.[31] The individual person is an instantiation of the "organic unity" constituted by an ontologically prior corporate reality, not in a metaphorical or symbolic sense, but in terms of what one scholar refers to as a "single group consciousness."[32] This is the principle of corporate personality; it is a reference to the idea that the "one" represents the "many" and the many are contained in the one.[33] That is, the individual stands as *both* the one and the many. The community is *literally* embodied in the individual whose own existence renders present (in real time and space) both past and future generations.[34]

---

30. Dr. Atkinson argues that the idea of the "corporate personality" is the most promising principle for grasping the anthropology at work in the Old Testament; see Atkinson, *Biblical and Theological Foundations of the Family* (Washington, D.C.: The Catholic University of America Press, 2014), 163. I am immeasurably indebted to Dr. Atkinson for both his work and his guidance in this area. For a thorough treatment of the meaning of the Hebraic principle of corporate personality and a comprehensive review of the literature on the topic, see ibid., 161–92. The definitive text on this topic is a work by H. Wheeler Robinson, *Corporate Personality in Ancient Israel* (Philadelphia. Fortress, 1967).

31. Dr. Atkinson offers an analysis of the evidence from scripture in chapter 6; Atkinson, *Biblical and Theological Foundations*, 170–73.

32. Ibid., 164, here quoting Robinson.

33. Ibid., 165.

34. Ibid.

In this account, the individual is neither absorbed into the community nor ontologically cut off from it. He does not suffer a loss of personal identity; it is intimately and organically connected to the community. He is indeed an expression of the "corporate personality." The Semitic worldview thus held the "personal and corporate aspects of the person in a dynamic, positive tension."[35] It is a form of "biblical personalism which proclaims the integrity of the individual person in relation to the group, while at the same time admitting that the individual person can ... represent the entire group."[36]

This vision of the person as a reflection of a corporate personality is grounded in the Hebrew account of the soul (*nepesh*). In this view, the soul is not "infused" into the body of an individual in the sense that two "parts" come together to form one whole, as more modern formulations of the soul in relation to the body tend to express. Instead, the person, in his total essence, *is his soul*, which is itself organically linked to the ontological reality of the entire community, past, present, and future. It is the Hebraic account of the soul that allows for the tradition's further claim that the individual person always exists as part of a much larger reality, which is constitutive of his existence and of which he is the concrete expression.[37] Here we see clearly that, in biblical anthropology, the "oscillation" between the one and the many takes place at the level of the concretely existing person, instantiated as he is by a human soul that is itself organically united to the whole community.

This admittedly brief excursus into Hebraic anthropology prepares us to return to our text and consider the meaning of *adam* and *ha'adam* in light of these two principles. We will take up the term *adam* first.[38] We find it at Genesis 1:26, when God says, "Let us make man (*adam*) in our image." We now know that the translation of *adam* as "man" does not

---

35. Ibid., 168.

36. Ibid., 166–67. Dr. Atkinson is citing Jean de Fraine, *Adam and the Family of Man* (Staten Island, N.Y.: Alba House, 1965), 14–15. The original quote is from A. M. Dubarle, "Melange Lebreton," *RSR* 39, no. 1 (1951/53): 59.

37. Atkinson, *Biblical and Theological Foundations*, 173–75. See also Johannes Pedersen, *Israel: Its Life and Culture* (London: Oxford University Press, 1959), i–ii, 99.

38. It is important to note that, though we have always thought of the main characters in these first two chapters of Genesis as Adam and Eve, only Eve is ever actually named—and even then, not until after the fall. The reference here is most certainly *not* to Adam, the husband of Eve.

adequately capture the actual meaning of the term. Indeed, as we will see in a moment, the only thing that comes close to its meaning in English translation is the signifier "man *as such*" or the familiar "man per se." The Hebrew author of Genesis 1 is referring here to *adam* (itself taken from *adama*, or earth) as an instantiation of the "corporate personality" referenced earlier. The creation of *adam* signifies the creation of the whole human race rather than merely an individual. But while *adam* contains all members of the community, it also retains connotations of personhood and concreteness. Here we see the significance of the "oscillation" between the one and the many so essential to biblical personalism. But unlike the signifier "man per se," it is not an abstraction; the Hebraic reference is always to a concrete existent and therefore includes a bodily existence. And since this moment in the text is a reference to the creation of the first human being (and again, not the abstraction "man per se"), it must be interpreted to mean that the first human being was male. However, as we have seen, simultaneously contained within that existent, indeed, already present within *adam*, is the first woman. And while the connotation of *adam* extends to all of humanity, this reality can only take on a concrete existence through the creation of the first woman, something made clear in the very next passage.[39]

At Genesis 1:27 we read, "So God created man (*ha'adam*) in his own image, in the image of God he created him (*otho*); male and female (*zâchâr* and *nikevah*) he created them (*otham*)."[40]

The meaning of *ha'adam* is easily stated: *ha'* is a definite article, and

---

39. Though '*adam* can be used to designate the individual man so called, and another individual man, what is meant in a particular passage would be clear either from the context or from the use of the definite article with it: viz., if the reference is to *hâ'adam*, it would refer back to some man already indicated from the context. In Genesis 1:27, the "man" already indicated from the context is precisely the individual man who also stands for the collective: the word '*adam* mentioned in v. 26 is without the definite article and therefore can be said to indicate man *as such*. Thus, '*adam* is a reference to man per se, not to an individual or particular human being. A different word—either *hâ'adam* or *'ish*— would have been used (both these terms are used in both the first and second creation accounts) if the intention were to refer to the individual man or that particular man whom the tradition has come to refer to as Adam, the husband of Eve. So, it is really not going too far to say that if there were a reference to the notion of man *qua* man in Hebrew, it would be '*adam*.

40. *Otho* is a contraction of the untranslatable object marker (*oth*) and the masculine pronoun (*o*). *Otham* is the object marker contracted with the masculine plural pronoun (*am*). The grammatical gender is masculine, which is the "default" gender for a mixed group of males and females.

the reference now is to *the* man. The text has introduced a new level of specificity to the creation of *adam* but has now declared *adam*'s existence as embodied in manifestly masculine and feminine form. Thus the priceless dignity afforded the first *adam*, created in the image and likeness of God, is extended to *zachar* and *nikevah*. It is *zachar* and *nikevah* who are instructed then to "be fruitful and multiply, fill the earth and subdue it" at Genesis 1:28. Here we can anticipate the differentiation that will become more explicit in the second creation account (Genesis 2:22); Genesis 1 reveals that it issues out of a unity that already existed in the original "one."[41] And so, though there is an order to creation that places man in the position of primacy, this in no way compromises the dignity or ontological status of woman. This order will repeat itself in Genesis 2, where it will become even more clear that woman possesses a value that mirrors that of man.

We are now prepared to consider John Paul's claim that the first creation account is a reference to man in the "objective" sense—that is, man *qua* man, or man in the abstract. Does the text support such an interpretation?

The metaphysical anthropology of St. Thomas Aquinas, though grounded in experience and observation of the human person, his powers, and his acts, employs the method of abstraction—that is, it prescinds from the individuating conditions of matter to arrive at more general, universal principles. All existing things are reflections of two principles, form and matter (if inanimate), soul and body (if living). Man *as such*, though an abstraction, is understood to be a union of these two principles, a union of both body and soul, possessing a rational nature, intellect, will, and freedom. This is "man" in the universal sense, and every individual instantiation of a rational soul, both male and female, is an expression of this universal human nature.

We have seen that ancient Semitic thought did not have the concept of a universal human nature or the notion of a "substantial form," that which makes something what it is essentially. These were terms intro-

---

41. Atkinson, *Biblical and Theological Foundations*, 171. Dr. Atkinson is here referring specifically to Genesis 2, but given (as we will see) that similar terms are used, this can also be applied to Genesis 1.

duced by the Greeks. But given what we now know about the meaning of *adam* as an expression of a "corporate personality" containing all of humanity, we can argue that it is perfectly legitimate to say that if there were a reference to the notion of man *qua* man in Hebrew it would be *'adam*. In this context *adam* is clearly a reference to man in the *universal* sense. So, when God says, "Let us make *adam* in our image," we can safely say that the reference is an approximate equivalent of our concept of man per se. That is, it can serve as an approximation of or reference to the creation of the instantiation of the "substantial form" that constitutes the human creature.[42]

The significance of this conclusion, in light of contemporary concerns for the "equality" of men and women, would be hard to overstate. It shows definitively, now in philosophical terms, that scripture *itself* reveals man and woman to be equally human. Man and woman, here at the level of the species, are both instantiations of the same substantial form and are therefore equally endowed with intellect, will, and freedom. All men and women who, together, comprise the human species, are equally human in every respect. They are both ontologically absolute subjects, possessing individuality, human agency, and the powers and potencies definitive of the rational soul.

This analysis has shown that John Paul II is justified in arguing that Genesis 1:26–27 is concerned with the creation of man in the objective sense, a formulation that, though it corresponds to the categories employed in the metaphysical anthropology of the Aristotelian-Thomistic tradition, finds a correspondence in the Hebraic account of the person. Both approaches demonstrate from scripture that man and woman are equally human reflections of the principle of equal dignity. But this is

---

42. The word *'ish*, on the other hand, designates specifically the male, the concrete individual man, because the word *zâchâr* is the one used in an adjectival sense for "male" (it is related to the word for "remember," perhaps because of the computation of genealogy through the male line). Sometimes *'ish* is also used in the sense of "each one, each man." The word *'ish* is not used at all until Genesis 2:23, right after the woman is created and Adam is naming her *ishshâh*—while saying this is because she is taken from the *'ish*. To avoid any illegitimate leaps in interpretation, the best way to maximize care and precision would be to say that, of all the terms available in Hebrew, the one that would have to be adopted to designate what later philosophy would refer to as man in the abstract would have to be *'adam*. It is this word that stands for "man" as the English language has traditionally and collectively used the word; it corresponds to the Greek *anthrôpos*, the Latin *homo*, the German *Mensch*, or the Polish *człowiek*.

not to say that they are interchangeable. We still need to consider that which differentiates them, a topic taken up in the next section of the essay.

Genesis 2

The first account has established that man and woman are equal in dignity. In the second account, we begin to see what differentiates them. It is here that, according to John Paul II, God creates man and woman in their personal subjectivity. At Genesis 2:7, man (referred to here as *hâ'adam*, or the man) is fashioned from *adama*, from the earth; he is the first human being; we know now that he is a reflection of both the one and the many. Gradually he realizes that he is alone. And so, in a separate, creative act at Genesis 2:22, woman is *made* or *built (banah)* out of one of the man's ribs (*tsela*). Here God brings forth woman from the already existing ha'adam, who is himself made in the divine image. And thus both become the bearers of that image, both possess absolute value and dignity. The man declares "here at last is bone of my bone, flesh of my flesh." He recognizes woman as a person like himself. Indeed, she is his mirror image and, with her appearance, ha'adam awakens to his own subjective existence. Both God and the man are finally content that a proper helper (*ezer*) has been found.[43] But what must get our attention immediately is the fact that *it is not until this moment in the text* (Genesis 2:22) that the sacred author refers to man and woman *for the first time* as concrete subjects of existence, as real existing persons. They are *only* now *'ish* and *ishshâh*: man and woman as *actual*. As John Paul II points out, there is no *'ish* without *ishshâh*, for it is not until *ishshâh* appears that the man, previously referred to *ha'adam*, is finally referred to as *'ish*. Though man maintains the place of primacy (*ishshâh* is made from *'ish*), the plain meaning of the text is clear: there is no concretely existing man without a concretely existing woman; they appear in the text together, at least in terms of their specific identity. It is ultimately these two persons who will be referred to as Adam and Eve.[44]

---

43. Atkinson, *Biblical and Theological Foundations*, 170.
44. This is a somewhat different interpretation of this passage from that of other scholars, in

In philosophical terms, when viewed through the lens of Aquinas's anthropology, this second account of creation can be seen as a description of the moment when signate matter and the principle of individuation have entered the picture. Man and woman (the 'ish and the ishshâh) of the second creation account are the result of particular matter (earth; rib) being introduced; the substantial form or soul that makes man what he is *absolutely* (adam) illuminated in the first account has now found individuation and differentiation via the designated (common) matter that the form animates in the second. The complementarity that characterizes *the nature as such has now been embodied in two concretely existing beings, differentiated by two distinct but related kinds of matter.*

A comprehensive explanation of this would take us too far from our purpose. It will have to suffice to say that, from this analysis, we can conclude that both man and woman are equally human, since both are an embodiment of a substantial form common to the species *humanum*. Both must be seen to be distinct instantiations of the species, made as they are of different matter and animated by souls that are "commen-

---

particular that of John Paul II in his *Theology of the Body*. There he argues that the reference to man at 2:7 is a reference to man in the abstract or collective sense. But my reading of the text and its use of *ha-adam* to refer to "man" in that passage leads to the conclusion that it is a reference to a specific "human being," in this case a man. As stated previously, in the Hebrew, *adam* without the definitive article *ha*, can refer to man in the collective sense (see Gen 1:26). But when the definitive article is used, it is a reference to a specific "human being," and, in this case, according to the narrative that follows, one who is male. And indeed, the narrative goes on to reveal that it is from the man's (*ha'adam*) rib that the woman (*ishshâh*) is created. It seems clear from the passage that the reference is to the man, that is, the concrete person of the *ha-adam*, while a specific individual, is at the same time representative and as it were 'contains' the whole of humanity, an interpretation that is very much in accord with Semitic thinking. However, it is essential to affirm as well that John Paul II is absolutely correct to point out that it is only with the creation of *ishshâh* (the concretely existing woman we have come to refer to as Eve) that *'ish* (the concretely existing man we have come to refer to as Adam) appears. There is no *'ish* without *ishshâh*. Some scripture scholars want to argue that Genesis 2 must be interpreted in light of Genesis 1's reference to *adam* and that woman and man are created simultaneously from *adam* in both accounts. Along with Brevard Childs, I dispute this interpretation. The Hebrew text is clear and direct in this instance. Gen 2:22-23 states that the matter from which the woman (*ishshâh*) is formed is from the *ha-adam* and that the woman (*ishshâh*) was taken out of the *'ish*. See Brevard S. Childs, *Old Testament Theology in a Canonical Context* (Philadelphia: Fortress Press, 1985), 189-194. A careful reading of both the text and the narrative reveals the clear meaning of Genesis 2. The author is indebted to her colleague Dr. Mary Lemmons for suggesting that this point be clarified, and to both Monsignor Michael Magee and Dr. Joseph Atkinson for their expertise in helping to confirm this interpretation.

surated" or adapted to their individual person.⁴⁵ This "commensuration" reflects both the universal structure of male and female and the personal structure of any one particular man or woman. Gender is not reducible to matter; it has an ontological component, since gender is the type of accident that is attributed to the subject *qua* subject—that is, to the whole composite of soul and body that constitutes the subject as a unity.⁴⁶ And so, here offering woman as our example, though matter is one of the things that differentiates woman from man, since woman is composed of both body and soul and since the soul of each individual woman is meant for her (that would be commensuration), she is in some essential way a woman. Her woman-ness does not reside in her merely in the matter of which she is made—it is who *she is*, as John Paul II states, both physically and ontologically. And these same things can be said of man: he is in some essential way a man. Men and women are equal, composite creatures and, at the level of the individual person, differentiated by both the matter of which they are made and the soul that animates them. This is true of both.

The implications could not be more important. For here we have a demonstration, grounded in scripture, that neither the male nor the female of the species can be considered normative for the species. This

---

45. In the creation account found in Genesis 2, we are no longer speaking of man in the abstract (*adam*) but individual persons. The Hebrew text includes reference to both *ha-adam* ("the human being," which, in Genesis 2, is a reference to a male at the level of the species, and *ish* and *ishshâh* (which refer to a concretely existing man and woman). At this point, matter (dust, man's rib) enters the picture. And, as Aquinas states, thus we enter the realm of accident. Aquinas explains gender as a type of (inseparable) accident; see Thomas Aquinas, *De Ente et Essentia*, chapter 6, trans. Armand Maurer (Toronto: Pontifical Institute of Mediaeval Studies. 1963), 68. But since this type of accident is said to be something attributable to the species, the categories of male and female, while certainly inseparable from the essence of the person, cannot be attributed to the species per se. To be "male" and "female" is a special kind of inseparable accident, perhaps even in a category all its own; see John Finley, "The Metaphysics of Gender: A Thomistic Approach," *Thomist* 79, no. 4 (2015): 585–614.

46. Aquinas, *Summa contra Gentiles* II, ch. 81, para. 8. I am indebted to Sister Prudence Allen and Monsignor John Wippel for pointing me to this passage. Though it does not deal directly with the distinction between genders but with the individuation of the human soul and its continuing individuation after it is separated from the body at death, it is here that Aquinas introduces the notion of the commensuration of each soul to each body. "Commensuration" is a term that means literally to have the same measure. Aquinas means here that each body is adapted or accommodated, even interpenetrated in an equal measure by the soul intended for it. See also Aquinas, *De veritate*, q. 5, a. 10, where Aquinas states, "The soul when joined to a body imitates the composition of that body."

means that women don't have to act like men to be considered human any more than men have to act like women to be considered human. There is absolutely no risk to the "equality" of men and women in understanding their nature in this way. Woman and man are equally human but different, a fact immediately discernible in human experience and accessible to scientific analysis.[47]

Though it is certainly a matter disputed by some—and though it may have faded from view during some historical periods—in her core teachings, the church has always affirmed the equality and dignity of man and woman.[48] The example set by Jesus Christ, especially as reflected in his relationships with women and the profound regard he had for them, would make any other position ultimately insupportable.[49] The truth about man revealed by sacred scripture affirms that men and women are both "equal" and different.

Genesis 1:27 and 2:22 Taken Together

This somewhat foreshortened analysis of Genesis 1 and 2 does establish both the equality of men and women and their difference. But there is

---

47. Though it will not be possible to include it here, it should also be noted at the outset that scientific research regarding what distinguishes men and women supports many of the conclusions found in the work of John Paul II as well as in this chapter; see Steven E. Rhoades, *Taking Sex Differences Seriously* (San Francisco: Encounter, 2004), 22–26; Anne Moir and David Jessel, *Brain Sex: The Real Difference between Men and Women* (New York: Delta, 1991), 68–112. For additional sources and a critique of brain organization theory as a whole, see Rebecca Jordan-Young, *Brainstorm* (Cambridge, Mass.: Harvard University Press), 2010. The author's general argument is that there are risks associated with attributing sex differences to hormones and that brain organization theory (found in these other sources) cannot account for all of them. I agree with her critique. Philosophy and theology must make their contribution.

48. Certainly, some feminists have disputed this point, and not without reason. The error can be traced to Aristotle's argument that woman is a defective male whose capacity for reason is inferior to man's. Aquinas does not fall entirely into this trap, but the flawed biology of Aristotle has made its way into the Western intellectual tradition in various ways. I offer a corrective to these errors in my essay "The Nature of Woman in Relation to Man"; see note 8. On the specific question of the church's teaching on the role of women, please see Sister Sarah Butler, "Catholic Women and Equality: Women in the Code of Canon Law," and Lisa Schiltz, "A Contemporary Catholic Theory of Complementarity," in *Feminism, Law, and Religion*, ed. Marie A. Failinger, Elizabeth R. Schiltz, and Susan Stabile, 345–70 and 3–24, respectively (Burlington, Vt.: Ashgate, 2013).

49. See John Paul's profound account of Jesus' relationships with women in *Mulieris Dignitatem*, chapter 5. It reveals that Jesus not only had respect for women, it was to women that he revealed himself. And it was women, in particular, who grasped who he was and is.

more to be found in these texts. Considered together, they allow us to illuminate more fully the meaning of the second creation account and its significance for our question here.[50] Let us turn to a fuller consideration of what can be discovered now.

In Genesis 1, the sacred author seems to lay out a particular hierarchical order in which God creates. God begins with the heaven and the earth, then light, he then divides the waters, then creates dry land, then vegetation, day and night. He goes on to create swarms of living creatures: birds, monsters, cattle, and things that creep. This all culminates in the creation of *adam*, human nature created male and female. This is clearly a hierarchy that is on its way *up*, from lower life forms to higher.[51]

In the second account we read at 2:7 that a particular man (*hā'adam*) is made from the dust of the earth. When, at Genesis 2:18, God sees that the man is alone, God forms every creature and brings them to the man to be named. Then God, realizing that none of the creatures correspond to the man's own being and that it is not good for him to be alone, decides it is necessary to make a fitting helper (the full text is *ezer kenegdo*) for him[52]—then puts him into a deep sleep and forms the

---

50. These two Genesis accounts of creation are clearly very different, with male and female created seemingly simultaneously in the first chapter, but sequentially in the second. Scripture scholars have long argued that this seeming contradiction can be attributed to the "Documentary Hypothesis," viz. that the two accounts were written at different times by different authors; see Antony F. Campbell and Mark A. O'Brien, *Sources of the Pentateuch* (Minneapolis: Fortress, 1993), 1–20. This is an interesting theory and perhaps even true (though there is a certain turning away from this hypothesis now; see Thomas B. Dozeman and Konrad Schmid, eds., *A Farewell to the Yahwist?: The Composition of the Pentateuch in Recent European Interpretation*, Symposium Series 34 [Atlanta: Society of Biblical Literature, 2006]), but it has never satisfied the systematic theologian's need to reconcile the meaning intended by what is ultimately and arguably a decision inspired by the Holy Spirit to juxtapose these two accounts in this way. Indeed, none other than scripture scholar Brevard Childs has affirmed such an approach; see Childs, *Myth and Reality in the Old Testament* (Naperville, Ill.: Allenson, 1960).

51. Brevard Childs argues that these passages reveal that God's work of creation "was toward an end. It was not done for divine amusement" but in order that salvation and righteousness would "sprout forth"; Childs, *Old Testament Theology in a Canonical Context* (Philadelphia: Fortress, 1985), 32. Scripture scholars argue that the narrative reveals that these passages reveal a preexisting unity out of which comes the diversity of creation. The same can be said to be true for the creation of man and woman.

52. The word *ezer* is translated in many different ways: a "suitable helper," "suitable partner." Perhaps the best is found in the Jewish Tanak—a "fitting helper."

woman (*ishshâh*) from man's (*'ish*) rib (*tsela*).[53] Upon awakening, Adam says, "This at last is bone of my bones and flesh of my flesh." As John Paul II points out, man recognizes in woman another *person*, a being equal to himself, a someone, not a something—a someone he can love, to whom he can make of himself a gift and who can reciprocate in kind. This seems fairly straightforward.

But there are several additional and important points to glean from considering these two chapters together. First, only when we come to the making of Eve do we see the final significance of the order introduced in the first account and brought to completion in the second.[54] Adam is made from the earth (*adama*) but Eve is made from Adam. Though it has troubled feminists forever—and is arguably the root of the historical misinterpretation of this passage—the fact that Eve is created second is not to make her subservient. She is, in fact, made on the way *up*—the last creature to appear, a creature made, not from earth, but from Adam—that is, from something that arguably *already* contains a greater degree of actualization than dust or clay. It does seem as though she is made of "finer stuff." In any case, because of the order suggested by reading the accounts together, Eve can be seen as the pinnacle of creation, not as a creature whose place in that order is sub-

---

53. Though the word *tsela* is traditionally translated as "rib," it is not at all clear that this is correct. The basic meaning of the word in Hebrew is ambiguous, and there are quite a few possibilities, including "plank," "side," and references to geographical and architectural terms. There have been many hypotheses concerning the word, but the only thing that is really clear is that, if it does mean "rib," it does so only in this one passage. Several possible interpretations have particular appeal: if it is taken to mean "side" or "plank," it could be thought to be the source of the expression that woman is man's "better half"; or, given its proximity to the heart, it has been taken to stand for human inwardness. Perhaps the most satisfying possibility is that it is a reference to sacral architecture, since in some contexts *tsela* refers to the side portions of the sanctuary that are necessary for its stability and function. The conclusion can be drawn that the Yawhist author of the passage used terminology "designed to evoke associations with the construction of the sanctuary" to suggest that human beings "come to fulfillment for which they are destined by creation only as man and wife and as God's temple"; see *Theological Dictionary of the Old Testament*, ed. G. Johannes Botterweck, Helmer Ringren, and Heinz-Josef Fabry (Grand Rapids, Mich.: Eerdmans, 2003), 12:400–404. St. Thomas Aquinas argues that the creation of Eve from Adam's rib anticipates the birth of the church when the thrust of the Roman soldier's lance brought forth blood and water from the side of Christ at the Crucifixion; *ST* I, q. 92, a. 3.

54. This interpretation is supported by Brevard Childs, who states that "the creation of the woman, which is sequential in time, foreshadows a climax to the creation which resounds with joy at the close of the chapter"; see Childs, *Old Testament Theology in a Canonical Context*, 191.

servient or somehow less in stature than that of Adam. For with her creation, human community appears for the first time—and enters into human history. Without man, woman has no place. But without woman, man has no future.

This proposition is reinforced when we consider that the Hebrew word usually translated as "helper" is *ezer*, which does not mean servant or slave.[55] When this word is used elsewhere in scripture, it *has the connotation of divine aid*.[56] Used here to express "helper" or "partner," it indicates someone who is most definitely *not* a slave or even remotely subservient—there is the sense of an equal, a partner, help sent by God.[57] Thus, Eve is not to be his servant—a different word would have been used if that were the intention—but someone who can help him to live.

An additional insight appears when we consider the full meaning of this moment in the text. Woman is described as *ezer kenegdo*; *kenegdo* is a preposition that means "in front of," "in the sight of," "before" (in the spatial sense). Thus, we can conclude *from the text* that woman is not "below" man in the order of creation, nor is she above him. She stands in front of him, before him, meeting his gaze as it were and sharing in the responsibility for the preservation of all that precedes them. Thus, woman and man are equal, and both constitute the "other" for each other. Woman's place in the order of creation reveals her true nature

---

55. This point is also made by Joseph Cardinal Ratzinger in his 2004 "Letter to the Bishops of the Catholic Church on the Collaboration of Men and Women in the Church and in the World," when he points out that "the term here does not refer to an inferior, but to a vital helper." See notes 5 and 6. I am using the word "servant" here as it is usually meant—as someone who occupies a lower rung on the ladder in any particular context. A different interpretation of the word "servant" is associated with being a follower of Christ, which, at this point in salvation history, cannot be invoked. But I do not mean to imply that woman is not to serve man. As St. Paul says in Ephesians 5, both men and women are to submit to one another out of reverence for Christ. The question of the headship of the man in the family is not under scrutiny here and is a topic for further research.

56. Excellent examples can be found in the Psalms: e.g., Psalm 30:11b, "The LORD will be *a helper* ('*ezer*) to me," or Psalm 121:1, "I will lift up my eyes to the mountains, whence comes *my help* ('*ezri*). The name of the great scribe "Ezra" of the restoration of Israel under the Persians, namesake of the biblical book, seems to be the Aramaic masculine form of the same word.

57. In his very fine translation of these texts, Robert Alter translates *ezer kenegdo* as "sustainer" rather than helper, a word with a much closer meaning to that intended by the sacred author in my opinion. I refer here to "helper," since that is the more traditional term used in most translations and makes my dispute with the usual interpretation more precise.

and mission—that of help sent by God. And thus is another misunderstood element in the tradition—that woman is subservient to man, sent to be merely his servant—revealed in its full meaning.

The man and the woman, now 'îsh and ishshâh, stand face to face with one another, poised to offer themselves as a gift to each other. They both possess intellect, will, and freedom, as well as the capacity for action and receptivity. But their gift of self is made possible by the very differences that characterize them. And the different gifts that each brings to the tasks of human living will be necessary to fulfill the mission, given to both at Genesis 1:27, to subdue the earth and fill it.

The Genius of Man and Woman

We are ready to turn our attention to what might constitute the particular "genius" of man and of woman. My claim is that both can be derived from the passages in Genesis 2 that describe their creation; we will consider that first. Then, since I will treat the genius of man more substantively shortly, I will offer a brief analysis of the genius attributable to woman. This will allow us to contrast her genius with that of man and to illuminate the complementary nature of their particular charisms.

First, it is notable that man is (apparently) in the Garden alone with God for some period before the appearance of woman, something that has important implications for the place he occupies in the created order and the traditional understanding of man as the head of the household.[58] But aside from this special relationship with the Creator, it can be said that man's first contact with reality is of a horizon that otherwise contains only lower creatures, what we might call "things" (res); this is what leads God to conclude that the man is incomplete and alone and ultimately leads to the creation of woman.[59] I will argue that this seems to provide a point of departure for the well-documented observation that men appear to be more oriented toward things than toward people. We will return to this in our investigation of the genius of man.

---

58. See also M. H. McCarthy, "'Headship': Making the Case for Fruitful Equality in a World of Indifferent Sameness and Unbridgeable Difference," Religions 11, no. 6 (2020): 295.

59. Properly speaking, the Hebrew word here is banah and actually means "building."

But in contrast and of special significance is the quite legitimate claim that, since woman comes into existence after man, her first contact with reality is of a horizon that, *from the beginning*, includes man—that is, it includes persons. One can imagine the woman, a person endowed with intellect and free will, who, upon seeing the man, would recognize another like her, an equal, while the other creatures and things around her appear only on the periphery of her gaze. The self-evident fact about woman's creation is that she has *never lived in a world uninhabited by persons*. This exegetical insight seems to provide a starting place in scripture for the equally well-documented phenomenon that women seem more naturally oriented toward persons.

In *Mulieris Dignitatem*, John Paul argues that the feminine genius is grounded in the reality that all women have the capacity to be mothers—and that this capacity, whether fulfilled in a physical or spiritual sense, orients her toward the other, toward persons.[60] I do not dispute his claim in any way—for surely we can agree that there is plenty of evidence to demonstrate it. And in every sense, Eve is certainly the mother of all humankind. But my point is that, in addition to her capacity to conceive and nurture human life, indeed *prior to it*, her place in the order of creation reveals that—from the beginning—the horizon of all womankind includes persons, includes the other.[61] This may explain why girls and women seem to know—from the beginning—that they are meant for relationship, while it takes men a bit longer to look up and realize they are lonely for something they only just realized was missing and to look for the one who can complete them.

The genius of woman is found here. While man's first experience of his own existence is of loneliness, woman's horizon is different, right

---

60. Pope St. John Paul II, *Mulieris Dignitatem*, nos. 4 and 29. However, grounded as it is in the undeniable fact that all women have the potential to be mothers, his work is vulnerable to the criticism that it risks a kind of biological determinism regarding the role that women can and ought to play in human society. See, for example, Elizabeth A. Johnson, "Imaging God, Embodying Christ: Women as a Sign of the Times," in *The Church Women Want*, ed. Elizabeth A. Johnson (New York: Crossroad, 2002). Obviously, this was neither his meaning nor his intention. I am arguing that there is actually a prior point of departure for an account of the feminine genius, one unencumbered by the risk of such criticisms.

61. And, as revealed at the foot of the cross, God has entrusted all of humanity to Mary's—and therefore to woman's—care; John Paul II, *Mulieris Dignitatem*, 14.

from the start. From the first moment of her own reality, woman sees herself in relation to the other. The fall will result in a disorder in this inclination; Eve's desire will now be for relationship with man, even when she knows he is using her as an object. But the preceding analysis has shown that this capacity—to include the other—*is not a lesser quality*. It is not something that only unnecessarily complicates things, diverting us from an otherwise clear line of sight to achieving results. Nor does it compromise woman's fundamental intelligence, her competence, her ability to get things done. Woman's mission is grounded in her particular genius; she is to keep constantly before us the fact that the existence of living persons, whether in the womb or walking around outside it, cannot be forgotten while we frantically engage in the tasks of human living. Woman is responsible for reminding us all that *all human activity* is to be ordered toward authentic human flourishing.[62]

And so, in these brief sketches, we see the outline of a starting place for both the genius of man and of woman. Scripture, like science and experience, suggests what differentiates men and women: men seem more oriented toward things; women seem more oriented toward persons.[63] These claims do not in any way preclude men attending to persons—or women having dominion over things. But Genesis 3 offers further evidence, as we learn that man and woman will suffer particular and distinct forms of alienation as a consequence of the fall.[64] Adam will now fight with creation; Eve will encounter disorder in her relationship to man. These seem to confirm that, in their original innocence, woman and man were in a right relationship to things (man) and persons (woman). I will return to these elements shortly. I turn now to a more thorough exploration of the masculine genius.

---

62. Angelo Cardinal Scola argues that the father introduces the child to the "law of exchange [work] as the law of growth in life," while the mother introduces her to the "law of gratuity [love]"; see Scola, *The Nuptial Mystery* (Grand Rapids, Mich.: Eerdmans, 2005), 242.

63. Rhoades, *Taking Sex Differences Seriously*, 134 and 193. Indeed, the entire book is full of scientific evidence and real-life examples in support of this conclusion.

64. Genesis 3:16–19.

The Genius of Man

In what follows, I provide an exegesis and interpretation of several passages from Genesis 2, laying the groundwork for the subsequent discussion of what might constitute the genius of man. I have limited myself to what I think are the essential elements for our account. But before we return to the Genesis text, let us pause briefly to consider why an account of the masculine genius is so needed at this time in history.

At least in the West, relationships between men and women are characterized by confusion and disorder. In the United States in particular, the radical feminist movement that marked the latter half of the twentieth century, while not solely responsible for the situation, has left men and boys in a quandary about who they are and what is expected of them. Dr. Meg Meeker, author of *Boys Should Be Boys*, states that "you can't have a revolution without casualties and in the feminist revolution the casualties were boys."[65] In fact, there is plenty of evidence that there is an actual war going on, a war on boys and on men.[66]

Consider the following facts: compared to girls, boys are less likely to graduate from high school, less likely to go to college, more likely to be diagnosed with a learning disability. Boys are more likely to commit suicide, use illegal substances, and engage in risky sexual behavior. Their struggle is due in part to attempts by well-intended feminists to help girls get ahead—not a bad thing in itself—but certainly leading educators to change the way they teach in the classroom and to establish school schedules that favor female learning.[67]

But by far the biggest factor is the absence of men from young boys'

---

65. Emily Stimpson, "We Must Let Our Boys Be Boys," *Our Sunday Visitor*, May 31, 2009, 5.

66. See Christina Hoff Sommers, *The War against Boys: How Misguided Feminism Is Harming Our Young Men* (New York: Simon and Schuster, 2000); Kay S. Hymowitz, *Manning Up: How the Rise of Women Has Turned Men into Boys* (New York: Basic Books, 2012); Dr. Leonard Sax, *Boys Adrift: The Five Factors Driving the Epidemic of Unmotivated Boys and Underachieving Young Men* (2007; repr. New York: Basic Books, 2016). Another important new study by political economist Nicholas Eberstadt documents the astonishing number of men who are now without work and no longer seeking work; see Eberstadt, *America's Invisible Crisis: Men without Work*.

67. Centers for Disease Control, "Youth Risk Behavior Surveillance," 2005 and 2007; quoted in Dr. Meg Meeker, *Boys Should Be Boys: 7 Secrets to Raising Healthy Sons* (New York: Ballantine, 2009). See also Sax, *Boys Adrift*.

lives. Half of all boys grow up without a father in the home. They have fewer male teachers and fewer real heroes. More than 30 million children in the U.S. do not have a father living with them; 90 percent of all runaway and homeless children are from fatherless homes, as are more than 71 percent of high school dropouts. At least 85 percent of all youths in prison grew up in fatherless homes.[68]

We live at a time when boys are told over and over that men are responsible for all the evils in the world. All the great heroes have been deconstructed, and boys have few real life and historical male role models. In the absence of such models, they turn elsewhere and open themselves up to misdirection from male peers, gang leaders, and worse. Fathers and men in general are disinvesting in family structures and the persons within them, even though evidence shows that such involvement provides men with a way toward real perfection and happiness.[69]

Even from this necessarily abbreviated account, we can recognize that humanity urgently needs a deeper understanding of the genius of men. We will see that without that genius humanity would not have survived to this point—and that without it, humanity is radically impoverished.

The Scriptural Foundations

To grasp what might constitute the genius of man, we return, once again, to the opening chapters of Genesis, beginning with Genesis 2:7–9 and the creation of man, referred to here as *hā'adam*, literally "the human being," the male of the species, man qua male. It reveals

---

68. David Popenoe, *Life without Father* (Cambridge, Mass.: Harvard University Press, 1999). See also Mitchell Pearlstein, *Broken Bonds: What Family Fragmentation Means for America's Future* (Lanham, Md.: Rowman and Littlefield, 2014), and his earlier work, *From Family Collapse to America's Decline: The Educational, Economic, and Social Costs of Family Fragmentation* (Lanham, Md.: Rowman and Littlefield, 2011).

69. David Blankenhorn, *Fatherless America: Confronting Our Most Urgent Social Problem* (New York: HarperCollins, 1995), 25–38, and Timothy Fortin, *Fatherhood and the Perfection of Masculinity* (Rome: Pontifica Universitas Sanctae Crucis, 2008): 442–55. Fortin's research, as well as that of Father Carter Griffin, *Why Celibacy?: Reclaiming the Fatherhood of the Priest* (Steubenville, Ohio: Emmaus Road, 2019), bear further investigation for fatherhood as perfective of masculinity in both the natural and priestly spheres.

that man's (that is, the male person's) proper place is in the midst of creation.

> Then the Lord God formed man of dust from the ground, and breathed into his nostrils the breath of life and man became a living being. And the Lord God planted a garden in Eden, in the east; and there he put the man whom he had formed. And out of the ground the Lord God made to grow every tree that is pleasant to sight and good for food.

The next passage of significance for our question provides an insight into Adam's personal mission as well as his role in the fall. At Genesis 2:15–17, we read:

> The Lord God took the man and put him in the garden of Eden to till it and to keep it. And the Lord God commanded the man, saying "You may freely eat of every tree of the garden but of the tree of knowledge of good and evil you shall not eat, for in the day that you eat of it you shall die."

This particular passage has profound meaning for our understanding of human work, since, clearly, Adam is placed in the Garden to do exactly that. But it also reveals that the instruction not to eat the fruit of the tree of knowledge is given directly to the man. We will come back to these themes shortly.

Finally, at Genesis 2:18–23, we learn that the man is tasked with naming all the living creatures, including the one made a "helper" (*ezer*) for him:

> Then the Lord God said, "It is not good that the man should be alone; I will make a helper fit for him." So out of the ground the Lord God formed every beast of the field and every bird of the air, and brought them to the man to see what he would call them; and whatever the man called every living creature, that was its name.

Having given names to every beast, yet still not encountering a fitting helper, God puts the man into a deep sleep and fashions the woman (*ishshâh*) out of the rib of the man. When she is brought before him by the Lord God, the man declares, "This at last is bone of my bones and flesh of my flesh; she shall be called Woman, because she was taken out of Man."

These passages reveal several important things about the masculine genius. First, although we have already established that woman does not occupy a subservient role simply because she comes into existence after him, man is clearly first in the order of creation. He is first to know God, and, when woman is brought to him, both the man and the Lord God recognize her for who she is—a person and his partner. The man's prior relationship with God prepares him in a special way to introduce the woman to God and to the things of creation. The origin of man's role in the family can be traced to this fact, as well as to the revelation that woman is herself created out of man. In a sense, man provides the material for the generation of woman and, it could be said, thus establishes his place as the active or generative principle.

But the heart of my hypothesis concerning the masculine genius is found at Genesis 2:15–23. Here we learn that man's place is in the midst of the created order and, further, that his task is to care for it. He is put in the Garden to till it. Though it is not insignificant that, in the first account, both woman and man are instructed to "fill the earth and subdue it," to have dominion over the earth, only man is given a specific task. And his task is to work, to care for the things found in God's creation. This becomes more evident when we consider that, as God searches for a partner for the man, he brings to him all the things of creation to see what *he will name them*. One by one, the man gives each a name—that is, *he takes dominion over them*.[70]

Now, in order to name things well and take dominion over them, man would have to gain some kind of direct knowledge of them and to possess a certain familiarity and sophistication with things. Indeed, Aquinas argues that Adam must have received an additional preternatural gift, infused knowledge, to be able to name all the animals brought before him. And it is here that we come to the core of what I propose is man's genius: he learns that he excels at discovering what things are, how they are to be distinguished from one another, and what they are for. This is his gift.

---

70. *ST* I, q. 94, a. 3. And though it is from an entirely different tradition, I find it so interesting to consider that one of Lao-Tze's more famous aphorisms is, "The beginning of wisdom is to call things by their right names."

From this account we are justified in at least proposing that man's capacity to name things, to determine what can be predicated of something and what cannot—and an ability to arrive at a systematic way of judging the matter—might be said to be the gifts men bring to the tasks of human living. It is this capacity that is the provenance of many of the achievements of Western civilization. As Professor Anthony Esolen points out in his own reflections on the masculine genius, "Without this literal 'discernment,' there can be nothing so intricate as law, the government of a city, higher learning, a church—not to mention philosophy and theology."[71] When considered along with the fact that man's mission is to work in the Garden, to care for God's creation, we are able to draw a further conclusion: that the genius of man is found in his capacity to know and to use the goods of the earth in the service of authentic human flourishing.

Two further points must be made in this regard. First, it is equally important to point out that the first man's capacity to know and use things does not mean that he is *only* oriented toward things. In truth, his first contact with reality includes the Lord God. He is, in the first instance, aware of his dependence upon his Creator, and he is truly marked by that relationship forever after. It is within this context that he encounters the woman. Until the woman is brought to him, both to name and to love as he can love no other, he has no "other" like himself. He knows immediately that the woman is *not* a thing; she is a person. Without hesitation he declares that she is "flesh of his flesh, and bone of his bones." And, while he can and does name her, he cannot have dominion over her in the same way he has over everything else. She represents for him his highest good, the greatest gift God has given him, and, as a consequence, the value of all the rest of creation is reordered. From and through his encounter with the woman, the man realizes that the Lord God has revealed to him the nature of the reciprocal relationship of the gift of self. And he must realize as well that his own gift—that of caring for and using the goods of creation—is a gift to be exercised in

---

71. Anthony Esolen, "An Interview with Zenit," http://www.zenit.org/en/articles/finding-the-masculine-genius. Though Professor Esolen admits he doesn't exactly have a theory, his thinking is very helpful.

service to her authentic good. As we shall see next, this gift will become clouded by the effects of the fall. But in the state of original innocence, man well understood the right ordering of creation and the place he occupied in it.

Last, the rather well-documented proclivity of men to attend more to things than to persons is often criticized, in many cases legitimately so, distorted as it can be by the effects of original sin. Nonetheless, I maintain that we are justified in seeing it as a reflection of man's genius once it is established that it is in virtue of this gift that man in particular contributes to the good of humankind. However, a further proposition is required to support this claim: we must recall that the goods of creation, like persons, have ontological status also. They are created by God, held in existence by God, endowed with a telos that orders them toward a final end according to God's design.[72] Thus, though the constant moral context of all human action is the fact that the highest value is and always will be the authentic good of human persons—the only creatures created for their own sake—man's orientation toward "things" is also an orientation toward creatures. In fact, it is this orientation that makes him most properly their steward.

Rightly understood, the particular genius of man has proven throughout history to be an essential gift in sustaining families and creating social order—indeed, it has been the key to the very building up of civilizations.[73] Of all the creatures in the material world, humans are the only ones who actually have to work to master their environment and create conditions that support human flourishing.[74] With-

---

72. For a fuller account of this reality, please see Savage, "The Metaphysics of Creation as the Foundation of Environmental Stewardship and Economic Prosperity," *Nova et Vetera* (English ed.) 12 (Winter 2012): 233–52.

73. Even a well-known mainstream feminist seems to agree with this point. See Camille Paglia, "It's a Man's World and It Always Will Be," *Time Magazine*, December 16, 2013, http://ideas.time.com/2013/12/16/its-a-mans-world-and-it-always-will-be/. For a different and very disturbing proposal concerning the role men have played and are destined to play in human history, see Konner, *Women after All*. Konner's analysis will have to be reckoned with and will be the subject of future research. But for additional reflection on this very question, please see Savage, "Adam's Gift: Man in the Order of Creation," *Humanum: Issues in Family, Culture, and Science* 3 (2016), http://humanumreview.com/articles/adams-gift-man-in-the-order-of-creation.

74. Mieczylaw A. Krapiec, *I-Man* (New Britain, Conn.: Mariel, 1983), 29–38. Father Krapiec points to the fact that of all the creatures on earth, man is actually a kind of alien in his environment. He does not possess fangs or a pointed snout that permits him to smell out and tear apart

out the specific genius of man, the human species would not have survived.[75] We owe men a debt of gratitude even if we must also remember that all of us—man and woman alike—are forever under the sway of the effects of original sin. It is the logic of sin that confuses us, that "needs to be broken [so that] a way forward can be found that is capable of banishing it from the hearts of sinful humanity."[76] But as our faith reveals, self-knowledge is an important weapon in our constant battle with the forces that seek to defeat us. To understand the masculine genius in this way is to equip man with the knowledge he needs to strengthen his own struggle with the effects of original sin, which now can be seen in a new light.

The Consequences of the Fall

Of course, so far all of this is in reference to what John Paul II terms the state of original innocence. It is a description of what God *meant* things to be before the fall. And so it is necessary to make a few comments about the fall from innocence. Though a full treatment of the nature of original sin itself is beyond the scope of this present study, the previous analysis does provide us with a framework within which to consider the significance of the ways it manifests in woman and man.[77] In fact, the account of the fall at Genesis 3 provides further evidence of the plau-

---

his food. He does not have fur to protect him from the harshness of his surroundings. This analysis is also reflected by Aquinas, *ST* I, q. 76, a. 5. In short, as John Paul II illuminates so beautifully in the introduction to his encyclical *On Human Work*, "Man is made to be in the visible universe an image and likeness of God himself, and he is placed in it in order to subdue the earth. From the beginning therefore he is *called to work*. *Work is one of the characteristics that distinguish* man from the rest of creatures, whose activity for sustaining their lives cannot be called work. Only man is capable of work, and only man works, at the same time by work occupying his existence on earth."

75. There is an interesting connection to be made and explored between this aspect of the genius of man and Angelo Cardinal Scola's argument that the father introduces the child to the "law of exchange (work) as the law of growth in life"; see Scola, *Nuptial Mystery*, 242.

76. Joseph Cardinal Ratzinger, "Letter to the Bishops on the Collaboration of Men and Women in the Church and in the World," 8.

77. A disordered relationship to things or the proclivity to use persons as objects is a manifestation of how original sin affects men in particular—and women have their own difficulties. The question of how original sin affects either gender is an interesting one and bears much more study.

sibility of the theory we have been investigating and provides a critical point of leverage as we consider the larger aims of this endeavor.

Aquinas argues that the soul itself "is the subject of original sin chiefly in respect of its essence."[78] From this it follows that since both men and women are instantiations of the same substantial form—that is, the same soul—they would also both be equally burdened with its effects. But the account of the fall at Genesis 3 makes manifestly clear that they will suffer differently as a result of their sin. The woman will endure greater pain in childbirth; nonetheless her yearning will be for her husband, who will, in spite of her desire, lord it over her. The man will now struggle with creation; those things he named as his own in Genesis 2 will now only yield their fruits with suffering and toil (Genesis 3:16).

The place both had occupied in the state of original innocence has now been turned upside-down. In light of the previous analysis, this can only mean that, instead of somehow occupying a place of honor (while nonetheless man's equal) woman will now be dominated by the man. As for man, instead of occupying the place of secure and confident steward of God's creation, he will now have to fight with it. The effects of original sin will (and clearly do) manifest quite differently in men and in women. We will consider the contours of this reality here.[79] And we will begin with the moments leading up to the act of disobedience itself.

First, let us take up anew the age-old question of why the serpent approached woman first with his temptation. There have been only a few interpretations of this, mostly variations on the same theme—that woman, being weaker and more vulnerable, was the easiest prey. But if I have shown that woman is man's equal in that she is fully human and therefore endowed with a rational soul and the powers of intellect, will, and freedom, we are no longer able to hold to that position. Woman is most certainly innocent, but she is not without intelligence. However, she is at a disadvantage: she knows little about the world of things,

---

78. Aquinas, *ST* I-II, q. 83, a. 2.

79. More research is called for into the obvious connections between this more properly theological account and the results of psychology's investigations of the ways in which men and women manifest their particular woundedness.

whereas man's relationship to the things of the Garden is much more sophisticated. He had named them; he knew God much more intimately than did woman. And so, yes, woman was easy prey.

But woman was sent to man as a kind of divine aid; she is man's equal while somehow occupying pride of place in the created order. This means that, in approaching woman, the serpent is executing a very clever strategy: his intent is to corrupt the entire hierarchy of creation, and so he begins, so to speak, at the "top." He knows that if he can get to woman, he will soon have man. As John Paul II tells us, woman is first in the order of love; she was sent to safeguard man's heart.[80] Woman was the greatest point of leverage—because it was and still is her primary charism to attend to the other, to keep man focused on the end toward which his work is ordered, the flourishing of human persons. And when woman loses her place, when she is corrupted—so is the family, the culture, the nation, indeed the world.

At the same time, Adam also had a job to do. He was first in the order of creation and on intimate terms with the Creator. His prior relationship with the Lord God and his sophistication with things has revealed that his horizon included a greater grasp of the created order and the way it came to be. In relation to man, woman is rather unsophisticated about "things"; she has heard that they are not to eat of the tree at the center of the Garden, but it was man who heard it directly from God. And it is worth noting that man appears to be more or less at her side at the critical moment of decision (Genesis 3:6). His task is to be the first line of defense against the serpent, to protect Eve from the threats to her person. And he failed her. In fact, it is in this very passage that we see man fail in what will be an essential element of his charism—that of protector. He knows firsthand what God has instructed; he has superior knowledge of things. It is his place to stay the hand of the woman as she reaches for the forbidden fruit. Instead, when God calls to them "in the cool of the day" and asks if they have eaten of the tree, man's response is to blame it on the woman *and* on God. He says, "The woman *you* gave me gave me the fruit of the tree, and I ate." Thus is man's guilt in the fall exposed. His mission was to ensure that the

---

80. Karol Wojtyła, *Mulieris Dignitatem*, no. 30.

goods of creation would be used for woman's *good*. He failed to exercise dominion over creation at a critical moment in salvation history.[81]

So we must conclude that both are complicit in this act of disobedience. Nonetheless, as we see in Genesis 3:16–19, the consequences of the fall from grace take very different shapes for each of them. In fact, the narrative that describes the aftereffects of the fall does seem to confirm the validity of the theory presented so far: it results in a distortion of the particular gifts given to each. Man will struggle with creation; woman will struggle with relationships.

Since it was her act that brought them to disgrace, God turns to woman first at Genesis 3:16 and says, "I will greatly multiply your pain in childbearing; in pain you shall bring forth children, yet your desire shall be for you husband, and he shall rule over you."

Woman's sin thus leads to a distortion of her own natural gifts. Her capacity to bear and nurture life will now be a source of physical anguish and suffering. Her capacity for relationship and her natural orientation toward persons will now be a source of confusion and torment. She is told that her desire will be for her husband, even in light of his tendency to dominate her. Here "husband" should not be taken too literally; woman's desire will be for man, even when she knows he is using her, even when she understands that the result of their union could be the pain of childbirth.

Our contemporary context certainly reflects these factors. The confusion in relationships between men and women that has manifested over the last fifty years is well documented.[82] Certainly it can be said that women manifest a disordered inclination in relationships. It is often the case for many women that their desire is for "the other" even when he treats her as an object, even when he dominates and uses her. The evidence is all around us; it takes shape in the widespread phenomenon of

---

[81]. Is that not so even today? Though many of us will deny it, women are in very great need of protection now—they have lost their way in large measure, not because they seek to fulfill their own creative potential through work outside the home, but because they insist on doing that within a social and economic context that reduces their natural capacity to bear life to an inconvenience and their natural orientation toward persons to an unnecessary complication. The evidence is all around us that both men and women have lost their orientation in the cosmic scheme.

[82]. See especially Mary Eberstadt, *Adam and Eve after the Pill: Paradoxes of the Sexual Revolution* (San Francisco: Ignatius Press, 2012).

the unwed mother, though we now call them "single" mothers. It shows up in the form of domestic abuse, prostitution, and sex trafficking.[83] Instead of expressing the natural authority that belongs to woman in the order of creation, she becomes anxious in her pursuit of relationships and love, clingy, needy, and fearful of abandonment.[84]

God turns to man next. At Genesis 3:17–19, the man is told that *because he listened to his wife*,

> cursed is the ground because of you; in toil you shall eat of it all the days of your life; thorns and thistles it shall bring forth to you; and you shall eat the plants of the field. In the sweat of your face you shall eat bread till you return to the ground.

The nature of man's sin must be made clear. His sin was not precisely that he ate of the forbidden fruit; it was "because he listened to his wife." From this we are not to conclude that men err when they listen to their wives![85] Its subtext must be understood: God is saying to the

---

83. For an extensive and well-cited summary of the statistics on domestic violence and its frequency and impact on women, see http://www.wewillspeakout.org/wp-content/uploads/2013/03/domestic-violence-statistics-2009.pdf. According to the United Nations Office on Drugs and Crime's "Global Report on Trafficking in Persons," women and girls make up 70 percent of all victims of trafficking worldwide; the full report is available at http://www.unodc.org/documents/data-and-analysis/glotip/GLOTIP_2014_full_report.pdf. And according to the most recently available census figures (2013) 36 percent of those living below the poverty level in American are women; 31 percent of households headed by single women were living below the poverty line. This is more than five times the poverty rate for families headed by a married couple (5.8 percent). It also contrasts with the 15.9 percent of male-headed households living in poverty during the same period; see U.S. Census Bureau, *Income and Poverty in the United States: 2013*, 16, https://www.census.gov/library/publications/2014/demo/p60-249.html. For evidence that fatherlessness is a predictor of poverty, see Sara McLanahan, "Family Structure and the Reproduction of Poverty," *American Journal of Sociology* 90, no. 4 (January 1985), 873–901. For more recent data supporting this claim, see http://www.fathers.com/statistics-and-research/the-consequences-of-fatherlessness/.

84. See Carol Garhart Mooney, *Theories of Attachment: An Introduction to Bowlby, Ainsworth, Gerber, Brazelton, Kennell, and Klause* (St. Paul, Minn.: Redleaf, 2010). An analysis of the particular personality disorders described by the DSM-5 and found more frequently in women includes "instability in interpersonal relationships, seriously unstable affects, fear of abandonment," and others. For a more complete account, please see chapter 5, by Dr. Paul Vitz, "Men and Women: Their Differences and Their Complementarity," in this volume.

85. One wonders if this has anything to do with the frequent report that, in general, men seem reluctant to listen to women, their wives in particular. It is funny, but sadly true. And it can be said to be the reason women, we must admit, do tend to become rather shrill at times. Perhaps if men listened better, women would not feel they needed to raise their voices in order to be heard.

man that, *because you listened to your wife—and not to me*, you have lost your place in the order I established. It is a clear indication of Augustine's dictate that all authority *comes from God*; man may seek to fulfill his role as the head of the family, but only if he never forgets that his first act is always an act of obedience to that which is above him.

But it is clear that the man's sin will now result in the need to struggle to realize the specific feature that characterized him in his original innocence. His natural relationship to the things of creation will now be fraught with difficulty, forever after burdened by confusion and backbreaking work. That he is told, specifically, that as a result of his sin he will have to struggle with creation only confirms the uniqueness of man's relationship to the things of creation. Original sin can be said to affect man in particular in his tendency to forget that all is gift, that his first obligation is toward his Creator. Most devastating for human relationships, he forgets what he knew in the first instance of his encounter with the woman: that she is *not* an object. This forgetfulness leads to a disordered relationship to things, for now everything and everyone is an object, something to be dominated and used as he sees fit. This manifests for some men in a quest for power over people and nations—and their possessions—frequently leading to actual war (which is, by the way, almost exclusively started by men), or to hostile corporate takeovers, or to plain everyday Machiavellian manipulation in the workplace. It has led men in particular to forget that the created order is itself a gift, given to him to "till and to *keep*"; instead they seek to exploit it, and the result has been environmental degradation. It leads to a compulsion for work and acquisition that leads them to forget themselves and the real purpose of human existence.

Here, again in brief sketches, we can grasp the significance of this account for our understanding of man and woman and the path ahead for both. The scriptural account reveals that the very things that had been the natural charisms of man and woman are now the source of suffering and struggle. These gifts are, at one and the same time, both our greatest weaknesses and our path to redemption.

In sum, the masculine genius is grounded in the scriptural account of the first man, which reveals that his fundamental gift is to know creation and to discover in it the goods that will permit him to contribute to the good of his family and of all humankind. He thus is oriented toward generative activity that leads him to create things *outside of himself*, things that can be brought to bear on man's highest good, that of human flourishing. But because he is marked by the burden of original sin, he often forgets that his donation of self in the act of making of himself a gift is something that can only be given to another person. One cannot make of oneself a gift to a bottom line or a project, no matter how important; on the other end of the donation of self is *always* another self. His particular blindness, the result of the fall, leads him constantly to forget this fact.

The feminine genius is grounded in the scriptural account of the first woman, which reveals her to be, first of all, a gift sent by God to all of humankind. She is, above all, *ezer*, divine aid, and her fundamental gift is an orientation toward the other that ensures that the primacy of persons is never forgotten or denied. She is meant to "keep humanity from *not* falling," and her mission is to remind man that the gift of self can only be made to another person, to keep this fact constantly before us by affirming and expressing what she understands through her own genius: that all human activity must be ordered toward the good of persons.

Though many men fail to live up to the potential found in their own genius, surely an equal number of women fail, as well. This is not surprising. Both the masculine and the feminine genius are in fact both natural and supernatural realities that, though they can manifest on the level of nature, require participation in the life of grace to reach full expression. The men, the fathers in our lives, are quite often engaged in superhuman efforts to lead, protect, and support their families. We should all be grateful for the masculine genius. Though certainly, we can acknowledge that mistakes have been made, unquestionably, it has ensured the well-being of families and cultures for millennia.

On the other hand, we have seen that the genius of woman is an equally evident reality, one that perhaps has not yet found full expression in the life of our culture, in spite of the progress of the past 150 years. This is surely due, in part, to a devaluing of the nature of woman qua woman in many aspects of our culture, both a vestige of the past and a result of the mistaken anthropology that grounds the radical feminist movement. For many reasons, women often face challenges, even obstacles, in giving voice to the gifts they offer and the wisdom they bring, not only in the home, but in the public arena. But they must persist, for the stakes are very high. As John Paul II tells us in *Evangelium Vitae*,

> In transforming culture so that it supports life, women occupy a place, in thought and action, which is unique and decisive. It depends on them to promote a "new feminism" which rejects the temptation of imitating models of "male domination," in order to acknowledge and affirm the true genius of women in every aspect of the life of society, and overcome all discrimination, violence and exploitation.[86]

Women are thus tasked with a very special mission, something the church has been aware of for almost a century. As Pius XII said to a group of Catholic Women's organizations in 1945, "The fortunes of the family, the fortunes of human society, are at stake—and they are in your hands."[87] These sentiments are even more clearly stated in the more recent *Compendium of the Social Doctrine of the Church*, where we find the following declaration: "The feminine genius is needed in all expressions of the life of society, therefore, the presence of women in the workplace must also be guaranteed."[88]

It seems clear that if we are to recover our culture we must take much more seriously St. John Paul II's claim in the *Letter to Women* that it is "to this unity of the two God has entrusted not only the work of procreation and family life, but the creation of history itself."[89] It would be impossible to overstate the importance of the conclusion we are led to by this investigation: the key to our future as a civilization is a deep understanding of the nature of woman and man *in relation to one another*—that is, a robust theology of complementarity, grounded in both scripture and tradition, that lifts up and acknowledges the genius that both men and women bring to our mission to return all things to Christ.

---

86. John Paul II, *Evangelium Vitae*, 99.
87. Pius XII, Address to Catholic Women's Organizations, 1945.
88. *Compendium on the Social Doctrine of the Church*, no. 295.
89. *Compendium of the Social Teaching of the Church*, no. 147, quoting John Paul II, *Letter to Women*, no. 8.

St. Joseph as an Icon of the Masculine Genius

There is but one more step in this investigation, and that is to consider a way forward. John Paul has told us that the icon of the feminine genius is the person of Mary, the Mother of God. And he has offered a full account of the way in which this is so in his Apostolic Letter *Mulieris Dignitatem*. Our task here is to consider who might offer us a similar insight into the nature of the masculine genius. It is no doubt tempting to suggest that Jesus himself provides the model for an understanding of the charism of men, and surely Our Lord offers us a fitting example to follow. But it must be acknowledged that Jesus is the model for both men and women—and he was, of course, both human and divine. If Mary, the perfect human, is the model for woman, there can really be only one choice fitting as a model for man—at least at the level of nature. And that would have to be her spouse and Jesus' earthly father, St. Joseph. I will argue that he is our prime example of the embodiment of the masculine genius in a concretely existing human person.

Though limitations of space do not permit an extended treatment of St. Joseph himself, Pope St. John Paul's Apostolic Exhortation on Joseph, *Redemptoris Custos*, points us toward that particular manifestation of the masculine genius found in fatherhood. It is a role that both reflects and serves to perfect his masculine nature.[90]

St. John Paul is quick to point out that St. Joseph is not a mere bystander in the events surrounding the Incarnation. Mary is already betrothed to Joseph at the time of the Annunciation, and Joseph is "the first to be placed by God on the path of Mary's 'pilgrimage of faith.'"[91] He is chosen to assure fatherly protection for the child when, as Mary's spouse, he is introduced to the mystery of Mary's motherhood by the messenger in his own "annunciation." It is to Joseph that the messenger returns, "entrusting to him the responsibilities of an earthly fa-

---

90. The work of Timothy Fortin and Father Carter Griffin will be important in pursuing this proposal.

91. Pope St. John Paul II, *Redemptoris Custos*, no. 5.

ther with regard to Mary's son."[92] Joseph thus becomes, together with Mary, the first guardian of this divine mystery.[93] Joseph is "called by God to serve the person and mission of Jesus Christ directly through the exercise of his fatherhood," and his entire life is lived in service to the mystery of the Incarnation.[94] But since salvation comes through the humanity of Christ, it is theologically significant to note that this humanity is revealed in Joseph's assumption of fatherly responsibility over his son. Joseph is the overseer of Jesus' birth and the guardian of his private, hidden life.

Thus Joseph would have had to possess the genius of man to a greater degree than most. For Mary would have encountered Joseph as a *person* and, since she was unencumbered by any hint of blindness because of original sin, would have recognized in Joseph—albeit inchoately perhaps—a man whose very being mirrored the qualities worthy of her sinless state. He is an icon of the masculine genius, and his example bears further investigation.[95]

For now, I will simply point to several aspects of Joseph's role in the life of the Holy Family that correspond in concrete ways to the account of the masculine genius proposed in this chapter. First, the generations listed at the beginning of Matthew's Gospel are according to the genealogy of Joseph; it is from Joseph's line that we understand the connection with the heritage of David and with the many prophesies associated with the coming of the Messiah. But, in light of our previous analysis, two aspects of Joseph's role bear particular mention. First, it is Joseph who is told to name the child, the first of the new creation, just as the first man named everything of the old.[96] And second, and in stark contrast with the first man's failure to keep woman safe, it was

---

92. Pope St. John Paul II, *Redemptoris Custos*, no. 3.
93. Pope St. John Paul II, *Redemptoris Custos*, no. 5.
94. Pope St. John Paul II, *Redemptoris Custos*, no. 8.
95. St. Joseph, as Mary's "most chaste spouse" and Jesus's earthly father, also points to his embodiment of the masculine genius as in some way analogous to Mary's embodiment as Virgin and Mother. This bears further exploration, especially in light of Father Louis Bouyer's very interesting analysis of the distinctions between the "virginity" of men and of women and the nature of fatherhood. See Bouyer, "Woman and God," in *Women in the Church* (San Francisco: Ignatius Press, 1979), 29–39.
96. Bouyer, "Woman and God," 7.

Joseph who learned in a dream of the threat Herod posed to his family and immediately "took the young child and his mother by night and departed for Egypt."[97] Joseph's actions reveal the genius of man as the head of the family and its protector.

But above all, Joseph obeyed, and in silence.[98] The gospels do not record a single word he may have spoken. At his own "annunciation" he says nothing; he simply does what the angel tells him to do. And, St. John Paul tells us, this became the beginning of "Joseph's way," a way marked by his silent witness to the meaning of the just man.[99] In this regard, Joseph's signature quality reflects that of the first man: he was a man who worked. This word, St. John Paul says, "sums up Joseph's entire life," revealing at the same time the possibilities of sanctifying the quotidian rhythms of daily life.[100] Joseph makes of himself a total gift of self, of his life and work; he "turns his human vocation to domestic love into a superhuman oblation of self."[101]

Even this brief treatment reveals that the figure of St. Joseph embodies and personifies the masculine genius in ways that approach its full expression. His example reflects the courage, loyalty, and tireless efforts of many men who serve their families and populate our communities. And for them, we give thanks.

Conclusion

We have come a long way. But there is one more essential point that must be made if we are to illuminate the way forward. For while the masculine and feminine genius can be spoken of on the level of nature, they are in fact both supernatural realities whose full expression cannot be realized without the action of grace. Both the feminine and

---

97. Matthew 12:13–14. I am grateful to Dr. Paul Vitz for pointing out this passage and its significance to me.
98. And, I would add, in keeping with our previous analysis, Joseph's first act always was to *listen* to the source of all authority, the word of God.
99. Bouyer, "Woman and God," 17.
100. Bouyer, "Woman and God," 22–24.
101. Bouyer, "Woman and God," 8.

masculine "genius"—if we can call it that—begins as a *potency in nature*, one that certainly can be actuated, observed, and spoken about on that level. But, in truth, if woman and man are to manifest this genius in its fullness, it will require them to enter into the life of grace and be sustained by it if they are to arrive at the level that represents a more perfected state. The fact that Mary and Joseph provide us with the models we need to emulate in order to arrive at a complete embodiment of the genius of woman or of man is a clue that grace and participation in the sacramental life of the church will be required.

For it is one thing for women to laugh about the fact that they seem to be able to remember where their husband left his glasses or his keys or to keep track of the many details that go into the life of the family. Certainly, it must be admitted that women tend to feel a sense of superiority when it is clear that they seem better equipped to "multitask." On the other hand, men may feel superior when they express their frustration at the ways in which women may seem to complicate matters with their apparently inexhaustible need for dialogue. But it is another thing entirely to exercise the virtue of charity in the home that, let us admit, often requires nothing less than an almost supernatural act—in order to serve each other as queen and king of the domestic church—to share in the royal dominion we both are called to exercise over the life of the family—and the world.

For this joint call to exercise royal dominion extends beyond the family, to every facet of contemporary life, including the workplace, politics, even academia. Both men and women need to be encouraged to bring their particular gifts to the challenge of living out the instruction both were given in the Garden. If it is true that this complementarity is what gives us our actual *mission*, then we must face our very real challenges with full and explicit awareness of our status as equal partners, not adversaries. The difficulty is that the effects of original sin are not left at the door; they accompany us wherever we go. Only a self-conscious awareness of this reality will ensure that the necessary partnership is forged. Both men *and* women will each need to acknowledge their own blind spots and work together to arrive at a comprehensive vision of what constitutes the authentic progress of the community and of humankind. It is, after all, the sacred task of the laity to transform the temporal order.[102] Only men and women, working side by side in the fullness of truth, will be able to bring that about.

Perhaps it goes without saying that there are signs all around us of the descent of man. The world is in desperate need of *both* women and men who understand and live out the complementarity that characterizes their fundamental relationship. For without question the future of humanity is in our hands—and not just theoretically. To live out the mission that is ours in virtue of our complementarity will take humility and courage—the humility to remember that original sin affects us all—and the courage to refuse to be caught up in the logic of sin, to try to see the truth about the other, to recognize their gifts, to understand their need for recognition and healing. In short, to become saints—because clearly that is what we are called to be—and humanity—in particular, our young people—deserve no less from us.

---

102. For further reflection on complementarity as mission, see Savage, "Man, Woman, and the Mission of the Laity," *Church Life Journal*, October 24, 2016, http://churchlife.nd.edu/2016/10/24/man-woman-and-the-mission-of-the-laity/.

CHAPTER 4

Michelangelo and the Shrine to Complementarity
The Sistine Chapel

Elizabeth Lev

Calling to mind the Sistine Chapel, some might spontaneously think of a band of male prelates who gather in the space to elect the successor to St. Peter during a conclave. Others could mentally evoke an overwhelming mass of exquisitely drawn male bodies, dubbed in its day as "fit only for a bathhouse or tavern."[1] Thinking scripturally, a few may envision the stories of Genesis starting from God the Father to the creation of the first man and concluding with Noah and his sons. At first glance, the Sistine Chapel would appear to be the least likely place in the entire ecclesiastical topography to look for male/female complementarity. It's been called patriarchal, male-oriented, verging on the homoerotic ... and yet ... it is quite the opposite.

St John Paul II, himself something of an artist, was the first to articulate the visual theme of complementarity between men and women in the Sistine frescos. During the inauguration of the newly restored chapel, the pope preached:

It seems that Michelangelo, in his own way, allowed himself to be guided by the evocative words of the Book of Genesis which, as regards the creation of the human being, male and female, reveals: "The man and his wife were both

---

1. Giorgio Vasari, *Lives of the Artists*, trans. George Bull (London: Penguin, 1987), 1:379.

naked, yet they felt no shame" (Gn 2:25). The Sistine Chapel is precisely—if one may say so—the sanctuary of the theology of the human body. In witnessing to the beauty of man created by God as male and female, it also expresses in a certain way, the hope of a world transfigured, the world inaugurated by the Risen Christ, and even before by Christ on Mount Tabor.[2]

What did he see in that space that art historians, critics, and tens of thousands of tourists were missing? The following pages will look at the complementarity encoded, or rather, enfrescoed, in the Sistine Chapel—a depiction of the cooperation between man and woman that started with Creation and continues to the present, reaffirmed in each generation. In every part of the 6,000 square feet of the ceiling, Genesis, heroes, prophets, and genealogies, men and women are depicted side by side, not interchangeably, but each complementing the other in their respective roles in salvation history. In depicting both men and women as actors in the divine plan, Michelangelo wove these varied threads together to illustrate the grand overarching picture of complementarity as envisioned by the church, promoted in a special way by Pope Sixtus IV, who built the chapel and dedicated it to Mary, bodily assumed into heaven. Despite the fact that she is depicted only once—in the Last Judgment painted twenty-odd years later—her presence permeates the chapel as both critical actor in the story of salvation and cooperatrix in human redemption.[3]

Although Michelangelo lacked the modern terminology, his pictorial language of the men and women of the Sistine Chapel illustrates what Sr. Mary Prudence Allen has called the "four principles of complementarity": clear differences (despite his use of powerful forms for both), the way that differing qualities aid in working toward the same goals (procreation, divination, salvation), sustained development over time, and, what is perhaps most surprising for the age, equal dignity.[4]

---

2. St. John Paul II, *Homily at Unveiling of Restored Sistine Chapel Frescos* (April 8, 1994), no. 6.

3. When the chapel was first inaugurated, Mary was represented both in the fresco of the Nativity and in the altarpiece of the Assumption on the altar wall. These were destroyed to make space for the Last Judgment.

4. The four elements of complementarity were laid out by Sister Mary Prudence Allen in "Four Principles of Complementarity: A Philosophical Perspective," in *Not Just Good, but Beautiful: The Complementary Relationship between Man and Woman*, ed. Steven Lopes and Helen Alvaré (Walden, N.Y.: Plough, 2014), 49–59.

Figure 4-1. Overview Image, Sistine Chapel Vault

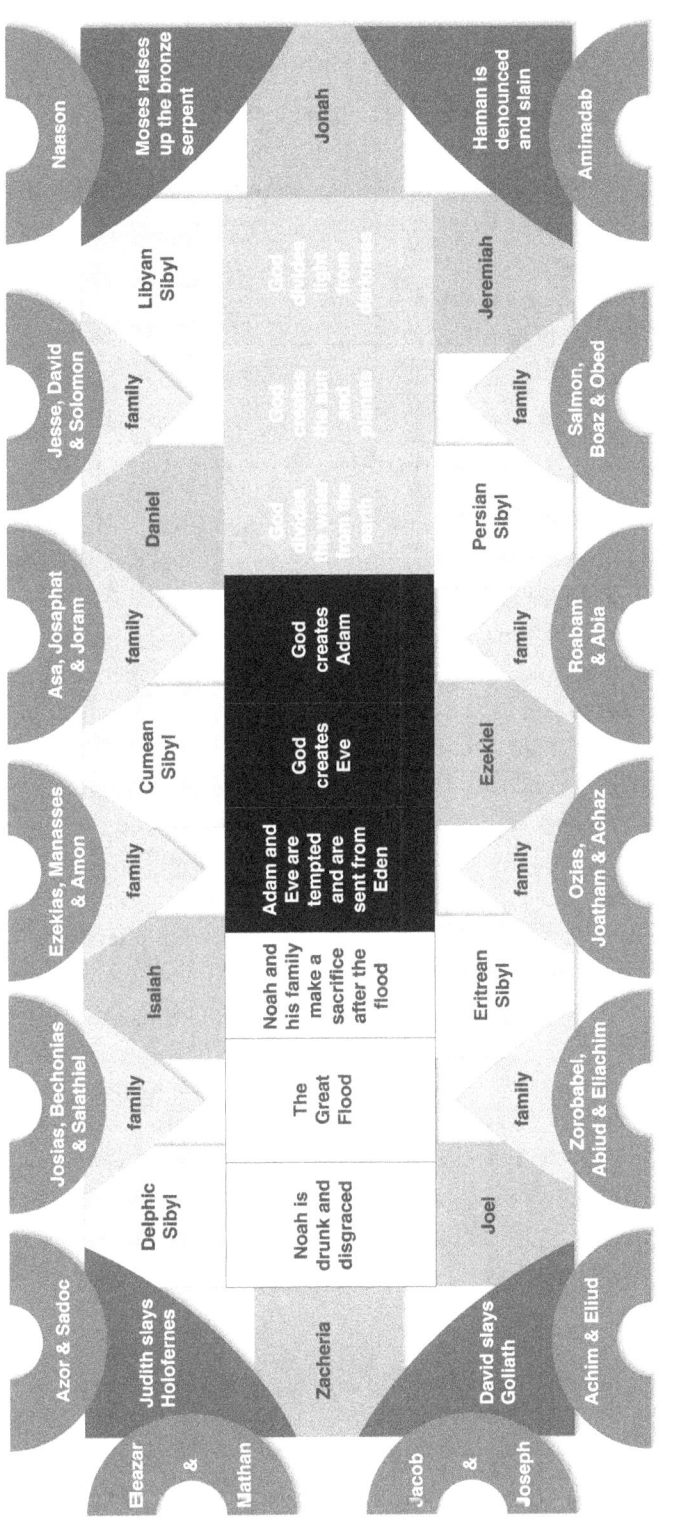

Figure 4-2. Diagram of Sistine Chapel

"In the image of God he created them; male and female he created them" (Gn 1:27)

By looking closely at the figures that people the Sistine Chapel ceiling, this chapter demonstrates that Michelangelo's vision of beauty was not revealed solely through the male form and establishes that the intended viewers were fully aware of this theme of pairing men and women in the story of salvation. Not only was his audience capable of appreciating his efforts, but they could also advise him as he assembled his compendium of complementarity.

A Daunting Task

In 1505, Michelangelo Buonarroti came to Rome with painting the furthest thing from his mind. The thirty-three-year-old sculptor had carved out a name for himself with the Roman *Pietà* in 1500 and then the colossal *David* in 1504. He was anticipating his most important assignment yet, a monumental tomb for the reigning Pope Julius II. Projected at twenty feet by forty feet with forty sculptures to adorn the marble structure, the tomb would have rivaled the wonders of the ancient world in scope and grandeur.

Politics, intrigues, and economics soon intervened, and the tomb project was indefinitely shelved. Michelangelo, however, was not dismissed, just reassigned to paint the Sistine Chapel ceiling, at the time frescoed with a starry vault. His instructions were simple (according to the artist): he should paint the "twelve apostles in the lunettes, and the remainder a certain division into parts filled with ornaments in the usual way."[5]

With limited experience in fresco painting, Michelangelo might have found the relatively straightforward task appealing, with little room for failure. Michelangelo had learned to fresco in the celebrated Florentine studio of Domenico Ghirlandaio, who, as it happens, had executed the panel of *The Calling of the First Two Apostles* in the same Sistine Chapel twenty-five years earlier. However, Michelangelo had

---

5. "Letter to Giovan Franceso Fattucci, Dec. 1523," in Michaelangelo, *Complete Poems and Selected Letters of Michelangelo*, trans. Creighton Gilbert, ed. Robert N. Linscott (Princeton, N.J.: Princeton University Press, 1980), 236.

abandoned his fresco training at age fifteen to join the sculpture academy formed in the garden of Lorenzo De' Medici. His talent had been honed to work in three dimensions, not two. The task of painting the apostles against a decorative ground, typical to most chapel ceilings, might appear a congenial task if a man were simply looking for a paycheck and a papal commission on his résumé.

But Michelangelo's hunger for glory, which drove him to accept the tomb commission in the first place, seems to have outweighed the fear of failure. He made an audacious counterproposal: not apostles, but stories of Genesis. Since the earlier masters like Ghirlandaio, Botticelli, and Perugino had covered the side walls with stories of Jesus and the life of Moses, why not depict the origin of all things?

Never had this type of painting cycle been attempted on a ceiling, and here Michelangelo played to strengths he knew he uniquely possessed. As a painter he had been trained to fill frames with busy scenes of people and places, but as a sculptor he had learned to think reductively, chipping away at a block of marble to reveal the form within. By using single dynamic figures to recount a story, the body became his language, while movement, energy, and form made up his vocabulary.

Only Michelangelo could have thought in these terms, as he also possessed the exceptional ambition to rise to such a challenge—it is his unique and very personal contribution to the ceiling. The selection of scenes and figures and the particular details of concordance and typology were likely suggested by theologians, but the vault became a personalized vision of a universal story. The ceiling is neither the work of a lone maverick making up theology as he goes along nor a painter simply coloring in lines marked out for him by theological advisors. Michelangelo chose to put his singular gifts at the service of a great narrative.

Michelangelo's formation in the Medici garden was not merely training in a craft. He was exposed to theology, philosophy, and poetry at the heart of the Medici circle. As a boy he had listened to the sermons of Fra Savonarola, and as a young man spent time with Fra Mariano da Genazzano, the general of the Augustinian order and famous adversary of Savonarola. Fra Genazzano often frequented the Medici circles where young Michelangelo was learning to sculpt. Angelo Polizano, who tutored the Medici children and offered inspiration to Botticelli, philosopher Pico della Mirandola, and theologian Marsilio Ficino were all on hand during those formative years in the informal academy of the Medici. In Rome, Giles of Viterbo, another Augustinian, has been credited with the lion's share of the theological heft of the Sistine ceiling. It should also be noted that Michelangelo's association with the Franciscans, from his childhood parish to his burial in the habit of the member of the third order, indicates a strong Franciscan spirituality alongside his Augustinian and Dominican sensitivities.

The finished ceiling, inaugurated on All Saint's Day, 1512, "brought him so great a reputation that it set him above all envy."[6] Michelangelo depicted nine stories from Genesis, from the *Separation of Light and Dark* to the *Drunkenness of Noah*, a cycle that stretched from altar to entrance. Immediately under these scenes a series of seven enthroned prophets and five sibyls form a visual foundation for the narrative. The four corners of the vault recount the deeds of two heroes and two heroines—Moses, David, Judith, and Esther—while the undercroft reaching to the windows contains the illustrated genealogy of Christ as described in the Gospel of St. Matthew. In analyzing these images it becomes clear that the choices made by both Michelangelo and his advisors stress complementarity in an entirely new and innovative fashion (see figs. 4-1 and 4-2).

In Michelangelo's opening panels of Genesis, the viewer sees God acting alone, a massive figure painted with long, swift brushstrokes to indicate movement. The Creator is greater than all he creates—he dominates the pictorial space in every image, separating light from darkness, surveying the world, and even as he forms the sun, moon, and vegetable life, the Creator is physically larger than all of his creations combined. Only in the *Creation of Man* does God share the stage, occupying half the panel as Adam occupies the other half (fig. 4-3). Although Adam is more sizable than the other creatures depicted, he nonetheless remains passive and inert before the generative energy of God.

In this panel, where the anticipated contact between the human and

---

6. Ascanio Condivi, *The Life of Michelangelo* (University Park: Pennsylvania State Press, 1999), 39.

the divine so enthralls the viewer, it is easy to overlook an important aspect of the presentation: while one hand of God reaches out to "activate" Adam, the other curls warmly around a woman, Eve (fig. 4-4).[7] Nestled in God's arm, "on his mind" in a certain sense, Eve is clearly part of God's plan for humanity from the very beginning.[8] Furthermore, the hand of God curls beyond her to splay on the shoulder of a child—the exaggerated length of the finger intentionally forces our gaze to the infant Christ looking out toward the viewer, premeditated from the beginning of time for the redemption of humanity.[9]

As the eye travels from Adam to God to Eve to Jesus, the centrality of the role of woman in bringing about the Incarnation comes to mind, first through the *felix culpa* of Eve (sung in the Sistine Chapel during the *Exsultet*), and then through the heroic *fiat* of the Virgin Mary, the New Eve.[10]

Visually, the two figures of Adam and Eve are joined together by God, one in his arm, the other about to be touched. While they are two distinct creations and painted more vividly than the angels around them, they are drawn together through the design of the Creator.

Yet famous as it is, the *Creation of Adam* does not occupy the central panel of the ceiling. Underscoring more explicitly the relationship between Mary, Mother of God, and Eve, Mother of all the living, Michelangelo chose to decorate the central panel of the Sistine ceiling with the *Creation of Eve* (fig. 4-5). Adam's panel may be larger, but Eve occupies the heart of the work and is framed with distinctive yellow ribbons contrasting the olive color used for the other scenes.

In this panel, Eve is drawn as a bridge extending from the side of sleeping Adam to the standing figure of God. Her hands folded in a gesture of prayer already allude to intercession. Where Eve's disobedience will be the catalyst of the fall, Mary's obedience will ensure that all her

---

7. Heinrich Pfeiffer, *The Sistine Chapel: A New Vision* (New York: Abbeville, 2007), 214.

8. Dr. Frank Lynn Meshberger, "An Interpretation of Michelangelo's Creation of Adam Based on Neuroanatomy," *JAMA* 264, no. 14 (October 10, 1990): 1837–41.

9. Elizabeth Lev and Jose Granados, *A Body for Glory* (Vatican City: Edizioni Musei Vaticani, 2014), 68.

10. The *Exultet*, a hymn of praise sung before the Paschal candle at Easter with roots dating back to St Augustine, contains the lines "O truly necessary sin of Adam, destroyed completely by the Death of Christ! / O happy fault, that earned for us so great, so glorious a Redeemer!"

Figure 4-3. Creation of Man, Sistine Chapel

pleas are answered. In this image we see a privileged role of woman as intercessor between God and man, begun by Eve and perfected by Mary. This distinct and personal link to God is unique to woman in the ceiling, seen first in this panel and then twenty-seven years later in the Virgin Mary of the *Last Judgment*. Eve's direct corporal connection from Adam's side to the Lord, her position of supplication and her parted lips as if already at prayer anticipate the role Mary will have as the "new Eve" in the undoing of the disobedience of first woman. God creates, Christ judges, Noah makes a covenant, but only Mary and Eve form a physical connection between human beings and the Lord.

Flanking Eve's creation, Michelangelo chose to represent a prophet and a sibyl famed for their Marian prophecies. One side represents Ezekiel, who had written,

Figure 4-4. Detail of Creation of Man God/Eve, Sistine Chapel

Then he brought me back to the outer gate of the sanctuary facing east, but it was closed. The LORD said to me: This gate must remain closed; it must not be opened, and no one should come through it. Because the LORD, the God of Israel, came through it, it must remain closed. Only the prince may sit in it to eat a meal in the presence of the LORD; he must enter through the vestibule of the gate and leave the same way. Then he brought me by way of the north gate to the facade of the temple. I looked—and the glory of the LORD filled the LORD's house! (Ez 44:1–4)

From St. Ambrose in the fourth century to the Litanies of Loreto, not only were these words interpreted as a foreshadowing of the Virgin Birth, but they also cemented Mary's role as *porta caeli* or "gate to Heaven."

On the opposite side, the Cumean sibyl serves a similar prophetic

Figure 4-5. Creation of Eve, Sistine Chapel

purpose, but in this case directed toward the Gentiles. Considered the prophetess par excellence of the Savior's birth, the Cumean sibyl predicts the imminent arrival of a salvific child to Emperor Augustus in Virgil's IV Eclogue:

> The Virgin now returns, and the reign of Saturn,
> The new generation now comes down from heaven.
> Lucina, look with favor on this child,
> —Lucina, goddess, pure—this child by whom
> The Age of Iron gives way to the Golden Age.[11]

Nebulous words, as were most mantic declarations, but these came to be seen by Christians over the centuries as a foretelling of the coming of the savior to the emperor during whose reign—and under whose pax romana—would come the birth of Christ.

11. Virgil, *Eclogue* IV, trans. David Ferry (New York: Farrar, Straus and Giroux, 1999), 29.

Michelangelo's third panel, dedicated to the fall from grace of man and woman, illustrates Eve's turbulent loss of status in the post-fall world. On the left side of the *Temptation and Fall of Man* (fig. 4.-6). Adam and Eve appear as two halves of a whole, as if recalling the image of male and female from Plato's *Symposium*. Despite clearly defined differences, the two reach together for the forbidden fruit. Eve, more passive, extends a languid arm while reclining on the ground, while Adam, more impetuous, lunges forward. Their bodies are each rendered beautifully by the standards of ancient art. Eve is strong and lifts her torso effortlessly, while Adam leans over her like a protective mantle allowing her to flourish. The proximity of their two nude bodies brings them no shame or discomfort; it is an elegant conjoining of perfect forms. They are both luminous—he more ruddy, she with a creamier radiance. They fit together, effortlessly beautiful, in the ideal state of man and woman in harmony and partnership.

On the other side of the panel, that perfect pair's radiant beauty has faded in the tragedy of the fall. Their once-erect posture is now hunched over in shame and fear; the light drains from their bodies; gravity dogs these forms whose bodies appear to have become a burden to them and through them to humanity.[12] Furthermore, the nature of the easy interaction between man and woman has changed. Adam now crowds Eve with his shoulder and "blocks the light from Eve's body, so that her body seems darker than his."[13] The role of Eve seems to diminish after the fall, as she is destined to live in the shadow of the man, as foretold in Genesis:

I will greatly multiply your pain in childbirth, In pain you will bring forth children; Yet your desire will be for your husband, and he will rule over you. (Gn 3:16)

This image of the fallen Eve might appear to illustrate the pervasive belief at Michelangelo's time that woman was inferior to man, an attitude expressed, for example, in the work of Nicholas de Cusa. Nicholas elaborated a theory of gender polarity, based on the study of Greek

---

12. Lev and Granados, *Body for Glory*, 71.
13. Pfeiffer, *Sistine Chapel*, 205.

Figure 4-6. Temptation and Fall of Man, Sistine Chapel

philosophers and mathematicians, by which men were associated with light and unity and women were associated with otherness and darkness.[14] The transformation of Eve after the fall from grace seems to hint at this association of woman with darkness.

A brief glance at the final scenes of the ceiling might seem to further reinforce this perception of woman's inferiority to man. Women rally in the *Deluge* as they try to carry their children to safety or pensively wait for death, but they make merely a fleeting appearance in the *Sacrifice of Noah* and are entirely absent at the scene of the *Drunkenness of Noah*. It would appear that the great plan for complementarity in Eden has gone much awry.

14. I am very much indebted to the work of Sr. Mary Prudence Allen in *The Concept of Woman*, vol. 2, *The Early Humanist Reformation, 1250–1500* (Grand Rapids, Mich.: Eerdmans, 2002), 788, for the research done on the gender theory of Nicholas de Cusa.

Yet nothing could be further from Michelangelo's intention. As the history of humanity did not end with a Noah unconscious in his barn, neither does the divine vision of complementarity end with the fall. As the viewer's attention turns to the next series of panels in the vault, Michelangelo's composition will express the ongoing complementarity through the successive eras.

Men, Women, and Knowledge of Divine Will: Prophets and Sibyls

The new tenor of the story was set by Michelangelo's striking change in palette. The nine scenes of Genesis display a decided lack of color compared to the brilliant hues of the panels painted by fifteenth-century masters below them. Along with the patina of age and candle smoke from services in the chapel, Michelangelo's muted pinks, grays, and beiges fueled decades of theories that the artist was so attached to sculpture that he could not think in color.

Those theories were thoroughly discredited by the cleaning of the Sistine Chapel ceiling. The dull tones of the Genesis narrative were then revealed to contrast intentionally and violently with the bright jewel tones of the figures immediately underneath. The art of the fresco, applying pigment to wet plaster, required that Michelangelo work on conjoining sections. As he was painting the dark, almost dismal background of Noah's drunkenness, he was also preparing the dazzling pigments for the figures below. The figures that draw the eye out of the dim, discouraging scene of *Drunkenness of Noah* provide the next cycle of decoration in the chapel: the prophets and sibyls.

While the eastern and western walls are anchored by two male prophets for liturgical reasons, the side walls of the nave that delineate the processional journey are flanked by both men and women. The pairing of male prophets and pagan prophetesses was primarily intended to illustrate the story of salvation as revealed respectively to the Jewish people and to the Gentiles. Early Christian author Lactantius lauded the sibyls for their gift of communication with the Gentiles, "the testimonies of the oracles and the sacred verses, which are much more reliable."[15] In the chapel, the decision to use these female figures goes a step further and adds a dimension of visual complementarity to the space, with its measured antiphonal rhythm of male and female.

Michelangelo was certainly not the first to use the symbolic images of the sibyls, but he chose to depict them in a completely original fashion. The selection of prophetesses—Persian, Eritrean, Delphic, Cumean, and Libyan—represented the known civilizations from the shores of India to North Africa to nearby Naples. These women embodied the universal mission of the church. The strong differentiation, not only among the women themselves but also between the male and the female figures, visibly underscores a difference in how the men and women receive divine knowledge and react to the presence of God.

It was Michelangelo's painting master, Domenico Ghirlandaio, who first introduced this feminine imagery to Florence in the Sassetti Chapel executed between 1483 and 1485. The sibyls made their artistic debut in Rome in 1489 in the Caraffa Chapel painted by Filippino Lippi. They were welcomed into papal apartments in 1492 when Pinturicchio decorated the hall of the liberal arts for Pope Alexander VI with a pairing of sibyls and prophets in the lunettes (fig. 4-7). These fifteenth-century painters, however, painted these female figures to look virtually alike: all boast long flowing locks, lithe bodies, pale, oval, youthful faces—more like frolicking nymphs than women possessed of divine knowledge. While paired with their male counterparts, they had little by way of individual characteristics. The prophets were always depicted with great variation: young and old, clean-shaven and bearded, while the mantic women seemed like cloned starlets, mere pretty backdrops for the male protagonists.

Not so with the five women painted by Michelangelo. Each of his sibyls is startlingly, unforgettably different, as indeed is each of his prophets. Old, bowed Jeremiah is distinct from the young, energetic

---

15. Lactantius, *Divine Institutes: Books I–VII*, book I, chap. 6, trans. Sister Mary Francis McDonald, OP, Fathers of the Church 49 (Washington, D.C.: The Catholic University of America Press, 1964), 32. The final word in the translation has been amended so that "reliable" is used in place of the unusual choice of "specific" for the Latin word certiora. See an older translation at http://www.newadvent.org/fathers/07011.

Daniel, who in turn contrasts with the proud, contemplative Joel. The same is true of these women, each one conveying her history and experience in her appearance and demeanor and complementing her male counterpart across the vault.

The Cumean sibyl must be considered the most venerable, as the woman who brought prophetic gifts, originally found only in Greece, Persia, and eastern civilizations, to ancient Rome. Dionysius of Halicarnassus claims that the Cumean sibyl was a foreign woman who sold books of prophecy to the Etruscan king Tarquinius, thus beginning the tradition of consulting the sibylline tomes in moments of peril for the city. Virgil dedicated book IV of the *Aeneid* to this formidable figure, who knew how to navigate Aeneas to the underworld and back. As the centuries passed, she became so associated with the Incarnation that in the *Jesse Tree* of the thirteenth-century Ingeborg Psalter, the Cumean sibyl takes her place immediately underneath Ezekiel. This pairing paved the way for Michelangelo to use the same two prophetic figures as a cornice for the *Creation of Woman*.

Michelangelo's depiction of this well-known oracular figure is shockingly new. Occupying a central section of the ceiling, her sheer size and hulking figure command attention. No slight sprite of Filippino Lippi here, she is gravitas personified. Alluding to the Ovidian myth in which Apollo offered the youthful Cumean sibyl endless life, but then withheld eternal youth when the girl refused to exchange it for her virginity, Michelangelo paints her as a leathery, aged woman. The crevices in her visage are visible from the floor, the flowing hair of maidenhood is bound in a veil, and her legs are pressed tightly together, still protecting her modesty. Michelangelo captures in pigment her prophetic power, so vividly described by Virgil.

> Before their eyes, she grows tall, something not mortal
> Enters, she is changed by the breath of the god
> Breathing through her. "Aeneas of Troy," she demands,
> "Your vows and your prayers, why do you wait? Pray,
> For until you have prayed, the jaws of this cavern
> Won't echo or open."[16]

16. Virgil, *Aenead*, book VI, trans. Seamus Heaney (New York: Farrar, Straus and Giroux, 2016), lines 74–79a (Latin lines 47–53), 9.

She makes a contemplative complement to the active prophet Ezekiel, who shares the bay with her. Where the male prophet of the many visions seems the more ecstatic, disregarding his scroll and turning sharply to face an angel pointing upward, the female oracle appears more composed as she consults her books and scrolls. Ezekiel is draped in fiery scarlet while cool azure swathes the sibyl. Both powerful predictors of the Virgin birth, they complement each other in their modes of receiving divine knowledge.

The Eritrean sibyl, traditionally distinguished by a flame, was praised by Lactantius as "held to be more renowned and more noble than the others."[17] As the supreme pagan prophetess of monotheism, her writings also explicitly referred to Christ. In *The City of God*, St. Augustine declared, "This sibyl of Erythrae ... wrote some things that clearly concern Christ."[18] Inscribing her prophecies on leaves, she is credited with creating the acrostic, the most famous being ΙΧΘΥΣ for Ἰησοῦς Χριστός, Θεοῦ Υἱός, Σωτήρ, "Jesus Christ, Son of God, Savior."[19]

Michelangelo boasts a startlingly varied palette in this figure, draped in layers of many hues and textures (fig. 4-8). Classically elegant, the sibyl's modeled features resemble the Grecian statues from the Ionian islands whence she came. As she studies her text she receives illumination, as evidenced by the soft light that bathes her face. This radiance was painted so as to appear to come from the altar, in recognition of Christ as light.[20] The revelation to the sibyl is less direct than that to her counterpart, Isaiah the prophet, who turns toward and engages a cherub-like figure, indicating future events.

Still different is the Persian sibyl: shrouded in a rose-colored mantle and heavily robed, she hides from view. Often referred to as the He-

---

17. Lactantius, *Divine Institutes: Books I–VII*, 34.

18. St Augustine, *The City of God*, books XVII–XXII, trans. Gerald G. Walsh, SJ, and Daniel J. Honan, Fathers of the Church 24 (Washington, D.C.: The Catholic University of America Press, 1954), book XVIII, chap. 23, p. 114.

19. St Augustine, *The City of God*, book XVIII, chap. 23, p. 114.

20. Each of the prophetic figures of the Sistine Chapel ceiling is illuminated by a direct light painted into the fresco by the artist that is made to appear to come from the direction of the altar. The luminosity increases on the prophet or sibyl (as does the size) as the figure draws closer to the altar. It is the system with which Michelangelo was able to draw the eye away from the dark scenes at the far end of the chapel to the most important space of the sanctuary and altar.

Figure 4-7. Eritrean Sibyl by Bernardino Pinturicchio, Borgia Apartments

brew sibyl, she is the most modest of the prophetesses, with only a faint glimpse of her face and hands bared before the viewer. She peers at a small book, turning away from the altar. The light emanating from the sanctuary space bathes her robes, but her face remains in darkness.

Not so with her counterpart, Daniel, once a citizen of Judah, who spent years in captivity in Persia. The complementarity between these two figures plays on the Judeo-Persian crossover of revelation. Daniel does not turn away but projects dramatically into the light, and his knee shines like the sun as it thrusts toward the viewer. As he reads and writes, the prophetic visions seem to swell within him. Again in this pairing, the contemplative role falls to the female figure, while the active stance defines the male.

The Delphic sibyl delights viewers as the most charming and animated of the prophetesses. As the oracle who presided over the temple

Figure 4-8. Eritrean Sibyl, Sistine Chapel

at Delphi, she enjoys the same youthful perfection in face and form as Apollo does in statuary. Michelangelo displays an almost playful virtuosity by baring the arm below the shoulder, demonstrating his flawless anatomical drawing. Her dynamic pose, looking backward while turning forward, underscores her pivotal role in redirecting the viewer toward the altar. The shining carnelian, lapis, and peridot robes draw the eye away from the murky scenes of Noah's drunkenness toward the promise of light. She outshines her partner Joel, who wears a muted lavender, contrasting the sibyl's "green of hope, which is held together by the promise of a divine golden future" with the "violet garment of penance" worn by Joel, illustrating the two themes of Advent and Lent, hope and repentance.[21] Her idealized face, drawn from classical statuary, contrasts with the almost portrait-like Joel, who "looks like a living person,"[22] with his concerned focus accentuated by his high forehead and furrowed brow.

The prophet and sibyl that close the journey toward the altar showcase Michelangelo's most dramatic use of color and draftsmanship. His depiction of the Libyan sibyl, representing the northern shores of Africa, was universally acclaimed in his own day as a masterpiece (fig. 4-9). Giorgio Vasari marveled at

the lovely figure of the Libyan sibyl who, having written a great volume drawn from many books, is about to rise to her feet in an attitude of womanly grace; and at one and the same time she makes as if to rise and to close the book, something most difficult, not to say impossible for anyone but the master to have depicted.[23]

The daring of this unusual representation, a figure drawn from behind, shown with her arms outstretched, grasping the edges of her tome, awed Michelangelo's contemporaries. Although from his preparatory drawing it is clear that that the model was male (as was the norm in most Renaissance workshops), the delicacy of the position, the cinched waist and the flame-colored robe tantalizingly unfastened and held together only by a slight celeste band, renders the figure strikingly feminine for all of her obvious physical power. Her heavy rose robe flips up over the knee to reveal her legs through a sheer gossamer drapery. She sits across from Jeremiah, another of the most virtuoso figures on the vault, who hulks out of the ceiling, lost in contemplation of dark portents (fig. 4-10). His tunic, rose and flame-colored like that of Libyan

---

21. Pfeiffer, *Sistine Chapel*, 154. Indeed, some art historians have suggested that it is a portrait of Donato Bramante, Michelangelo's colleague and rival.

22. Vasari, *Lives of the Artists*, 358.

23. Vasari, *Lives of the Artists*, 358.

Figure 4-9. Libyan Sibyl, Sistine Chapel

sibyl, draw the two together even as their gestures set them apart. This time it is *she* who is active, closing her book and rising, while he sits in contemplation. They both gaze down upon the people beneath them, but she, the prophetess of hidden things revealed, looks with tender compassion, while he, the prophet of the capture and loss of Judah, his face lost in shadows, seems to portend those sad events.

None of these sibyls are the ethereal creatures depicted by earlier artists. Michelangelo imbued each one with physical presence and power, lending a visual gravitas to the prophetesses who revealed the will of the Lord to the Gentiles. But this master storyteller expanded his

Figure 4-10. Jeremiah, Sistine Chapel

characters yet further, painting each sibyl with a distinct appearance and identity that would complement her male counterpart. Where the male figures appear more active in their reception of knowledge, the women appear more contemplative. As destiny comes to fruition in the final panels toward the sanctuary, the woman expresses compassion and the man expresses solemn studiousness. These, the largest figures of the Sistine Chapel ceiling, guide the viewer's eye toward the altar, the site of the fulfillment of all prophecies, a visual synergy between Jew and Gentile, sibyl and prophet, and man and woman.

Heroes and Heroines

The thundering figures of sibyls and prophets are given grand trompe l'oeil niches as part of the quadrature firmament that anchors the chapel. The four corner pendentives, however, link the lofty world of Creation and prophesy with the sturdy walls of the earth-bound chapel. In these corners, Michelangelo chose to buttress his ceiling with images of Old Testament heroes and again chose to pair men and women in the great endeavor of protecting their people. Two heroes, David and Moses, are paired with two heroines, Judith and Esther. David and Judith destroyed their enemies through decapitation, while Moses and Esther saved their people by means of a cross.

The two champions splayed over the entrance arch are David and Judith; they are also the first figures Michelangelo completed as he began the task of painting from this side of the chapel. Fully aware of his fame as the sculptor of the colossal David of Florence, Michelangelo departed from the heroic nudity and psychological interiority of his earlier version and depicted David about to deal the final blow to his enemy (fig. 4-11). Sword raised, David straddles Goliath as the giant endeavors to rise in vain. Michelangelo's hasty brushstroke captures the action-packed moment of the kill.

These strokes grow more precise, and the depiction more detailed, in the tale of Judith. As in the depiction of David, Judith is placed at the very center of the triangular field, and, again like her counterpart, a plain white background emphasizes the Jewish widow as the drama's protagonist (fig. 4-12). But in this depiction, the deed is already accomplished, and Judith and her maidservant are escaping with the head of Holofernes, the Assyrian general. On the right, the decapitated body lies in the shadows as if frozen in a final death throe. On the left a soldier sleeps heavily on his shield. The maid holds the head on a tray; she stoops to allow Judith to cover it. Judith is the only dynamic figure in the group. Her foot elegantly poised like that of the Libyan sibyl, she steps away from the tent, but then turns abruptly as if she hears something. Her heroic action is already complete, but she remains alert. In this pairing of scenes, Michelangelo adopts two analogous ways of rep-

Figure 4-11. David and Goliath, Sistine Chapel

resenting similar action-packed stories: David is in the midst of the ugly business of murder, while Judith is portrayed as having already performed the same deed, with the brutal moment of death in the past. Michelangelo's storytelling is enhanced by complementing the aggressiveness of David with the anxiousness of Judith.

In this pairing of heroes it can also be seen that Michelangelo chose to linger over female fashions far more than he did over those of the men. Goliath may wear a few golden stripes on his tunic, but the ribbons and décor of Judith's robes reveal an appreciative eye. Her hair is bound in a pearl-encrusted lapis-colored cap, and as she turns sharply her long neck is exposed. A melon-color sash crosses her iridescent green robe, hemmed with a golden fringe that draws attention to

Figure 4-12. Judith and Holofernes, Sistine Chapel

a breast visible in profile. The figure of Judith is coyly attractive, her clothes flattering and fashionable; no wonder Holofernes lost his head when faced with such a remarkable woman! It would appear that Michelangelo himself was not impervious to her appeal, if the persistent rumor indeed be true, that he depicted his own portrait as the head of Holofernes on the tray.

Esther and Moses span the corners of the altar space. Here, the heroes are no longer center stage, but hidden away from the main action. Moses does not appear at all in the scene of the Brazen serpent—many suffer and several are saved, but the great figure of the venerable patriarch is nowhere to be seen.

Esther, on the other side, is almost lost in the crowd around the couch of Ahasuerus. The center stage is occupied by the gigantic nude body of Haman, stretched out on his cross in a tour de force of foreshortening. His broad bare chest is echoed in the figure of Ahasuerus, reclining and pointing back toward the figure of Haman. In the middle of this circle, formed of the two powerful characters, Esther, slight and youthful, emerges from the shadows clad in a scarlet mantle. Although her hair is bound like that of a matron, the face of Esther, wide-eyed with her heavy draperies, accentuates the delicate youth of her visage. Barely noticeable at first glance, this heroine, irresistible to Ahasuerus for her beauty, subtly makes her presence felt from behind the scenes. Esther is content not to be the protagonist, just as Moses no longer appears after he has raised the brazen serpent. Their duty as intercessors completed, they silently exit the stage.

The behavior of Michelangelo's heroes and heroines draws on the patterns of differences between men and women noted by Renaissance theorists and modern neuroscientists alike. To defeat his enemy, David needed decisive action, whereas Judith considered how to catch her enemy unawares before destroying him. (They are of course both dependent on the help of the Lord, but that is the point of the story.)[24] Moses furthers salvation by the construction of an object, the brazen serpent, while Esther gently uses interpersonal relationships to achieve a similar goal. The complementary differences between men and women present in the Old Testament accounts are given life and color by Michelangelo on the Sistine ceiling.

By his images of heroes and heroines, Michelangelo created two formidable, complementary "teams": Moses and Esther, unobtrusive intercessors, and Judith and David, fierce defenders of their people. From these isolated characters, the story then shifts to an ever-increasing population. A chosen people, taken out of Egypt, brought to their promised land, attacked and then exiled, provides the drama for the final cycle of images, propelling the narrative into the culmination of salvation history.

---

24. The recognition of behavior traits distinct to men and women comes from Simon Baron-Cohen, *The Essential Difference: Male and Female Brains and the Truth about Autism* (New York: Basic Books, 2003), cited in chapter 5 of this volume: Paul Vitz, "Men and Women: Their Differences and Their Complementarity: Evidence from Psychology and Neuroscience."

Visualizing the "Gen" in the Generations before Christ

The fictive architecture of Michelangelo's trompe l'oeil ceiling design rests on a series of sturdy arches along the side walls, with a triangular field at the apex of each arch thrusting its way into the narrative cycle above. In these spaces, where the lofty structures of the ceiling connect with the viewers' domain, Michelangelo chose to represent a cycle not of heroes or prophets, but the families that drove human history forward toward redemption. By depicting the ancestors of Christ, the artist brings the story into the world of ordinary men and women, struggling from generation to generation. As a result, these figures seem more approachable, often more similar to candid family photographs than a studied exercise in artistic virtuosity.

The genealogy of Christ traces the bloodline of Jesus from the patriarch Abraham to Joseph, husband of Mary. It opens the Gospel of Matthew and counts forty generations. In the biblical passage, each member of the male line is noted, while only a scant five women are named: Tamar, Rahab, Ruth, Bathsheba, and Mary. Michelangelo's version, already innovative as an iconographical decision, pairs each of the scriptural male figures with female counterparts, producing a unique decorative cycle where every father of the genealogy corresponds to a mother. The addition of twenty-two female figures, defined by their motherhood, provided the artist a surprisingly creative outlet for costumes, poses, and even personalities. Michelangelo even added a boisterous display of children climbing, sleeping, nursing, and playing, forming a refreshing ribbon of domesticity around the weight of the more formal scenes.

In supplementing the written genealogy with his own inventions, Michelangelo produced a groundbreaking iconography in the history of art. This was hardly unusual for the ambitious artist. But in previous works he had plenty of precedents to wrestle with. The series of the ancestors of Christ, however, complete with fathers and mothers, had never been done before. This not only left the artist a certain freedom to invent, but also added a much-needed current of naturalism to the often-overwhelming monumentality of his historical and allegorical figures.

Despite a certain neglect from modern scholars, these paired images are also remarkable from a formal point of view in their swift execution and almost ad hoc approach, similar to a snapshot. They also represent a startling development in religious art, not only in depicting Christian ancestors, but also in capturing the interaction between mothers and children. The most surprising aspect of all, however, remains his depiction of these twenty-two mothers; young, old, active, or sedate, they are a far cry from the studied artifice of his other figures.

While at first glance these images may seem hastily dashed off in comparison with the somber Genesis narratives above them, closer inspection reveals a personal and thoughtful ideal of family, which in turn reflects Michelangelo's era and above all the artist's own interiority.

Close study of the genealogy reveals a facet of Michelangelo's artistic vision rarely explored in art: a respect and even delight in mothers and motherhood. The depiction of ordinary mothers, already common to Michelangelo during his years of training, blossomed into an exaltation of maternity in the Sistine ceiling. Through it we can trace a theological thread from Eve, the first mother and the central figure of the ceiling, to Mary, the mother of God, to whom the chapel was dedicated.

Images of lineage were not uncommon in ecclesiastical art, beginning with depictions of papal succession. Ever since the fifth century, parades of papal portraits had graced many a sacred space. They would draw an unbroken line, a "family tree" of popes from St. Peter, the first pope, to varying moments in history, thus underscoring continuity in papal successions. The Sistine Chapel vaunted the likenesses of thirty-two pre-Constantinian popes from St. Peter to St. Marcellus, and St. Paul's "outside the walls" contains an array of portraits up to the present day. When Michelangelo arrived in Siena in 1501 to work in the cathedral, the project to decorate the cornice with papal portrait busts was in process, having begun just six years earlier.

Two gospel accounts trace the lineage of Christ: one, the aforementioned Matthew with its forty-two generations; the other, a longer version in Luke containing a full seventy-seven progenitors tracing back from Joseph to Adam of Genesis. Mary's family line was also reverenced through the Tree of Jesse, perhaps the most common type of genealogical image in art, which focused on the line of King David, Jesse's youngest son. Giotto's Arena Chapel had also employed images of Christ's ancestors in the decorative bands around the vault scattered amid prophets, saints, and a few sacred stories.

But until Michelangelo's vault, no artist had ever brought the viewer through time and lineage with a series of families, replete with wives and infants. The common thread in every previous illustration of the passage of time through generations, whether by means of popes or patriarchs, was male-oriented imagery. The Tree of Jesse, while generally following the line laid out by Matthew, only showed male progeny and of those males, mostly the royal relatives. Jesse's Tree had graced dozens of medieval manuscripts; in Santa Croce, Michelangelo's family church, Taddeo Gaddi had painted a monumental Jesse Tree above his Last Supper. Michelangelo's representation of ancestry distinguished itself from all other precedents in its inclusion of mothers. Moreover, he did not depict them as regal, distant icons of motherhood, but rather as busy, everyday women tending to toddlers, toilette, toys, and tasks.

Michelangelo's startling decision to place mothers and fathers side by side on the vault illustrates what Sister Mary Prudence Allen has called "gender reality" and was implicit in the design of the ceiling.[25] Illustrating the passing of generations, whether in Genesis or Matthew, necessarily emphasizes the begetting of children. Sister Prudence writes,

The root "gen" from the beginning of Judaism establishes the significance of the history of a people living in continuity generation after generation. It incorporates the act of sexual intercourse, of a male and a female, of a man and a woman who become father and mother through their synergetic union. Thus we can also say that the concept of sex is inherently included within the concept of the root of generation, or "gen."[26]

---

25. Allen, "Gender Reality," *Solidarity: The Journal of Catholic Social Thought and Secular Ethics* 4, no. 1 (2014): 25.

26. Allen, "Gender Reality," 25.

Michelangelo's pairings in his genealogy is in itself the picture of the essential complementarity required for a population to form and a people to grow.

Michelangelo suffered through the activity of painting, although certainly not in silence. Standing with his head thrown back as he reached up to paint the nine panels of Genesis and the crucial passages of the prophets and sibyls must have caused him exceptional discomfort.[27] The design of the scaffold, planned by the painter himself, involved a flat platform lifted to a few feet from the ceiling and then stairs descending on either side to allow access to the spandrels and lunettes. In these lower sections, painted after the travails of the vault, he could sit, rest his neck, and lean forward.

That physical liberation makes itself felt in the speed and ease of these figures. Analysis of the ceiling during the restoration from 1981 to 1989 has revealed that painting the vault took at least 520 *giornate* (the term for a day's work in fresco) spread over two campaigns, the first from 1508 to 1511 and the second from 1511 to 1512, when the artist was under massive pressure to finish quickly.[28] Michelangelo started, however, not above the altar, which is where the actual narrative begins, but near the entrance, a smaller section of the chapel reserved for those not of the papal court or "family." Therefore, his last paintings were those closest to the altar. Although the artist progressed much more rapidly during the second period of work, a certain pattern emerges in the time spent on each section of the ceiling. The Genesis narratives were the most time-consuming: twenty-four *giornate* for the panel of the *Deluge* and sixteen for the *Drunkenness of Noah*, although the numbers grew smaller as Michelangelo reached the final panels. The prophets and sibyls required extensive labor, ranging from ten to eighteen *giornate*, but the lunettes and spandrels of the ancestors were

---

27. This is testified to by a poem written by Michelangelo to Giovanni of Pistoia during the ordeal of the ceiling, replete with a drawing with the artist standing with his head bent back. This is kept in Casa Buonarotti, and the translation by Creighton Gilbert is in the *Complete Poems and Selected Letters of Michelangelo*, 5.

28. Gianluigi Colalucci, "Tecniche di restauro" [The Technique of the Sistine Ceiling Frescos], in *La Cappella Sistina. I Primi Restauri: La Scoperta del Colore*, edited by Marcella Boroli (Novara, Italy: Istituto Geografico De Agostini, 1986), chapter 9.

executed in large fields of five-and-a-half square yards, employing at most three *giornate* and occasionally only one.

Also distinguishing this section from the rest of the vault is the execution without preliminary drawings or cartoons. No marks of incision or pouncing technique were found on any of the twenty-two extant panels, indicating that they were done freehand.[29] (The lunettes containing the images of Abraham, Isaac, Jacob, Judah, Hezron, Perez, and Ram were destroyed in 1534 to make room for the Last Judgment.) The variations of the brushstrokes and the speed of the execution manifest Michelangelo's passion for drawing from life, as he varies parallel strokes, staccato swipes, cross-hatching, and reinforced contours to capture fleeting gestures and expressions. The vivid colors visible in the surprising accents and use of the shot silk (*cangiante*) technique are almost entirely absent in the Genesis panels. This color technique, which involves creating shadows and highlights with other contrasting colors, served to direct attention to figures that would otherwise be hidden in the shadows of the undercroft of the vault. In these scenes, remarked the restorers, "the practice of drawing and painting fuse into a single moment."[30] The result of this rapid execution is that more than any other images on the ceiling, the depictions of these ancestors have the immediacy of photography. The artist's experiences from daily life seem transposed directly onto the wall without the customary filters of antique sculpture, complex studio poses, or quotations from previous masters.

The male figures display a wide variety of poses and types as well as a great deal of wit. Michelangelo's penetrating eye was swift to notice character actors in the crowd, and here, released from the monumental confines of the story of salvation, he indulged in a few clever observations. Boaz (reportedly a caricature of Pope Julius II) gazes at his mirror image carved in the knob of his walking stick;[31] stylish Aminadab sports earrings and a jaunty head scarf; Abijah sleeps, a familiar sight in any Roman tavern; and Naason slouches in relaxation. The latter

29. Colalucci, "Tecniche di restauro," chapter 9.
30. Fabrizio Mancinelli and Anna Maria de Strobel DeLuca, eds., *Michelangelo: Le Lunette e le Vele della Cappella Sistina; Liber Generationuis Jesu Christi* (Rome: Leonardo-De Luca, 1992), 8.
31. Pfeiffer, *Sistine Chapel*, 122.

could allude to the artist himself, sitting, as was possible for him only when painting the lunettes, completing the final section of the monumental task.

Humor, however, is replaced with warmth and tenderness when Michelangelo turns to portray the mothers. They are surprisingly stylish, as opposed to the heroic nudes of the principal narrative and the classicizing draperies of the sibyls; it seems that Michelangelo could occasionally spare an eye for contemporary fashions. In the earlier figure of Mary, closest to the door, he spent more time on sartorial details, such as a rainbow-colored shawl or an elaborate pearl-speckled headdress. Michelangelo would never replicate the skillful rendering of the pleated, beribboned, and diaphanous veils that distinguished the ethereal women of Botticelli and Filippo Lippi but would favor more sculptural head coverings such as the architectonic coifs of Pollaiuolo. In the successive lunette, the wife of Eleazar wears the *gamurra*, the typical stitched overdress of a Florentine woman over a simple white *camicia*, embellished with the trademark changeable sleeves (fig. 4-13). She wears a shorter, simpler cap in keeping with her sterner and more masculine features. Eleazar's wife borrows a page from male fashions, wearing the purse and key customary to the man of the house. Indeed, her husband looks almost startled by her vigor as she holds up her son, surveying him solemnly. As was the case in many Tuscan households, here it is evidently the wife who calls the shots.

The strict architectural framework of the ancestor series repeats the motif of the fictive niches painted by the Quattrocento masters in the Gallery of the Popes, and, at the same time, these more detailed outfits create a visual link with the finery in the narrative panels of the previous Florentine painters. Michelangelo's costumes become more "antique" and classicizing in the sibyls and prophets, before giving way to the triumph of the nude in the Genesis series. But in almost every pairing in the genealogy, the mothers' clothes are far more attentively rendered than those of the fathers. Achim's bride wears a bodice that dips invitingly beneath her shoulder blades, cinched tightly at the waist before flowing into a cascade of stylish drapery. Azor's wife wears a cummerbund in the color of copper patina accentuating her breast caught in the asymmetrical neckline of her overdress. The voluminous mustard skirt and mauve shawl on Jedidiah, mother of King Josiah, falls away to reveal an olive dress with a striking back panel that complement the intricate rolls and knots of her silver and periwinkle turban. By contrast, the breasts of Hephzi-ban are accentuated by the brilliant white of her thin chemise tucked into a wisp of ribbon around her shoulders. The veiled Maacah emphasizes her pregnant belly with a cornice of gold, teal, and scarlet drapery, while Rahab, the former prostitute, is enfolded in modest drapery with a front slit common to nursing mothers. For someone raised in a household of men with four brothers, Michelangelo displays an astonishing knowledge of the variety of women's braids, turbans, veils, and headbands.[32]

Certainly, Michelangelo must have picked up some of his acumen for costume design during his apprenticeship with Ghirlandaio, whose ability to render the finest styles in Florence made him one of the city's most popular painters. Known for illustrating the fabulous fashions in his many portraits, Ghirlandaio (according to Vasari, the son of a celebrated maker of women's headgear) excelled in rendering women's clothing, a skill that brought great profit to his studio. Although never sharing Ghirlandaio's interest in depicting sartorial minutiae, Michelangelo seems to have honed the ability to observe and depict a broad gamut of attire.

One of Michelangelo's earliest sonnets, written at the outset of the Sistine project, playfully describes women's wear in a brief moment of erotic whimsy. The poem demonstrates a spirit of observation both of female finery and physique as well as a natural male reaction to the female form.

> All through the day that dress is well contented
> That binds her breast, and then seems to be stretch
> And what they call the filigreed gold has touched
> her neck and cheeks, and cannot make an end.

---

32. Both Edward Maeder, in his essay "The Costumes Worn by the Ancestors of Christ," chapter 6 in *The Sistine Chapel: A Glorious Restoration*, ed. Pierluigi De Vecchi (New York: Abradale, 1999), and Heinrich Pfeiffer, *Sistine Chapel*, discuss Michelangelo's interest in contemporary dress at length, albeit from different perspectives.

Figure 4-13. Eleazar's Wife, Sistine Chapel

> But happier still, that ribbon seems delighted,
> Having a golden tip made in a manner
> To press and touch the breast that it has yoked.
> And I believe the simple sash that's knotted
> Says to itself, I'd fashion here forever!
> How would it be then that my arms would act?[33]

In this section of the Sistine Chapel depicting Christ's ancestry, Michelangelo appears to have allowed himself a pause from the formal and monumental figures of the ceiling and from his quest for ideas and inspiration amid Pope Julius's collection of antique sculpture. The majority of these details of attire were not gleaned from ancient statuary or archaic descriptions, but from the piazzas and hearths of Florence, snapshots from home in the midst of courtly, masculine Rome. Though

33. *Complete Poems and Selected Letters of Michaelangelo*, 4.

his artistry was forged amid the muscular Greek statues or the sinewy studio hands who served as models, Michelangelo also could appreciate the voluptuous bodies of the women around him.

Families were part of piazza décor, especially during the grand public christenings in the Florentine baptistery, where a steady stream of infant citizens were inducted into their Christian and civic inheritance as soon as possible. Also, the unprecedented number of domestic scenes rendered in everything from birth trays to monumental fresco cycles took advantage of the holy births of Mary and John the Baptist to bring the viewer into contemporary birthing chambers. Aged thirty-three when embarking on the Sistine Chapel commission, Michelangelo would have been expected to take a wife (indeed, Raphael was compelled to at about the same age),[34] and thus it would not be strange that the idea of marriage and fatherhood made his eye keener to such scenes.

Many of Michelangelo's thoughts on wives and mothers would have been forged by the leading manual for up-and-coming families, *I Quattro Libri della Famiglia*, or *On the Family*, written by Leon Battista Alberti in 1440. Alberti, an illegitimate member of an aristocratic family, wrote a great deal about painting, sculpture, and architecture, but also composed the books on family life. To ensure circulation among the middle class of Florence, Alberti wrote this treatise in Italian instead of scholarly Latin. Michelangelo would have already been interested in Alberti's artistic thought, but the book on the family served as a manual for how to advance in society. Many of Alberti's ideas find expression in Michelangelo's depiction of Christ's ancestors. Wives are not meant to be chosen for looks or money alone but for overall "virtue," defined by Alberti as "aesthetic balance and harmony."[35]

Michelangelo's mothers balance care for their dress with virtuous poise, as if illustrating Alberti's treatise. Alberti warns of the "danger to babies in hard hands of men . . . let him sleep in his mother's lap."[36] The women have exclusive care of infants in the ceiling, whereas the

---

34. Vasari, *Lives of the Artists*, 319.
35. Allen, *Concept of Woman*, 2:18.
36. Leon Battista Alberti, *I Libri della Famiglia* (Turin: Einaudi, 1994), 59.

men play with the more boisterous toddlers, the age Alberti claims "is full of delight and is accompanied by general laughter ... the child makes known his wishes and the sparkle in child's face and words are comfort and delight of fathers."[37] In the swaddling age of children, Michelangelo's infants are assigned to women's quiet care rather than to the active attention of men. The playful toddler Shealtiel clambers onto his father's lap, and other boys vie for their fathers' attentions, but the infants nestle in the quiet warmth of their mothers. The continuity between Michelangelo's art and the writings of Alberti indicate not only thought, but study of what constitutes a good family and noble ancestry.

Very few preliminary drawings remain from the Sistine ceiling. A low estimate suggests that the artists produced some 300 to 400 detailed drawings from models, of which only sixty-five drawings of any sort remain. Of these, thirteen are dedicated to the scenes of the ancestors. The extant drawings were produced on a large sheet folded to become a sort of transportable sketchbook of eight pages, to be kept on hand for street scenes and figures that might inspire the artist.

These sketches show an endless variety of poses, taking the Florentine repertoire of composing figures in round, square, or rectangular frames and exponentially increasing the variations by arching the men, women, and children over and around the lunettes. Of Michelangelo's very few remaining sketches for the ancestors, none has the finer finished qualities of some of the *ignudi* or sibyls, but are comprised of swift lines that allow the ink to blot at crucial junctions where muscles contract or relax. Like memos sketched from life, one figure slouches, another sleeps, and a few lines indicate the action. The imagination must do the rest. On one faded sketch of a mother and child, the artist wrote, "dalgi bere," the germ of his idea to represent these mothers in action, whether nursing or working, as in further down on the same sheet where he portrays a figure holding a spindle. In a black chalk sketch of the Cumean Sibyl kept in the Royal gallery of Turin, the recto shows two seated female figures both engaged in caring for children. These are sketches for Amon's wife, Jedidah. Both drawings were meant to capture the most intimate moments between mother and child and

---

37. Alberti, *I Libri della* Famiglia, 59.

are rendered in delicate lines of chalk as if hoping not to disturb the serenity of the scene. The final figure is a masterpiece of peaceful activity. Meshullameth, wife of Manasseh, cradles her swaddled son while rocking another infant in a cradle with her foot (fig. 4.-14.). This maternal multitasking, alien to the papal palace but familiar in the home, was immortalized in the Sistine Chapel.

Michelangelo would have been able to find some inspiration for his busy women in the Sistine panels of the life of Jesus and the life of Moses. Executed by the previous generation of Florentine masters, these panels also make room for families and activity. One was done by Ghirlandaio himself, no doubt evoking for Michelangelo his early days of fresco painting in the Tornabuoni Chapel. Only three of the history panels are devoid of women. The *Delivery of the Keys* by Perugino depicts only men because this image bears direct reference to the conclave, the all-male event that took place among the cardinals in the chapel. Botticelli's *Punishment of Korah* alludes to the precedent of conferring the authority of priesthood, another male-only activity. The last image to leave out women is Cosimo Rosselli's *Last Supper*, the institution of the Eucharist that was re-presented in the enclosure around the altar where only men would be able to stand. The remaining images, whether by Botticelli, Luca Signorelli, or Perugino, are enlivened by women, in particular by mothers tending to their children.

Among Michelangelo's families of the ancestors, the women are considerably more active than the men. Over twice as many women as men are engaged in some task, whether subduing unruly offspring or tending to domestic chores. Azubah, the wife of Asa, appears to have fallen asleep with her spindle in hand, exhausted by her work. Only five male figures read, write, or care for children, whereas twenty-three women are working. Bathsheba spins, Rahab cuts fabric, and the wife of Amminadab combs out her golden hair in the sun, a common trick used among Renaissance beauties to keep their blond locks shining.

Michelangelo's observed reality of families from the hearths of Florence reflects the concepts of complementarity between mothers and fathers in raising children, noted by Alberti and reinforced by modern neuroscience, and breathes life and color into science and theory.

Figure 4-14. Meshullameth, Sistine Chapel

No greater image of motherhood in action exists in Renaissance art than a mother nursing her child. From the development of Medieval *Madonna Lactans* to the allegory of charity, the ultimate image of self-giving—second only to the crucifix—was the breastfeeding mother. While many children were sent out to a wet nurse, as was the case of Michelangelo himself, authors from Plutarch to Leon Battista Alberti advocated breastfeeding as a way to allow mothers to increase their love for their children and for children to receive good health and good habits.[38] Sewing, cooking, and cleaning were all fine accomplishments, but children were the most important activities of mothers. Michelangelo's first *Madonna and Child* showed the infant Jesus, who appears to have just fallen asleep at his mother's breast, and the artist would return to the theme again and again. Among the industrious mothers of Michel-

38. Alberti, *I Libri della Famiglia*, 128.

angelo's Sistine lunettes, two are engaged in nursing children. One, Jerusha, bride of Uzziah, nurses little Jotham, who lurches toward his mother; meanwhile, the wife of Josaphat wrestles with one boy leaping on her back, while she cradles another and a third greedily nurses. No inert motherhood here: nurturing and feeding involve a full physical engagement.

Far from passively posing for roll call, these women, captured at work, become doers on the Sistine ceiling. They find their greatest complement in God the Father and his creative dynamism in separating light and dark, bringing forth the sun and moon, and bestowing life upon man. It is not only the male who is created in the image and likeness of God; mothers emulate him in their capacity to bestow life and their activity in nurturing it.

Adding to the domesticity of these scenes is the accumulation of objects, household family items that women gather to make a home. Renaissance marriage chests were laden with objects that newlywed women would bring to make their homes. The Sistine vault is remarkable for its lack of "stuff"—even the creation of vegetable life is represented by just a few tufts of grass, and the Garden of Eden is strikingly barren. The sibyls and the prophets may hold books, scrolls, or torches, but they are short on the accessories and everyday objects of Renaissance life. By contrast, Michelangelo emphasizes an element of hominess in his depictions of these mothers by adding plates, spindles, combs, mirrors, cradles, and footstools. The settings, albeit stark and architectural, are made more familiar by the addition of these objects.

Michelangelo here not only evokes the "virtuous woman" of Proverbs 31:10, whose value "is far beyond pearls" and whose work and warmth are "to be praised," but also draws these many often anonymous mothers closer to Eve, the first mother and central figure of the Sistine ceiling. Bocaccio, the enormously popular fourteenth-century author, penned a widely distributed series of biographies of famous women. The series opened with Eve, the first woman, and offered an intriguing perspective on her nobility. "There while her husband tilled the soil with the hoe, this distinguished woman, famous for her above-mentioned deeds, discovered the art of spinning with the distaff. She experienced the pains of childbirth and also suffered the grief which tortures the mind at the death of children and grandchildren."[39] As these many women lived and suffered in the wake of the expulsion, they united their everyday family experience to the great epic of salvation history depicted on the ceiling. When writing on women, Alberti joined Boccaccio in praising the First Woman and drew out their complementary natures.

[Eve] did first find a roof under which to nourish and protect herself and her offspring. There she remained, busy in the shadow, nourishing and caring for her children. And since woman was busy guarding and taking care of the heir, she was not in a position to go out and find what she and her children required for the maintenance of their life.[40]

Michelangelo maintained this tradition of the heroic work of motherhood as he painted those brightly colored women in the shadows of the vault, nurturing, nursing, and caring for the generations that would lead from Eve's fall to Christ's redemption.

Mary: Mother, Heroine, Prophetess

The myriad women depicted on the Sistine Chapel ceiling demonstrate a vast range of ages, styles, poses, and costumes. Yet the qualities they represent—the pre-fall state, their ability to understand divine will, their willingness to intercede for their people, and the nurturing care of their families—all find their culmination in the Virgin Mary. Despite the fact that Mary now appears in the chapel only once in the Last Judgment and vaguely in the genealogy, the chapel was dedicated to the Assumption of the Virgin on August 15, 1477, and the altar piece of the same subject was painted by Perugino, the leader of the earlier team of fourteenth-century artists. That painting was destroyed to make room for the *Last Judgment*. But as we shall see, Michelangelo returned Mary to the focal point of the chapel in an even greater role than before.

39. Giovanni Boccaccio, "De Mulieribus Claris," in *Letteratura Italiana Storia e Testi*, ed. Pier Giorgio Ricci (Milan: R. Ricciardi, 1965), 9:721.
40. Alberti, *I Libri della Famiglia*, 128.

During his lifetime, Michelangelo portrayed Mary in many guises, a compendium of feminine imagery that ultimately represents the perfect form of complementarity. The four principles of complementarity noted by Sr. Mary Prudence Allen—equal dignity, significant difference, synergetic relation, and intergenerational fruition—are all found in the person of Mary and in her relationship to Christ.[41] From the New Eve who cooperates with the New Adam to steadfast heroines flanking the dynamic heroes; from prescient eyes and sealed lips alongside voluble prophets to the nurturing mother assisting the contemplative father, Michelangelo used Mary as the matrix of all his images of complementarity in the Sistine Chapel ceiling.

The Virgin Mary played an enormous role in the development of the young artist. Even as Michelangelo first honed his skills and taste for sculpting nude figures in action in the *Battle of the Lapiths and Centaurs*, he countered this violent drama by carving the *Madonna of the Steps*, where a peaceful Mary pensively nurses her son.

His breakthrough work, *The Pieta*, sculpted in 1500, already demonstrated a completely innovative interpretation of the centuries- old subject by changing the emphasis of the scene from Jesus to Mary.[42] His images of Mary would continue, always changing, always looking at the Mother of God from a different perspective, until his last work, the *Rodannini Pieta*. In the numerous representations he made of the Virgin—in tempera, fresco, or marble—the inspiration for each of the fascinating women of the Sistine Chapel ceiling becomes apparent.

The New Eve: Mary as Mother of All the Living

Identifying Mary as the new Eve dates back to the earliest church fathers. St. Irenaeus declared, "The knot of Eve's disobedience was untied by Mary's obedience. For what the virgin Eve had tied by her un-

---

41. Allen, "Four Principles of Complementarity."

42. Lev, "Reading Theological Context: A Marian Interpretation of Michelangelo's Roman Pietà," in *Revisioning: Critical Methods of Seeing Christianity in the History of Art*, ed. James Romaine and Linda Stratford (Eugene, Ore.: Cascade, 2013), 207–22.

belief, this Mary untied by her belief."[43] This dichotomy between Mary and Eve grew into a sort of slogan by the time of St. Jerome: "Death came through Eve, life through Mary."[44] Centuries of meditation on Mary's choice to obey the divine will deepened the church's understanding of her place in the history of salvation so that Mary would be perceived as having an increasingly active role in man's Redemption. Blessed John Henry Newman wrote,

As the history stands, she was a sine-qua-non, a positive, active, cause of it ... she was not a mere instrument in the Incarnation, such as David, or Judah, may be considered; they [church fathers] declare she co-operated in our salvation not merely by the descent of the Holy Ghost upon her body, but by specific holy acts, the effect of the Holy Ghost within her soul; that, as Eve forfeited privileges by sin, so Mary earned privileges by the fruits of grace; that, as Eve was disobedient and unbelieving, so Mary was obedient and believing; that, as Eve was a cause of ruin to all, Mary was a cause of salvation to all; that as Eve made room for Adam's fall, so Mary made room for our Lord's reparation of it; and thus, whereas the free gift was not as the offence, but much greater, it follows that, as Eve co-operated in effecting a great evil, Mary co-operated in effecting a much greater good.[45]

A few paragraphs later in the same letter, Newman draws from these thoughts the conclusion that Mary was Immaculately conceived, for "if Eve had this supernatural inward gift given her from the first moment of her personal existence, is it possible to deny that Mary too had this gift from the very first moment of her personal existence? I do not know how to resist this inference:—well, this is simply and literally the doctrine of the Immaculate Conception."[46]

The decision to place the Creation of Woman at the very heart of the vault as the central panel of the nine narratives, in a chapel dedicated

---

43. St. Irenaeus of Lyon, *Against the Heresies*, vol. 3, *Book 3*, trans. Dominic J. Unger, Ancient Christian Writers 64 (New York: Newman Press, 2012), 22:34, pg. 105.

44. St. Jerome, "Epistle 22 (*To Eustochium*)," *The Letters of Saint Jerome*, vol. 1, *Letters 1–22*, trans. Charles Christopher Mierow, Ancient Christian Writers 33 (New York: Newman Press, 1963), 154.

45. John Henry Newman, "A Letter Addressed to the Rev. E. B. Pusey, D.D., on Occasion of His Eirenicon," in *Certain Difficulties Felt by Anglicans in Catholic Teaching* (Pittsburgh: The National Institute for Newman Studies, 2007), 2:36.

46. Newman, "Letter Addressed to the Rev. E. B. Pusey," 2:36.

to Mary and built by Pope Sixtus IV, who put the feast of the Immaculate Conception on the universal calendar and commissioned two offices for the solemnity, underscores the fact that this was not merely Michelangelo's personal conviction, but a belief of the church promoted by the magisterium. Catholicism holds Mary in special veneration because of her cooperation with Christ in humanity's salvation; thus she is the archetype of complementarity.

Mary as Prophetess

An evident Marian matrix in the stories of creation might be expected; but one also finds Michelangelo representing Mary in the role of prophetess in several of his early works. The *Bruges Madonna*, carved between 1503 and 1505 immediately after his Roman *Pietà*, illustrates a different side to Mary, showing her to be possessed of foreknowledge. The voluminous draperies of her lap appear to frame the Christ Child, yet the Child steps away from their protective cover and prepares to walk out into the world. Her face somber, Mary looks beyond her son's feet as if seeing what the future will hold. This work was commissioned as an altarpiece, which means that Jesus would appear to be about to step onto the altar—the space where the church represents his self-sacrifice. Despite foreseeing the troubling events of the future, Mary allows her son to leave her nurturing embrace in order to fulfill his mission. In this depiction, her face, while sharing the rounded chin and oval lines of the Delphic sibyl, gazes solemnly in the same way that the Eritrean sibyl looks into her book of prophecies. Like the sibyls, Mary perceives and reacts to the divine will, but in her knowledge of revelation she remains contemplative.

Mary as Heroine

Mary as heroine is found in several different artistic interpretations in Michelangelo's oeuvre. While Mary is depicted as a dynamic figure in his *Doni Tondo*, painted in 1506, Michelangelo's greatest representation of the extraordinary strength of Mary was in his Roman *Pietà* of 1500. Still and silent, Mary contemplates the body of her son even as she offers it toward the altar. Unlike any previous image, Michelangelo chose to shift the focus of the work from the body of Christ to the face of Mary. Jesus' body, modeled after classical Greek statuary and gently sapped of life, compels the viewer to meditate on this moment through Mary's eyes, who knew her son as savior and experiences not only the loss of her child but also the apparent demise of the project of salvation. The triangular composition lends Mary the visual stability and endurance of the pyramids themselves, rendering iconic her heroic fiat to accept the divine will no matter what the cost. Thus, Mary becomes a heroine modeled after Esther, whose spotless beauty and willingness to submit herself to the will of the king saved her people.

In the twelfth century, St. Bernard encouraged Christians to pray daily to Mary. He wrote seven prayers to the Virgin, in which he praises her might and power, evoking her as a *mulier fortis*, a formidable woman.[47] This fortitude, unlike that of the sword-swinging warrior or the sinewy desert aesthete, is Mary's special contribution to the heroic imagination. She possesses the strength to stand fast in faith despite indications that all is lost. She chooses to continue to trust in God even when he appears to be dead. Giving herself entirely to God, she redefines the model of the hero. Greek heroes fight the will of the gods and flee divine mandates, whereas Mary remains steadfast in the will of the Lord.

Mary as Mother

Michelangelo's Mary never stops being a mother. Although his own mother died when he was six years old, Michelangelo seemed to have endless mental images of mothers to choose from for his works. His debut, the somewhat studied *Madonna of the Steps*, where Mary in sharp

---

47. Regina Stefaniak, *Mysterium Magnum: Michelangelo's Tondo Doni* (Boston: Brill, 2008), 59.

profile holds her nursing son as she gazes into the distance, developed into the *Pitti Tondo* (1506), where Mary looks indulgently at John the Baptist while the infant Christ scampers across her lap.

His *Doni Tondo*, however, presents the type of energetic, vivacious mother seen in the Sistine vault. In this private work, meant to celebrate the firstborn child of the wealthy and influential Doni family in Florence, Michelangelo experimented with a strikingly active vision of the Virgin. Seated between the knees of St. Joseph, already a surprising bit of iconographic intimacy not usually explored in art, she turns backward, demonstrating the exceptional skills in foreshortening that the young artist had already mastered. Joseph's knees project forward, and her arms arc behind her to receive her Son from her husband's hands. The movement pulls her sleeve away from her body, baring her arm to the shoulder and even dropping down to expose a sliver of bare torso, a motif that would reappear in the Delphic sibyl. This strong, slender Madonna wears a soft robe that drapes over her body and reveals the length of thigh and point of her knee under her skirt. She is iconic, yet fetching, a lovely mother with the energy to keep up with her boisterous little boy. The decorative brooch on her dress, like the complicated fold of her snood in the *Pitti Tondo* or the diadem of the *Taddei Tondo*, all hint at the Michelangelo who will be able to depict such a vast array of mothers and their costumes in the Sistine ceiling.

Mary's motherhood had been exalted long ago at the council of Ephesus when she was declared *Theotokos*, "Mother of God." The stiff, regal images associated with that title were replaced at the dawn of the Renaissance with pictures of the *Madonna Lactans*, a mother suckling her child. Michelangelo also executed several works of a nursing Mary, from the *Madonna of the Steps* to the *Madonna and Child* carved between 1521 and 1534 for the Medici Chapel.

In the gospels, Jesus twice addresses Mary as "woman." The first time was at Cana, when she pointed out the lack of wine during the wedding feast (Jn 2:4), and the second took place as Jesus hung on the cross and said, "Woman, behold thy son" (Jn 19:26). Returning to the theme of the new Eve, in Eden, Eve was known simply as "woman" until the fall when "the man gave his wife the name 'Eve,' because she was the mother of all the living" (Gn 3:20). At the cross Mary starts as Woman, but becomes mother—mother to John, to the apostles, to the martyrs, and to all those who live in Christ.

The myriad female images of the Sistine Chapel glitter with their bright colors like facets of a jewel. They reflect light but are merely a feature of the gem, not the stone itself. The diamond that holds these women together in the Sistine Chapel is the ever-present but barely depicted Virgin Mary. In her, Michelangelo found every woman, endless varieties of virtue, endless types of beauty, endless forms of goodness. Essentially, he created a compendium of feminine genius. In the *Letter to Women*, St. John Paul II wrote:

> The Church sees in Mary the highest expression of the "feminine genius" and she finds in her a source of constant inspiration.... Putting herself at God's service, she also put herself at the service of others: a service of love. Precisely through this service Mary was able to experience in her life a mysterious, but authentic "reign." It is not by chance that she is invoked as "Queen of heaven and earth."[48]

Mary as Queen of Heaven

Indeed, Mary finally appears in the Sistine Chapel as Queen of Heaven in the *Last Judgment* (fig. 4-15). Michelangelo had to destroy Perugino's altarpiece of the *Assumption of the Virgin* when preparing the wall for the gigantic fresco of the Last Judgment, commissioned by Pope Paul III almost twenty-five years after Michelangelo had completed painting the vault. The mood of the church had changed; the Reformation saw struggles both within and without church walls, and many of the pope's inner circle of bishops and cardinals had joined the new church of Henry VIII or one of the other Protestant causes. The *Last Judgment*, designed to call the leaders of the church to order, may seem at first a stern, pitiless painting with hundreds of bodies spiraling around a Christ who not only looks away but seems to cast the souls around him to the depths of

---

48. John Paul II, *Letter to Women* (June 29, 1995), no. 10.

perdition with his mighty hand. But a closer look reveals a pathway to salvation—Mary nestled by Christ's side: the gateway to Heaven.

Never before had Mary been given such a pivotal role in an image of the Last Judgment. Her usual placement put her across from St. John the Baptist, both on a slightly lower plane than Christ the Judge, who was invariably figured alone. Michelangelo carefully thought through the process of moving Mary from a side role to one of sharing the throne of judgment. Two existing preliminary drawings demonstrate that his first thought was to place her in the traditional spot seated to the lower right of Christ, but with her hands clasped and pleading as she rose from her seat. The second drawing grew even bolder: he planned Mary approaching her Son with arms open, showing him the breasts that nursed him as the souls crowded in her wake.

In the finished work, Mary cleaves to Christ's side, next to the wound opened by the spear during the crucifixion. In his catechesis to early Christians, St. John Chrysostom explained that since "the symbols of baptism and the Eucharist come from the side of Christ. It was from his side, therefore, that Christ formed His Church, just as he had formed Eve from the side of Adam."[49]

In this context Mary reveals herself as the new Eve, complement and coworker with the new Adam. He perfects the central imagery of the figure of Eve emerging from Adam's side and propending toward God by painting Mary, who, while gazing back upon faithful, returns to the side of the Lord.

The heroines of the ceiling find their apogee in Mary of the Last Judgment. She actively draws close to her Son, but her crossed hands and gentle expression illustrate her greatest heroic act, that of supreme obedience. The crossed arms, often wrongly interpreted as fear or impotence before the awe-inspiring presence of her Son, have instead a very different iconographic origin. Michelangelo's native city of Florence had a particular devotion to the Annunciation, so much so that each new year began on March 25, the feast day of Gabriel's announce-

---

49. St. John Chrysostom, *Catechesis* 3.17; SC 50:174–77. English translation: *Baptismal Instructions*, trans. Paul W. Harkins, SJ, Ancient Christian Writers 31 (Westminster, Md.: Newman Press, 1963), 62.

ment to Mary. Processions, celebrations, and the consecration of the monumental cathedral all evolved around this feast day. The plethora of images painted, sculpted, or drawn of this subject by the finest artists in Florence could be found not only in churches, convents, and homes, but also in public buildings and street corners. Biblically, the Annunciation consists of five lines of dialogue where the Virgin recounts her state of mind from surprise to inquiry to acceptance.[50] Artists enjoyed selecting a particular moment of the drama and recounting through composition and gesture which line of this momentous announcement was being captured. Far and away the most frequently represented was the *submitio*, when Mary declares herself to be "the handmaid of the Lord" and says, "May it be done to me according to your word" (Lk 1:38).[51]

From the frescos of Beato Angelico, the celebrated Dominican painter already recognized as saintly during his own time, to the illustrated prayer books destined for young aristocratic women, the representation of the *submitio* showed Mary bowed with her hands crossed over her chest. By replicating this gesture in the *Last Judgment*, Michelangelo extols the heroism of Mary's fiat already celebrated in his *Pietà* and prefigured in the scenes of Esther and Judith.

The heroic nature and monumental dimensions of Mary are contrasted by the lithe and graceful lines of her body. Mary is reminiscent of a blushing bride by the side of a groom. Jesus is bulky and vigorous, Mary gentle and coy. Her long legs, revealed by the drapery, cross delicately at the ankles with the feminine grace of the Libyan sibyl. As in the scene of the *Temptation*, we see the bodies of male and female conjoined and completing each other in a great celestial plan of complementarity. As Michelangelo used as inspiration two of the most impressive ancient sculptures, the *Belvedere torso* and the *Apollo Belvedere*, to fashion his Christ, he also found his model for the Virgin amid the collection of ancient statuary. Mary was modeled after the copy of *Bithynian Venus* by Doidalsas, a celebrated work from the first century

---

50. Michael Baxandall, *Painting and Experience in Fifteenth-Century Italy* (Oxford: Oxford University Press, 1988), 51.

51. Baxandall, *Painting and Experience*, 55.

capturing the goddess of love, beauty, and desire crouching seductively in her bath.[52] In Michelangelo's hands the profane nature of the model is cleansed away, leaving only the irresistibly lovely pose evoking imagery from the Song of Solomon, where the groom rejoices in the beauty of his bride. "How beautiful you are, how fair, my love, daughter of delights!" (7:7). As in the case of Esther, the queen's beauty is such that nothing can be refused to her.

If the forceful figure of Christ embodies justice, the gentleness of Mary represents mercy. This Mary, New Eve, Mother of the church and Bride of Christ, draws the viewer's gaze to the gentle gesture of Jesus' hand framing his wound and gathering souls to him, a sharp contrast to his emphatically raised arm. There, through Mary's intercession, souls find salvation and join a heaven imagined by Michelangelo as peopled with men and women of exceptional strength, beauty, awareness, and humanity.

The Sistine Chapel and its denizens, designers, and decorators recognized that in this space there was the potential to encapsulate all of human history in a single room, creating a pictorial journey from the beginning of time to the end of the world. Its artistic beauty inspired the poet in St. John Paul II to pen this description:

> Here then—we look and we see
> the Beginning, which came forth from nothingness
> in obedience to the creative Word.
> It speaks from these walls.
> Yet it is the End that speaks even more powerfully.
> Yes, the Judgment is even more powerful:
> the Judgment, the Last Judgment.
> This is the road that all of us walk—
> each one of us.[53]

John Paul writes of a common journey, shared by men and women from Eden through the long ages of prophecies and expectations and

---

52. Bernadine Barnes, *Michelangelo's Last Judgment: The Renaissance Response* (Berkeley: University of California Press, 1998), 61.

53. John Paul II, "The First to See," book II, part 1, *The Poetry of John Paul II: Roman Triptych, Meditations*, trans. Jerzy Peterkiewicz (Washington, D.C.: USCCB, 2003), 15.

Michelangelo | 181

Figure 4-15. Mary and Jesus of Last Judgment, Sistine Chapel—Detail

rescued from perils by heroes and heroines along the way. Propelled through generations by mothers and fathers producing children in the hope of a brighter future, the project of human redemption finds its ultimate destiny and guide in the image of Christ and Mary: father and daughter, mother and son, bride and bridegroom, the deep-rooted complementarity ingrained by God, taught by the church and incomparably illustrated by Michelangelo.

CHAPTER 5

Men and Women
Their Differences and Their Complementarity
Evidence from Psychology and Neuroscience

Paul C. Vitz

The Three Major Models

There are now many ways to understand and treat sexual differences, some of which are identified by Sr. Mary Prudence Allen in chapter 2 of the current volume. However, at present, there appear to be only three *major* interpretations of these differences. First is the Unisex Model, which assumes that there are no important sex differences that impinge on personality and behavior in any significant way. But this assumption, common in society today, is contradicted by a large and growing amount of evidence to the contrary and thus constitutes a denial of important facts. It also overlooks an enormous amount of historical and cultural evidence that shows that male and female differences have been important markers for different roles in every society and culture we know about. Some of these worldwide social differences between men and women are identified by the evolutionary psychologist Anne Campbell, who, when discussing human universals, writes, "Of special interest to the study of gender we find [as universals]: binary distinctions between men and women, division of labor by sex, more child care by women, more aggression and violence by men, acknowledgement of differences between male and female natures, and domination of the public square by men."[1]

A second model or understanding of sex differences is the recognition that such differences do exist, accompanied by the belief that these differences imply that one sex is superior to the other. The common historical example can be called the "Macho" Model, where men dominate and are considered superior to women. In principle, there is also a "Femo" Model that reverses the Macho understanding. This seems to have been rare in the past, and as a social organization it is probably nonexistent, but it is propounded by some of today's feminists. In any case, the Macho Model has been strongly critiqued by feminists and others as unjust and as neglectful of women's obvious strengths and virtues. Many of these criticisms are valid. Accepting either the Macho or Femo model guarantees ongoing serious conflict.

A third alternative is the Complementary Model, which will be developed here. The Complementary Model accepts that men and women are often different in important respects, and it thus addresses the truth of such evidence. However, it also posits that men and women are equal in dignity as well as in moral and social importance. This position follows from a Judeo-Christian theological perspective. God created both men and women in his image, and thus it is when they are taken together that they represent a more complete image of their Creator. This model can be accepted on other than biblical grounds, but it certainly receives basic support from the book of Genesis and from much recent theological writing. John Paul II is especially known for his emphasis on complementarity, as expressed in his *Theology of the Body*.[2] It has also received secular support.[3]

An additional property of the Complementary Model will receive

---

[1]. Anne Campbell, *A Mind of Her Own: The Evolutionary Psychology of Women*, 2nd ed. (Oxford: Oxford University Press, 2013), 25.

[2]. John Paul II, *Man and Woman He Created Them: A Theology of the Body*, trans. Michael Waldstein (Boston: Pauline Books and Media, 2006). For other important sources, see Sr. Mary Prudence Allen, "Four Principles of Complementarity: A Philosophical Perspective," in *Not Just Good, but Beautiful: The Complementary Relationship between Man and Woman*, edited by Steven Lopes and Helen Alvaré (Walden, N.Y.: Plough, 2014).

[3]. K. K. Klein and W. B. Wilcox, *Mother Bodies, Father Bodies: How Parenthood Changes Us from the Inside Out* (New York: Institute for American Values, 2014).

development here. I propose that many of the weaknesses of each sex are matched by a complementary strength of the other sex. This complementarity also means that men and women can create a *synergistic* interaction that has a special fruitfulness. We observe this most commonly, of course, in the creation of a child and a family and then its future generations. Allen is especially known for this emphasis on synergy within complementarity. She states that "the four principles of complementarity are: *equal dignity*, *significant difference*, *synergetic relation* and *inter-generational fruition*."[4]

The development of the concept of synergy in understanding complementarity is based on constructive interactions between men and women, but we all know that often these differences lead to difficulties, conflict, and negative relationships. Men and women easily find each other irritating. The "battle of the sexes" probably goes back to the fall of Adam and Eve. Nevertheless, it is the case that an intelligent and wise understanding of male-female differences can greatly reduce this conflict and increase positive synergy.

Another important point should be emphasized before we proceed: the proposed differences between men and women are based on averages, and there are always a good many exceptions to the statistical average. For example, men, on average, are taller than women, but some women are taller than some men. One should therefore keep in mind when thinking about differences between the sexes that there are exceptions, and there is always some overlap. Let me add, however, that our present culture greatly emphasizes the supposed importance of the exceptions. A consequence of this has been the erosion of understanding and social support for the usual or typical person. One result is that large numbers of people feel confused and even attacked by this overemphasis on the rare cases, the atypical, the unusual.

Although the differences to be discussed are often on a continuum, this does not imply that human sexuality itself is best understood on a continuum. Human biology is, in fact, discrete and binary with respect to sexuality, and this difference must be acknowledged before we turn

---

4. Allen, "Gender Reality," *Solidarity: The Journal of Catholic Social Thought and Secular Ethics* 4, no. 1 (2014): 1 (italics in original); see also her "Four Principles of Complementarity."

to complementarity. (Androgynous people and those with XXY and XYY chromosome combinations are understood as anomalies and thus support the binary rule.) Also, each human cell is male or female; a human skeleton is of a man or a woman. Indeed, many of our organs have male or female characteristics that affect our health in different ways. It is well known that statistically men are more likely to have a heart attack than are women, but women also have heart attacks. Their heart attacks are different; the symptoms are often more ambiguous and harder to detect. Indeed, the hearts of men and women are rather different: a woman's heart is about two-thirds the size of a man's, its blood vessels have a smaller diameter, and it beats more rapidly.[5] The smaller size of the heart and blood vessels frequently makes surgery more difficult. There are also significant sex differences in other organs and in many diseases, such as diabetes. In addition, "sex hormones have a great impact on energy metabolism, body composition, vascular function and inflammatory responses."[6]

DeVries and Forger demonstrate pervasive sex differences in internal characteristics of the human body. In their review, they show "sex differences in muscles, adipose tissue, the liver, immune system, gut, kidneys, bladder and placenta that affect the nervous system and behavior."[7] In short, male and female bodies in a wide variety of ways are significantly different; and though apparently there is no "complementarity" at this level, there certainly are many unexpected biological differences, some of them documented only recently.[8]

---

5. Acibadem, "The Twelve Differences between a Woman's Heart and a Man's Heart," http://www.acibadem.com/en/12-differences-between-a-womans-heart-and-a-mans-heart, accessed February 6, 2019. See also Warren Rosenberg, "What Is the Difference between Male and Female Heart Rates?," https://www.livestrong.com/article/208145-what-is-the-difference-between-male-female-heart-rates/; and A. H. E. M. Maas and Y. E. A. Appelman, "Gender Differences in Coronary Heart Disease," *Netherlands Heart Journal* 18, no. 12 (2010): 596–602.

6. A. Kautzky-Willer, J. Harrieter, and G. Pacini, "Sex and Gender Differences in Risk, Pathophysiology and Complications of Type 2 Diabetes Mellitus," *Endocrine Reviews* 37, no. 3 (June 2016): 278.

7. Geert J. De Vries and Nancy G. Forger, abstract, "Sex Differences in the Brain: A Whole Body Perspective," *Biology of Sex Differences* 6, no. 1 (August 15, 2015), https://www.ncbi.nim.nih.gov/pmc/articles/PMC4536872/.

8. See De Vries and Forger, "Sex Differences in the Brain"; L. Ellis et al., *Sex Differences: Summarizing More Than a Century of Scientific Research* (New York: Psychology Press, Taylor and Francis

Nevertheless, the concept of important sex differences is today controversial. One sign of this is the recent use of the word "gender" for the prior, almost universal term "sex." The word "sex," precisely because of its traditional usage and its strong links to biology—and thus to a natural category—is now commonly avoided. The word "gender," because of its novelty and links to grammar and language and not to any natural biological reality, already implies the notion that gender's meaning is arbitrary and socially constructed. This, of course, is exactly what many postmodern and feminist intellectuals claim: a person's gender has no serious base in biological reality.

In contrast, the approach adopted here is "Gender Reality," as it is called by Allen,[9] as opposed to the social construction position, which she correctly calls "Gender Ideology." The beginning of the gender ideology position goes back in large part to Marxist philosophers who argued for the social construction of the new anti-capitalist and communist man. This general position has morphed into the new socially constructed, not biologically determined, gendered person.

In chapter 1 of this volume, Allen thoroughly documents the origin and spread of the gender ideology position. Drawing mostly on the work of Catholic philosophers, she concludes with a powerful rebuttal of the ideology position. "Gender Reality," although it derives from an older tradition, has solid support; this "reality" position now gets strong support from neuroscience, evolutionary theory, and psychological research.

The Importance of Sex Differences for Understanding Complementarity

It may seem obvious, but it needs emphasis: Sex differences are needed for complementarity to occur. If there are no important and reliable differences between men and women, then the sexes cannot comple-

---

Group, 2008); and Heather MacDonald, "Gender Is a Construct—Except When It's Not," *City Journal*, August 17, 2018, https://www.city-journal.org/html/gender-construct-16117.html.

9. See chapter 2, "Gender Reality vs. Gender Ideology," by Prudence Allen, in this volume.

ment each other. The fact that there are important sex differences has become much better understood in the last few decades, thanks to a large number of scientific studies and now book-length treatments.[10] This evidence, however, has not had much impact on the general culture, especially that of the liberal elites and the university world. These new findings, many in the texts just mentioned, will be often cited in this chapter, which follows male-female differences from infancy, childhood, and the teen years to adulthood.

Although the results are often very similar over these different ages, the point is to make clear how reliable and often complementary the differences are. Later there is a short treatment on a hyper-male and a hyper-female type, as these show sex differences in a more extreme form. The conclusion presents a set of proposed masculine and feminine psychological differences with both associated strengths and weaknesses and an implicit complementarity.

Boys and Girls: As Infants

The subject of psychological differences—and their implicit complementarity—really begins with the differences between infant boys and girls. From the start, girls are much more interpersonally oriented than boys. They look at faces more, smile and talk earlier, and are much more responsive to people in general.[11] Boys are relatively more in-

---

10. See, for example, Simon Baron-Cohen, *The Essential Difference: Male and Female Brains and the Truth about Autism* (New York: Basic Books, 2003); Louann Brizendine, *The Female Brain* (New York: Broadway Books, 2006); Brizendine, *The Male Brain* (New York: Broadway Books, 2010); J. Budziszewski, *On the Meaning of Sex* (Wilmington, Del.: ISI, 2012); David Buss, *Evolutionary Psychology: The New Science of the Mind*, 5th ed. (London: Routledge, 2015); Campbell, *Mind of Her Own*; Yves Christen and Nicholas Davidson, *Sex Differences: Modern Biology and the Unisex Fallacy* (New Brunswick, N.J.: Transaction, 1991); Ellis et al., *Sex Differences*; D. C. Geary, *Male, Female: The Evolution of Sex Differences*, 2nd ed. (Washington, D.C.: American Psychological Association Press, 2010); Michael Gurian, *Boys and Girls Learn Differently: A Guide for Teachers and Parents*, 10th ed. (San Francisco: Jossey-Bass, 2011); Doreen Kimura, *Sex and Cognition* (Cambridge, Mass.: MIT Press, 1999); Steven E. Rhoades, *Taking Sex Differences Seriously* (San Francisco: Encounter, 2004); Deborah Tannen, *You Just Don't Understand: Women and Men in Conversation* (New York: Ballantine, 1990); and Anne Moir and David Jessel, *Brain Sex: The Real Difference between Men and Women* (New York: Delta, 1991).

11. See E. B. McClure, "A Meta-Analytic Review of Sex Differences in Facial Expression

terested in things, especially things that move and make noise.[12] The frequently observed involvement of girls with dolls and their response to new babies are just two pieces of support for the difference.[13] Infant girls show more empathy than do boys. For example, Simner found that infant girls cried longer than infant boys when exposed to the cry of another infant, but there was no sex difference in such crying when babies were exposed to a loud artificial noise.[14]

Because so much work has been done on the differences between boys and girls, we provide a summary of some of the major texts. We begin with the social philosopher Michael Gurian, who has published extensively on this topic.[15] Table 5-1 shows some of the early significant differences.

Boys and Girls: As Children

Studies have found greater empathy in older girls as compared to boys.[16] This relative lack of empathy in boys may facilitate their early

---

Processing and Their Development in Infants, Children and Adolescents," *Psychological Bulletin* 126, no. 3 (2000): 424–53; Jeanette Jones Haviland and Carol Zander Malatesta, "The Development of Sex Differences in Nonverbal Signals: Fallacies, Facts and Fantasies," in *Gender and Nonverbal Behavior*, ed. Clara Mayo and Nancy M. Henley (New York: Springer-Verlag, 1981), 183–208; and Jennifer Connellen et al., "Sex Differences in Human Neonatal Social Perception," *Infant Behavior and Development* 23 (2001): 113–18.

12. Svetlana Lutchmaya and Simon Baron-Cohen, "Human Sex Differences in Social and Non- Social Looking Preferences, at 12 Months of Age," *Infant Behavior and Development* 25 (2002): 319–25; and D. McGuinness and K. H. Pribram, "The Origins of Sensory Bias in the Development of Gender Differences in Perception and Cognition," in *Cognitive Growth and Development: Essays in Memory of Herbert G. Birch*, ed. M. Bortner (New York: Brunner/Mazel, 1979), 3–56.

13. D. E. Sandberg and H. F. L. Meyer-Bahlburg, "Variability in Middle Childhood Play Behavior: Effects of Gender, Age, and Family Background," *Archives of Sexual Behavior* 23 (1994): 645–63.

14. Marvin Simner, "Newborn's Response to the Cry of Another Infant," *Developmental Psychology* 5, no. 1 (1971): 136–50, http://dx.doi.org/10.1037/h0031066.

15. For example, Gurian, *Boys and Girls Learn Differently* and *The Minds of Girls: 4 New Path for Raising Healthy, Resilient and Successful Women* (Spokane, Wash.: Gurian Institute Press, 2018).

16. See N. Eisenberg and R. Lennon, "Sex Difference in Empathy and Related Capacities," *Psychological Bulletin* 94 (1983): 100–131; M. L. Hoffman, "Sex Difference in Empathy and Related Behaviors," *Psychological Bulletin* 84 (1977): 712–22; and C. Zahn-Waxler et al., "Development of Concern for Others," *Developmental Psychology* 28 (1992): 126–36.

TABLE 5-1

Developmental Gender Differences and Tendencies: In the Uterus to about Six Months (summarized from Gurian, *Boys and Girls Learn Differently*, 33–36)

Boys	Girls
Develop testosterone	Develop estrogen
"Set" male brain immune to female hormones	"Set" female brain immune to male hormones
Fetus generally more active	Fetus generally less active
Cortex develops more slowly	Cortex develops more quickly
Six weeks in the uterus sexual identity begins to develop, and brain changes	Normal template of human brain appears to be female
At six weeks large dose of testosterone changes brain permanently	Lack of testosterone allows brain structure to stay the same
Brain is more lateral(ized)	Brain is less lateral(ized)
Less physically flexible	More physically flexible
Less internalized	Less externalized
Greater idling in brain stem (reptilian brain)	Greater idling in cingulate gyrus (limbic system)
Brain (mass) 10 percent larger	Brain (mass) 10 percent smaller
Smaller corpus callosum	Larger corpus callosum
Prefers mechanical or structural toys	Prefers soft, cuddly toys
Looks at objects for shorter but more active periods	Plays with objects for longer periods, but less actively
Gazes at mother half as long as girl does	Play is more cheerful
Motor activity more vigorous than girl's	At one week, able to distinguish another baby's cry from background noise
At four months of age cannot distinguish faces of known people in photographs	At four months of age is able to recognize faces of known people in photographs

TABLE 5-2

Important Developmental Differences: From about One Year to about Six Years (summarized from Gurian, *Boys and Girls Learn Differently*)

Boys	Girls
Speaks first words later than girls	Develops better vocabulary earlier than boys
By age four-and-a-half, 99 percent of speech is comprehensible	By age three, 99 percent of speech is comprehensible
Less able to multitask	Better ability to multitask
Better at math performance and at 3-D reasoning	Reads earlier, better
More able to separate emotion from reason	Better verbal ability
More likely to ignore voices, even parents'	Less likely to ignore voices, especially easily familiar ones

distinctive social behavior: studies "confirm that boys organize themselves into much larger social groups than do girls, engage in intergroup competition once such groups are formed, form within group hierarchies, and show within group differentiation and specialization."[17] Still other research shows that "boys begin to show a preference for group-level activities over dyadic ones as early as 3 years of age, show strong bias against members of competing groups by 5 years of age, and consistently form larger groups than girls by 6 years."[18]

Many of these differences have been clearly linked to hormone differences, which show up at a very early age. For example, Collaer and Hines commented, "Elevated androgen in genetic females . . . is asso-

---

17. Geary, *Male, Female*, 304. See also D. Eder and M. T. Hallinan, "Sex Differences in Children's Friendships," *American Sociological Review* 43 (1978): 237–50; and I. Lever, "Sex Differences in the Complexity of Children's Play and Games," *American Sociological Review* 43 (1978): 471–83.

18. Geary, *Male, Female*, 304. See also Joyce F. Benenson, "Greater Preference among Females Than Males for Dyadic Interaction in Early Childhood," *Child Development* 64, no. 2 (1993): 544–55; and A. J. Rose and K. D. Rudolph, "A Review of Sex Differences in Peer Relationship Processes: Potential Trade-Offs for the Emotional and Behavioral Development of Girls and Boys," *Psychological Bulletin* 132 (2006): 98–131.

ciated with masculinized and de-feminized play"[19] (see table 5-1 for hormone effects). Boys show a good deal more of what is called "rough and tumble" play.[20] But the strong presence of a male hormone (CAH) increases such play in girls.[21]

Boys and Girls: Differences in Learning

The following summaries and quotes are from Gurian, *Boys and Girls Learn Differently*, pp. 44–50.

Deductive and Inductive Reasoning

Boys favor deductive conceptualizations, beginning from a general principle.

Girls favor inductive thinking, beginning with concrete examples.

Abstract and Concrete Reasoning

Boys tend to excel at abstract reasoning, favoring philosophy and abstract principles.

Use of Language

Girls tend to prefer to have things conceptualized in everyday language, while boys find jargon and coded language more interesting.

---

19. M. L. Collaer and M. Hines, "Human Behavioral Sex Differences: A Role for Gonadal Hormones during Early Development?," *Psychological Bulletin* 118 (July 1995): 92.

20. See Irenäus Eibl-Eibesfeldt, *Human Ethology* (New York: Aldine de Gruyter, 1989); also B. B. Whiting and C. P. Edwards, "A Cross-Cultural Analysis of Sex Differences in the Behavior of Children Aged Three through Eleven," *Journal of Social Psychology* 91, no. 2 (1973): 171–88; and Whiting and Edwards, *Children of Different Worlds: The Formation of Social Behavior* (Cambridge, Mass.: Harvard University Press, 1988).

21. See S. A. Berenbaum and E. Snyder, "Early Hormonal Influences on Child-Sex Typed Activity and Playmate Preferences: Implications for the Development of Sexual Orientation," *Developmental Psychology* 31, no. 1 (1995): 31–42. Also see E. Vuoksimaa et al., "Having a Male Co-Twin Masculinizes Mental Rotation Performance in Females," *Psychological Science* 21, no. 8 (2010): 1069–71, for a similar effect.

Evidence

Girls tend to be better listeners, hear more of what is said, and are more receptive to detail.

Boys hear less and more often ask for evidence.

Boredom

Boys get bored more easily than girls, requiring more varied stimulants to keep their attention.

Girls are better at self-managing boredom.

Use of Space

Boys tend to use more space than girls when they learn, especially at younger ages.

Movement

Girls do not generally need to move around as much while learning.

Movement seems to help boys stimulate their brains but also manages and relieves impulsive behavior.

Settling Differences

Boys are much more likely than girls to use physical force to settle differences.

Sensitivity and Group Dynamics

Cooperative learning is easier for girls to master. "Girls learn while attending to a code of social interaction better than boys do. Boys tend to focus on performing the task well, without as much sensitivity to the emotions of others around them." Also, girls, as previously noted, show more empathy than boys.

Boys form pecking orders that are more important to them than the social strata of girls. Research has shown that a girl who finds herself lower in the pecking order is less likely to fail in school than a boy in the same situation. Males at the top of the pecking order secrete less cortisol. Cortisol, a stress hormone, can derail the learning process by forcing attention on emotional and survival needs.

Symbolism

Boys tend toward the use of symbolic texts, diagrams, and graphs. Pictures, which stimulate the right hemisphere, are more often relied on in male learning.

Learning Teams

Boys tend to create structured teams, while girls form looser organizations. Boys focus less on team process, jumping right to goal orientation.

Boys and Girls: Teen Years

The following are from Gurian, *Boys and Girls Learn Differently*, 36–37.

Boys are much more likely than girls to be involved in criminal behavior.

Boys are less likely to suffer clinical depression than girls, who are much more often depressed.

Boys with an extra female chromosome do less well at spatial reasoning than other boys; girls with higher than normal testosterone are better at spatial reasoning.

Social acceptance of boys is most often based on physical strength and athleticism. Not surprisingly, boys and men also show greater levels of physical activity.[22]

For girls, social acceptance is based more on peer relationships

---

22. W. O. Eaton and L. R. Enns, "Sex Differences in Human Motor Activity Level," *Psychological Bulletin* 100, no. 1 (1986): 19–28.

and beauty. Pursuit of power is a universal male trait; pursuit of comfortable environment is a universal female trait. Of the students in advanced-placement computer science classes, 85 percent are males; females outperform males in verbal and communication skills.

Boys and Girls: Teen Years

To summarize important specifics on how the female brain is changing and setting particular responses during puberty and adolescence, here are quotes from chapter 2 of Louann Brizendine's *The Female Brain*.[23]

We start with a long quote about the girl at puberty when the girl's

> pituitary gland has sprung into life as the chemical brakes are taken off her pulsating hypothalamic cells.... This cellular release sparks the hypothalamic-pituitary-ovarian system into action. It is the first time since infantile puberty that the girl's brain cells will be marinated in high levels of estrogen. In fact, it is the first time that her brain will experience estrogen-progesterone surges that come in repeated monthly waves from her ovaries.... The rising tide of estrogen and progesterone starts to fuel many circuits in the teen girl's brain that were laid down in fetal life. These new hormonal surges assure that all her female-specific brain circuits will become more sensitive to emotional nuance, such as approval and disapproval, acceptance and rejection.[24]

Brizendine continues by noting that, once females have entered puberty, their bodies and brains react to stress differently than do males'. Fluctuating estrogen and progesterone in the brain, especially in the hippocampus, are responsible for this different stress responsivity in females. Girls begin to react more to relationship stresses and boys to challenges to their authority.

The girl's brain circuits are arranged and fueled by estrogen to respond to stress with nurturant activities and the creation of protective social networks. She hates relationship conflicts. Connecting through

---

23. Brizendine, *Female Brain*, 31–56. (The actual studies these comments are based on are given in her "Notes" section for chapter 2, 193–96, and in her extensive references.)
24. Brizendine, *Female Brain*, 33.

talking activates the pleasure centers in a girl's brain. Sharing secrets that have romantic and erotic implications activates those centers even more.

Brizendine comments further, "At midcycle, during peak estrogen production, the girl's dopamine and oxytocin level is likely at its highest, too. Not only her verbal output is at its maximum but her urge for intimacy is also peaking. Intimacy releases more oxytocin, which reinforces the desire to connect, and the connecting then brings a sense of pleasure and well-being."[25]

Adult Men and Women: Differences

Physical Differences

We begin with simple physical differences. Much of this and later evidence is taken from David C. Geary, *Male, Female: The Evolution of Human Sex Differences*, and from David Buss, *Evolutionary Psychology: The New Science of Mind*. Both Geary and Buss are important evolutionary psychologists. Their central position, that men and women have many biologically based behaviors related to successful adaptation to the environment, is now widely accepted. Apparently, neither directly addresses the issue of complementarity, but often the complementarity is apparent. When we return to this topic, the relevance of their findings for complementarity will be made explicit.

We start with the commonplace fact that men are, on the average, considerably taller, bigger, and physically stronger than women.[26] It is

---

25. Brizendine, *Female Brain*, 37
26. "During childhood there are small to moderate differences favoring boys in tasks such as grip strength, jumping distance and running speeds, with large differences emerging during adolescence (Thomas and French, 1985); by 17 years of age more than 9 out of 10 boys outperform the average girl in these areas.... Substantial sex differences emerge in lower and especially upper body strength during adolescence and early adulthood"; Geary, *Male, Female*, 289–90. Many other studies show this, also; see A. V. Carron and D. A. Bailey, "Strength Development in Boys from 10 through 16 Years," *Monographs of the Society for Research in Child Development* 39, no. 4, serial no. 157 (1974); S. T. Pheasant, "Sex Differences in Strength—Some Observations on Their Variability," *Applied Ergonomics* 14 (1983): 205–11; and J. M. Round et al., "Hormonal Factors in the Development of Differences in Strength between Boys and Girls during Adolescence: A Longitudinal Study," *Annals of Human Biology* 26 (1999): 49–62.

interesting that men and women don't pair off randomly with respect to each other's height, weight, and age. As a rule, women prefer and usually marry men who are taller, bigger, and stronger, and also usually older, than themselves.[27] It appears that women want to feel protected from outside threats, and such male characteristics imply they will be. Women also prefer men whose status and power or wealth suggest they will be able to provide resources.[28] Sometimes a woman will marry a shorter man—but he is often a powerful, rich, or successful man who in these ways makes up for his shorter height.

Expression of Sexuality

In general, and not surprisingly, men's sexual desire and interest in sex are greater than women's, and they are more likely to spend money on sexual products and activities—for example, pornography and prostitution. Men also masturbate more frequently and at an earlier age. In addition, men's sexuality is more connected to visual stimuli. With men, aggression is also more strongly linked to sexuality than with women—as is clear in self-concepts, initiation of sex, and in coercive sex.[29]

Involvement in Relationships

As a rule, women are much more involved in personal relationships, and their sexuality is also more interpersonal.[30] This is hardly news! As the prominent psychologist Baron-Cohen puts it, "The female brain is predominately hard-wired for empathy."[31] And, of course, empathy is the basis for caring and interpersonal bonding. We have already seen good evidence for this in the research on babies, girls, and teenagers.

---

27. See Buss, *Evolutionary Psychology*, 112, 114, 127; and B. J. Ellis, "The Evolution of Sexual Attraction: Evaluative Mechanisms in Women," in *The Adapted Mind*, ed. J. Barkow, L. Cosmides, and J. Tooby (New York: Oxford University Press, 1992), 164–88.

28. See Buss, *Evolutionary Psychology*, 108–10, 123, and Barbara Smuts, "The Evolutionary Origins of Patriarchy," *Human Nature* 6 (1995): 1–32.

29. See L. Peplau, "Human Sexuality: How Do Men and Women Differ?," *Current Directions in Psychological Science* 12, no. 2 (2003): 37–40.

30. See M. B. Oliver and J. S. Hyde, "Gender Differences in Sexuality: A Meta-Analysis," *Psychological Bulletin* 114, no. 1 (1993): 29–51.

31. Baron-Cohen, *Essential Difference*, 1.

But this kind of evidence continues into adulthood. Women seek companionship and intimacy. Their spouses, their lovers, their children, their friends are central to their sense of well-being. It is not surprising, then, that women find social exclusion more disturbing and painful than do men.[32] For men, this is less so, and instead their status and their accomplishments are much more central to their sense of well-being.[33] Many other differences flow from these two basic differences—namely, that men mostly seek achievement in the outside world and women base their achievement in their positive interpersonal relationships. For example, women's well-documented higher verbal abilities and memory for faces and interpersonal events and men's greater risk-taking, aggression, systematic abstract thought, and most visual abilities all fit this picture with its implicit complementary nature.[34]

In short, there is now a large amount of evidence supporting the psychological generalization that adult women are much more people-oriented than are men. Perhaps more surprising is the support for such a claim to be found in biochemical and brain studies. Cozolino presents considerable evidence that a mother's attachment to her child is often a kind of addiction, since the biochemicals and brain structures involved in child-rearing are similar to those in drug addiction. He notes that research with primates suggests that the activation of the opioid systems of mother and child propels and regulates the attachment process. When female primates come together for contact, grooming, or play, endorphin levels increase in both parent and child.[35] Also, human mothers often report feeling distress, anxiety, and sadness when they are separated from their newborns. In large part, this response is caused by the precipitous declines in endorphin lev-

---

32. Joyce Benenson et al., "Social Exclusion: More Important to Human Females Than Males," *PLOS One* 8 (February 6, 2013), essay e55851, http://doi.org/10.1371/journal.pone.0055851.

33. For a recent study, see T. Kwang et al., "Men Seek Social Standing, Women Seek Companionship: Sex Differences in Deriving Self-Worth from Relationships," *Psychological Science* 24, no. 7 (2013): 1142–50.

34. A. Herlitz and J. Loven, "Sex Differences and the Own-Gender Bias in Face Recognition: A Meta-Analytic Review," *Visual Cognition* 21, no. 9–10 (2013): 1306–36.

35. Louis Cozolino, *The Neuroscience of Human Relationships: Attachment and the Developing Social Brain*, 2nd ed. (New York: Norton, 2014), 115–29.

els that are triggered by separation.[36] Many of a mother's rewards come from her behavioral responses to her children and to others, but it is clear also that much of the reward hinges on her body, specifically on endogenous opioid hormones.

For many fathers it has been an unexpected, generally positive surprise that their wives give so much time, attention, and energy to their babies and children. It is amazing how time-consuming babies and young children are! What is the reward? After all, babies don't seem to give anything back to their caretakers that could be interpreted as obvious "reinforcement." Nevertheless, strong nurturing behavior is commonly shown by mothers. Of course, in view of the vulnerability of human infants, a vulnerability that lasts for many years, good nurturing of the young has been absolutely essential since the first human beings for the survival of our species. Therefore, powerful predispositions and rewards for women have to be built in, or we humans would not be here. What is the reward? These built-in predispositions and hormonal and behavioral responses are the reward for a mother's nurturing behavior.

One of these rewards clearly is the positive effects of oxytocin. As noted earlier, oxytocin is a bonding hormone that also produces the experience of trust, a kind of anti-anxiety effect. It also increases a person's empathy.[37] Many other studies link oxytocin and related hormones to emotional states in humans.[38]

And it is not just that women and girls are more prepared for relationships in general; the female brain actually changes during preg-

---

36. Cozolino, *Neuroscience of Human Relationships*, 118–21.

37. J. A. Bartz et al., "Oxytocin Selectively Improves Empathic Accuracy," *Psychological Science* 21, no. 10 (2010): 1426–28; P. Y. Lin et al., "Oxytocin Increases the Influence of Public Service Advertisements," *PLOS One* 8, no. 2 (2013): 1–11; and R. Reidel and A. Javor, "The Biology of Trust: Integrating Evidence from Genetics, Endocrinology, and Functional Brain Imaging," *Journal of Neuroscience, Psychology and Economics* 5, no. 2 (2012): 63–91.

38. For example, see T. R. Insel, "Oxytocin: A Neuropeptide for Affiliation," *Psychoneuroendocrinology* 17 (1992): 3–35; Insel and L. J. Young, "The Neurobiology of Attachment," *National Review of Neuroscience* 2 (2001): 129–36; R. Landgraf, "Intracerebrally Released Vasopressin and Oxytocin: Measurement, Mechanisms, and Behavioral Consequences," *Journal of Neuroendocrinology* 7 (1995): 243–53; and J. Panksepp, "Oxytocin Effects on Emotional Processes: Separation Distress, Social Bonding, and Relationships to Psychiatric Disorders," *Annals of the New York Academy of Sciences* 652 (1992): 243–52.

nancy. The amygdala, so important in emotion and its regulation, as well as the brain areas involved in response to faces, actually get larger during pregnancy. This is part of what is sometimes called the "mommy brain."[39] Not only does the baby, once it is born, trigger positive nurturing from the mother, but the mother has, not surprisingly, positive effects on the baby's nervous system. The mother's presence has a positive effect on affect regulation and the amygdala in children.[40] There is recent evidence that pregnancy changes a woman's brain for up to two years.[41]

Male and Female Differences in Brain Function

Male and female brains also appear to be wired differently in a way that supports the general sex difference interpretation.[42] Women's brains were found to be more connected across the corpus callosum—that is, women are highly connected across left and right hemispheres. Men's brains are much more connected between front and back regions of the brain, and typically in only one hemisphere. The lateral connections support women as better at social skills, at remembering, and at multitasking.

Men seem wired for perception and coordinated physical actions and, not surprisingly, have a better sense of direction.[43] Boys tend to emphasize directions such as north and south or the connections of roads. This directional approach shows an understanding of space as a geometric system; the focus on roads is an understanding based on a transportation system.[44] However, women have a better memory for

39. See Brizendine, *Female Brain*, chapter 5.
40. See D. G. Gee et al., "Maternal Buffering of Human Amygdala-Prefrontal Circuitry during Childhood but Not during Adolescence," *Psychological Science* 25, no. 11 (2014): 2067–78.
41. E. Hoekzema et al., "Pregnancy Leads to Long-Lasting Changes in Human Brain Structure," *Nature Neuroscience* 20 (2017): 287–96, http://doi.org/10.1038/nn.4458.
42. M. Ingalhalikar et al., "Sex Differences in the Structural Connectome of the Human Brain," *Proceedings of the National Academy of Sciences of the United States of America* 111, no. 2 (2014): 823–28.
43. Carl W. S. Pintzka et al., "Changes in Spatial Cognition and Brain Activity after a Single Dose of Testosterone in Healthy Women," *Behavioral Brain Research* 298, part B (February 1, 2016): 78–90.
44. Baron-Cohen, *Essential Difference*, 77.

specific locations of things in the visual field. These differences may reflect skills needed in the traditional distinction between male hunters and female gatherers. Both activities are essential for good social survival, and the difference anticipates our treatment of complementarity in men and women.

Another example of this person-oriented female characteristic shows in a different male and female response to stress. The most typical response to stress has long been identified as "fight or flight," but recently a more female type of response to stress has been noted and called "tend and befriend"; it is discussed, for example, by Taylor, where she identifies the importance of the bonding hormone oxytocin in "tend and befriend" behavior as a response to stress.[45] This female emphasis on bonding and caring has received serious emphasis from the philosopher Eva Feder Kittay, in *Love's Labor: Essays on Women, Equality, and Dependency*,[46] which contrasts caring with the more common focus on individual autonomy and self-interest. The material presented here certainly supports much of her position. However, there are two major exceptions, clearly identified by Erika Bachiochi: Kittay fails to appreciate sexual difference and as a consequence fails to present the distinct contributions of fathers.[47]

Male and Female Memory Differences

Women have better memories for *episodic* events—that is, private events usually involving persons and their activities and interactions with others.[48] They also have better memories for faces. Men have a better *semantic* memory—that is, for usually public facts and abstract ideas, such as the capital city of every U.S. state or the value of pi to five

---

45. S. F. Taylor, "Tend and Befriend: Biobehavioral Bases of Affiliation under Stress," *Current Directions in Psychological Science* 15, no. 6 (2006): 273–77.

46. E. F. Kittay, *Love's Labor: Essays on Women, Equality, and Dependency* (New York: Routledge, 1999).

47. Erika Bachiochi, "Embodied Caregiving," *First Things* 266 (October 2016): 39–44.

48. A. Herlitz and J. Rehnman, "Sex Differences in Episodic Memory," *Current Directions in Psychological Science* 17 (2008): 52–56.

decimals.[49] Women also have richer, more detailed autobiographical memories of experiences,[50] and they tend to remember the dates of life events more accurately.[51] Again, we see evidence for women's superior people skills.

Father and Mother Differences

Kittay, as mentioned, clearly identified the importance of female caring for others;[52] however, she failed to present the distinct contributions of fathers.[53] This seems the place to mention briefly the benefits both mothers and children get from fathers and the rewards fathers get by being good fathers. These differences between father behavior and mother behavior also implicitly identify a kind of complementary style of parenting. Probably the single most widely and indeed now massively documented finding is the importance of fathers in preventing criminal and antisocial behavior in their sons. In the United States, which has a very large prison population, it has often been noted that its prisons are essentially buildings to house fatherless young men. Keep in mind that the United States has the largest prison population of any country and, I believe, the largest proportion of its population in prison of any country.[54] The economic and social costs of this are enormous. There are a very large number of studies showing the link between fatherlessness and criminal behavior and drug use. Many of these are noted by Vitz and McCall, who also identify the father as the

---

49. See Gurian, *Boys and Girls Learn Differently*, 27.

50. J. M. Andreano and L. Cahill, "Sex Influences on the Neurobiology of Learning and Memory," *Learning and Memory* 16, no. 4 (2009): 248–66; also D. B. Pillemer et al., "Gender Differences in Autobiographical Memory Styles of Older Adults," *Memory* 11, no. 6 (November 2003): 525–32.

51. John J. Skowronski et al., "Social Memory in Everyday Life: Recall of Self-Events and Other-Events," *Journal of Personality and Social Psychology* 60, no. 6 (1991): 831–43.

52. Kittay, *Love's Labor*.

53. As noted by Erika Bachiochi, "Embodied Caregiving."

54. Becky Pettit, *Invisible Men: Mass Incarceration and the Myth of Black Progress* (New York: Russell Sage Foundation, 2012); Tyjen Tsai and Paola Scommegna, "U.S. Has World's Highest Incarceration Rate," Population Reference Bureau website, last updated October 24, 2014, https://www.prb.org/us-incarceration/.

primary source of self-control or self-regulation in children.[55] The father teaches children, especially boys, to control impulses and to learn and respond to the laws and rules of society. There is even evidence of this effect with animal fathers and their young in the case of rodents.[56] In addition, this lack of impulse control has been found with young male elephants when they live only in groups without older male elephants, and can be corrected when older males are introduced to their group.[57]

Vitz and McCall also report studies showing that children with absent fathers experience greater mental problems, such as depression and lower cognitive skills. Cross-cultural research has shown that mothers in families where the father is present show better mothering than mothers in families where the father is not present.[58]

As for benefits and rewards for fathers, there are many, not the least that marriage by itself brings greater health and longevity.[59] In actual practice, for men the Complementary Model means that their natural masculine gifts of leadership, energy, strength, aggressive intelligence, confidence, and so on can be acknowledged, expressed, and valued as long as they are put in the service of others! If, however, men put these qualities in the service of the self, the macho has returned; if the masculine qualities aren't even there, the unisex wimp has resurfaced. But, when men put their abilities in the constructive service of others, neither women, nor children, nor communities complain.

---

55. P. C. Vitz and M. McCall, "The Importance of the Father for the Family: Research and Theory," unpublished paper (Arlington, Va.: Divine Mercy University, 2016).

56. Shirley. S. Wang, "This Is Your Brain without Dad," *Wall Street Journal*, October 27, 2009: B-7, 8, https://www.wsj.com/articles/SB10001424052748704754804574491811861197926.

57. "Delinquent Elephants," an interview with Rob Slotow, by Steve Curwood, *Living on Earth* website, December 15, 2000, https://www.loe.org/shows/segments.html?programID=00-P13-00050&segmentID=7.

58. Other important sources of fathers' contributions are Kyle Pruett, *Fatherneed: Why Father Care Is as Essential as Mother Care for Your Child* (New York: Broadway, 2000); P. Raeburn, *Do Fathers Matter? What Science Is Telling Us about the Parent We've Overlooked* (New York: Scientific American and Farrar, Straus and Giroux, 2014); and R. P. Rohner and R. A. Veneziano, "The Importance of Father Love: History and Contemporary Evidence," *Review of General Psychology* 5 (2001): 382–405.

59. Y-H. Hu and N. Goldman, "Mortality Differentials by Marital Status: An International Comparison," *Demography* 27, no. 2 (May 1990): 233–50.

Special Male Characteristics

Baron-Cohen states, "The male brain is predominately hard-wired for understanding and building systems,"[60] and he provides much evidence that men are better at systematic, abstract, and problem-solving tasks. Males are more interested in mechanical objects, which are, of course, systems.[61] This preference starts at birth when one-day-old boys look longer at a mechanical mobile than do girls; at twelve months, boys like looking at a video of cars more than girls do.[62] This decided preference continues through toddlerhood into adulthood.[63] In addition, male observers report seeing more mechanical objects and women more people in scenes where both were equally present.[64] In the fields of math, physics, and engineering, cross-cultural studies reliably show that boys perform better at problem-solving than do girls, although girls do better at the computational and calculating aspects of math tests, which may tap into their verbal abilities.[65]

These male interests and abilities show up in the adult workplace. Baron-Cohen notes that "some occupations are almost entirely male. Take, for example, metalworking, weapon-making, or crafting musical instruments. Consider the construction industries, such as boat building. These occupations are almost always carried out by men, and this sex difference is seen universally, not just in the Western World. This sex difference does not reflect the greater physical strength in males since, in many of these occupations (making a violin or a knife are good examples), strength is not a key factor. The focus of these occupations is on constructing systems."[66]

Men also generally show superior aptitude for many spatial tests such as mental rotation.[67] Many publications have identified the im-

60. Baron-Cohen, *Essential Difference*, 1.
61. Baron-Cohen, *Essential Difference*, 70.
62. Baron-Cohen, *Essential Difference*, 70.
63. Baron-Cohen, *Essential Difference*, 69.
64. Baron-Cohen, *Essential Difference*, 70.
65. Baron-Cohen, *Essential Difference*, 73.
66. Baron-Cohen, *Essential Difference*, 70. See also Martin Daly and Margo Wilson, *Sex, Evolution and Behavior* (Boston: Willard Grant, 1983).
67. See M. C. Linn and A. C. Petersen, "Emergence and Characterization of Sex Differences in Spatial Ability: A Meta-Analysis," *Child Development* 56 (1985): 1479–98; and D. Voyer, S. Voyer,

portance of such spatial abilities for success in science, technology, engineering, and mathematics.[68] Mental rotation is a major characteristic of spatial intelligence.[69] These differences, for example in mental rotation, show sex differences even in infancy.[70] This ability in males in infancy predicts both spatial and mathematical aptitude in later childhood.[71] There is evidence that female rotation performance is enhanced in females who were somewhat masculinized socially by having a male co-twin.[72]

In addition, men's brains are more modular than women's. Modularity means that men's brains appear to organize types of mental processing into more specific, localized brain areas than do women's.[73] This, combined with a tendency to function much more in one hemisphere, suggests, I propose, the reason men are also more irritated at being interrupted. They need to travel a longer internal neural distance to address the interruption as well as to escape from their focus in a particular task-based module. For women, crossing the corpus cal-

---

and M. P. Bryden, "Magnitude of Sex Differences in Spatial Abilities: A Meta-Analysis and Consideration of Critical Variables," *Psychological Bulletin* 117 (1995): 250–70.

68. D. L. Shea, D. Lubinski, and C. P. Benbow, "Importance of Assessing Spatial Ability in Intellectually Talented Young Adolescents: A 20-Year Longitudinal Study," *Journal of Educational Psychology* 93 (2001): 604–14; Jonathan Wai, David Lubinski, and Camilla P. Benbow, "Spatial Ability for STEM Domains: Aligning Over 50 Years of Cumulative Psychological Knowledge Solidifies Its Importance," *Journal of Educational Psychology* 101, no. 4 (2009): 817–35; and H. J. Kell et al., "Creativity and Technical Innovation: Spatial Ability's Unique Role," *Psychological Science* 24 (2013): 1831–36.

69. A. Frick, W. Mohring, and N. S. Newcombe, "Development of Mental Transformation Abilities," *Trends in Cognitive Sciences* 18 (2014): 536–42; and M. Hegarty and D. Waller, "Individual Differences in Spatial Abilities," in *The Cambridge Handbook of Visuospatial Thinking*, ed. P. Shah and A. Miyake (Cambridge: Cambridge University Press, 2005), 121–69.

70. See D. S. Moore and S. P. Johnson, "Mental Rotation in Human Infants: A Sex Difference," *Psychological Science* 19 (2008): 1063–66; and P. C. Quinn and L. S. Liben, "A Sex Difference in Mental Rotation in Young Infants," *Psychological Science* 19 (2008): 1067–70.

71. J. E. Lauer and S. F. Lourenco, "Spatial Processing in Infancy Predicts Both Spatial and Mathematical Aptitude in Childhood," *Psychological Science* 27, no. 10 (2016): 1291–98.

72. See Vuoksimaa et al., "Having a Male Co-Twin Masculinizes Mental Rotation Performance in Females."

73. Ingalhalikar et al., "Sex Differences in the Structural Connectome of the Human Brain"; Tunç et al., "Establishing a Link between Sex-Related Differences in the Structural Connectome and Behaviour," *Philosophical Transactions of the Royal Society B: Biological Sciences* 371 (2016): 16–88; and Ronald A. Yeo et al., "Cognitive Specialization for Verbal vs. Spatial Ability in Men and Women: Neural and Behavioral Correlates," *Personality and Individual Differences* 102 (November 2016): 260–67.

losum is much easier, and, being less module-based, they can more quickly move from one task to another even if they stay in the same hemisphere. Dealing with family life and dealing with people demands easily coping with interruptions and not showing irritation or hostility. Men's tendency to irritation and anger would upset the children and other adults—including the mother!

Sex Differences in Emotionality

Another distinctively female characteristic is greater expressed emotionality.[74] Again, this is hardly a new idea, but the recent evidence from neuroscience gives it a much firmer foundation in the adult female body. This expressed emotionality is there from the start in girls, but it is greatly increased during puberty and remains present as affected by a woman's monthly cycle; as noted, it also tends to increase during pregnancy. A variety of different behaviors has been reported to vary with a woman's monthly cycle as well as with other fluctuating hormones.[75]

Some might argue that although women are more expressive of emotion, men are just as emotional but don't express it. There may be some truth to this, but even so it demonstrates a major difference in the behavior of men and women. There is also some neurological evidence that men are, on average, in fact less emotional than women. We know that autism, much more common in men, reduces the ability to empathize and to understand that other people have emotions. In addition, psychopaths, also more commonly male, appear to have little capacity to empathize with others. The one major male emotion that may seriously qualify the generalization about women being more emotional

---

74. Ellis et al., *Sex Differences*, 247–50; Geary, *Male, Female*, 259.
75. See K. M. Durante, A. Rae, and V. Griskevicius, "The Fluctuating Female Vote: Politics, Religion, and the Ovulatory Cycle," *Psychological Science* 24, no. 6 (2013): 1007–16; A. B. Eisenbruch, Z. L. Simmons, and J. R. Roney, "Lady in Red: Hormonal Predictors of Women's Clothing Choices," *Psychological Science* 26, no. 8 (2015): 1332–38; C. N. Macrae et al., "Person Perception across the Menstrual Cycle: Hormonal Influences on Social-Cognitive Functioning," *Psychological Science* 13, no. 6 (November 2002): 532–36; G. Miller, J. M. Tybur, and B. D. Jordan, "Ovulatory Cycle Effects on Tip Earnings by Lap Dancers: Economic Evidence for Human Estrus," *Evolution and Human Behavior* 28, no. 6 (2007): 375–81.

than men is the emotion of anger, which seems to be much more commonly expressed in men.[76] Some men specialize, so to speak, in anger, but there is reason to believe that women experience anger as often as men, but less overtly express this particular emotion.[77]

Another aspect of female emotionality is that women can change their emotional state more easily than men. This characteristic is probably another effect facilitated by the corpus callosum. In addition, the female brain tends to rest (that is, when not actively involved in some behavior or thought) in the limbic system, which contains major emotional structures, while the male brain tends to rest in the medulla oblongata, which is less associated with emotion.

In understanding women's emotions, it is important to recall the bonding hormone oxytocin, which facilitates peaceful moods, trusting relationships, and interpersonal bonding. It is released during birth, nursing, and in most intimate interactions, including sexual relations. A woman's emotional life goes through a last hormone-induced change during and after menopause.[78] This latter change typically involves a decline in preoccupation with the immediate family, a greater interest in others outside the family, and more concern with the self.

Male and Female Aggressiveness and Some Other Differences

In terms of major psychological differences, men are reliably more aggressive, which has the advantage of their being able to protect and advance a family's welfare. (As just noted, this aggressiveness often involves expression of anger.) Men are also risk-takers, and this means

---

76. John Archer, "Sex Differences in Aggression in Real-World Settings: A Meta-Analytic Review," *Review of General Psychology* 8 (2004): 291–322.

77. See Ellis et al., *Sex Differences*, 249; Benenson et al., "Social Exclusion"; A. M. Kring, "Gender and Anger," in *Gender and Emotion: Social Psychological Perspectives; Studies in Emotion and Social Interaction*, ed. A. H. Fischer (New York: Cambridge University Press, 2000), 211–31. For studies on how women deal with expressing aggression toward other women, see J. A. Krems et al., "Is She Angry? (Sexually Desirable) Women 'See' Anger on Female Faces," *Psychological Science* 26, no. 11 (2015): 1655–63; and T. Vaillancourt and A. Sharma, "Intolerance of Sexy Peers: Intrasexual Competition among Women," *Aggressive Behavior* 37 (2011): 569–77.

78. See Brizendine, *Female Brain*, 137–38, 148–55.

that new approaches and ideas are more often pioneered by men.[79] On the down side, aggression, risky behaviors, and new ideas that are false, mistaken, or premature can result in death or personal failure. Men in many careers are more confident, or even more overconfident, than women in the same careers.[80] But the homeless are very typically men; women in such situations are much less common. Young men are especially prone to risk-taking, as shown in their much higher accidental death rates as compared to those of young women. If women had such characteristics they would jeopardize not only their own safety but also that of their actual or future children.

By early adulthood, men have moderate to large advantages in visual acuity, throwing accuracy, and ability to track and block objects thrown at them.[81] During puberty and adolescence there develops in males a lower sensitivity to pain and a greater risk of pain-related disorders.[82] Men have a higher threshold and greater tolerance for physical pain than do women on average.[83] Apparently, in the case of various illnesses, women feel more pain than do men.[84]

---

79. See Gary Charness and Uri Gneezy, "Strong Evidence for Gender Differences in Risk Taking," *Journal of Economic Behavior and Organization* 8, no. 1 (2012): 50–58; and C. R. Harris, M. Jenkins, and D. Glaser, "Gender Differences in Risk Assessment: Why Do Women Take Fewer Risks than Men?," *Judgment and Decision Making* 1, no. 1 (2006): 48–63.

80. See J. F. Schultz and C. Thöni, "Overconfidence and Career Choice," *PLOS One* 11, no. 1 (2016): e0145126, http://doi.org/0.1371/journal.pone.0145126.

81. See Rosemary Jardine and N. G. Martin, "Spatial Ability and Throwing Accuracy," *Behavior Genetics* 13, no. 4 (July 1983): 331–40; and Neil V. Watson and Doreen Kimura, "Nontrivial Sex Differences in Throwing and Intercepting: Relation to Psychometrically-Defined Spatial Functions," *Personality and Individual Differences* 12, no. 5 (1991): 375–85.

82. Greenspan et al., "Studying Sex and Gender Differences in Pain and Analgesia: A Consensus Report," *Pain* 132, Suppl. 1 (November 2007): S26–S45, http://doi.org/10.1016/j.pain.2007.10.014.

83. E. J. Bartley and R. B. Fillingim, "Sex Differences in Pain: A Brief Review of Clinical and Experimental Finding," *British Journal of Anaesthesia* 111, no. 1 (2013): 52–58; and A. H. Buss and N. W. Portnoy, "Pain Tolerance and Group Identification," *Journal of Personality and Social Psychology* 6, no. 1 (1967): 106–8.

84. Rachael Rettner, "Women Feel Pain More Intensely Than Men Do," *Scientific American*, My Health News Daily, January 22, 2012, https://www.scientificamerican.com/article/women-feel-pain-more-intensely/.

Male and Female Differences in Mental Pathology

A recent essay by Fossati et al. provides considerable support for many of the male-female differences documented earlier. In their thorough evaluation of the alternative model of personality disorders involving different kinds of measures (outlined in the American Psychiatric Association's *Diagnostic and Statistical Manual of Mental Disorders*, 5th ed.), they found many significant sex differences.[85] For example, men showed more restricted affectivity, more withdrawal, and more antagonism (e.g., callousness, grandiosity); they also scored higher in risk-taking, and they judged relationships as secondary. In contrast, women scored higher in anxiousness, emotional lability, agreeableness, neuroticism, and preoccupation with relationships.

Two clear examples of such mental health differences are the much greater tendency to self-injury (e.g., cutting or burning) in girls,[86] while mentally disturbed boys and young men show much more violence against others, as in the case of school shooters.[87] There is also significant neurological evidence for major differences in mental health problems, generally, supporting these distinctions.[88]

It is curious to note that some of the preceding male and female differences are apparently becoming more accentuated in recent years.[89] For example, Lueptow and Garovich-Szabo report, "Taken overall, a substantial body of research reveals a very clear picture in spite of widespread expectations and desires, the various aspects of gender differentiation are not disappearing, if anything there is an increase

---

85. A. Fossati et al., "The *DSM-5* Alternative Model of Personality Disorders from the Perspective of Adult Attachment," *Journal of Nervous and Mental Disease* 203, no. 4 (2015): 252–58, esp. table 1.

86. T. P. Beauchine, S. P. Hinshaw, and J. A. Bridge, "Nonsuicidal Self-Injury and Suicidal Behaviors in Girls: The Case for Targeted Prevention in Preadolescence," *Clinical Psychological Science* 7, no. 4 (2019): 643–67.

87. See Peter Langman, *School Shooters: Understanding High School, College and Adult Perpetrators* (Lanham, Md.: Rowman and Littlefield, 2015).

88. See Margaret M. McCarthy et al., "Sex Differences in the Brain: The Not So Inconvenient Truth," *Journal of Neuroscience* 32, no. 7 (2012): 2241–47; and A. N. V. Ruigrok et al., "A Meta-Analysis of Sex Differences in Human Brain Structure," *Neuroscience and Biobehavior Reviews* 39, no. 100 (2014): 34–50.

89. John Tierney, "As Barriers Disappear, Some Gender Gaps Widen," *New York Times*, September 9, 2008, https://www.nytimes.com/2008/09/09/science/09tier.html.

in sex-typing, especially with the pattern most expected to decline, the femininity of females."[90] The authors interpret this as evidence for an unchanging evolutionary understanding of sexual differentiation, in contrast to any sociocultural explanation.

The Hyper-Abstract and Autistic Male

One way to make sex differences even clearer is to identify extreme types of both sexes. In any population there is a variation around the mean, and it is often helpful to look at the extremes. When you have two distributions—for instance, men and women—there will be some extremely "male" men and likewise some extremely "female" women. These extremes shed light on the less extreme average distribution. Hence, the importance of hyper-male and hyper-female types, even if they come close to being stereotypes.

As already noted, there is good evidence that men are more abstract, logical, systematic, and hierarchical in their thinking, and they are usually more interested in the physical world than in people and relationships. This is an advantage for a scientist, mathematician, philosopher, theologian, or any kind of systematic thinker. Simon Baron-Cohen has recently described this kind of thinking as intrinsic to men—that is, natural to the male brain—and also as implicitly autistic.[91] He proposes that extremely autistic thinking is hyper-masculine, and, indeed, autism is much more common in males than in females, by about a 4 to 1 ratio.[92] The truly autistic person is one who is "mind-blind"—that is, incapable of understanding other people as having minds, in particular of having thoughts, feelings, and intentions. Some autistic people seem to be unaware that they even have such mental properties. Instead, people are just objects or things, like the rest of the inanimate world. Such a world is one that is cold, emp-

---

90. L. B. Lueptow and L. Garovich-Szabo, "Social Change and the Persistence of Sex Typing: 1974–1997," *Social Forces* 80 (2001): 16.

91. Baron-Cohen, *Essential Difference*.

92. It is interesting that oxytocin apparently stimulates the social brain regions in autistic children; see Pam Belluck, "Oxytocin Found to Stimulate Social Brain Regions in Children with Autism," *New York Times*, December 2, 2013: A18, https://www.nytimes.com/2013/12/03/health/-oxytocin-found-to-stimulate-brain-in-children-with-autism.html.

ty of interest in others, and without any relationships or emotions. In terms of what matters to most people, such "objective" knowledge is without any human meaning and therefore lacks most of what is of real interest to them. Of course, most scientists and abstract thinkers are not truly autistic, but being somewhat autistic probably helps.

Scientific disciplines reject emotion as bias, reject intention as inadequately knowable, and require logical connections, observable material facts, and systemic order. In other words, scientific disciplines such as physics and biology incorporate the underlying set of assumptions that also characterize autism. This understanding of science came in with Galileo, Francis Bacon, and Descartes, among others, and it has helped create the modern model of the lonely, empty, machine-like universe devoid of all but mechanistic meaning. By rejecting the relevance to science of a personal God and by rejecting as relevant to understanding the universe any property such as purpose (intentionality), they set up today's *autistic* scientific naturalism as conceptualized by the isolated objective observer. This kind of philosophy is also similar to today's libertarian worldview, with its emphasis on the autonomous individual and its rationale for what many call selfishness. It is no accident that libertarianism is so popular with men, especially those involved in technology.[93]

The Somewhat Hyper-Empathic and Relational Female

According to Baron-Cohen, there are moderately extreme female differences that parallel the extreme negative male type. One is the hyper-feminine mode of thinking that is the opposite of the pathological hyper-masculine autistic mode. This hyper-empathic woman is discussed by Baron-Cohen.[94] The hyper-empathic woman contrasts with the much more common basically empathic woman who often

---

93. See Julie Borowski, "No, Here's Why Libertarians Are Mostly Men" (blog post, 2015), retrieved from http://www.julieborowski.com/no-heres-why-libertarians-are-mostly-men/ (site discontinued); Kevin Drum, "Here's Why Libertarians Are Mostly Men," *Mother Jones*, June 5, 2015, http://www.motherjones.com/kevin-drum/2015/06/heres-why-libertarians-are-mostly-men; and Jocelyn Kelly, "In Search of Libertarians," Pew Research Center website, August 25, 2014, http://www.pewresearch.org/fact-tank/2014/08/25/in-search-of-libertarians/.

94. Baron-Cohen, *Essential Difference*, chapter 12.

is a very good psychotherapist, teacher, doctor, or nurse. Recently a large-scale test of the Baron-Cohen position was conducted in the United Kingdom using data from almost 700,000 people and very significantly supported greater empathy in females and greater systemizing in males.[95]

The Issue of Complementarity

After our extended sketch of male and female differences, we turn to how their differences can function in a complementary fashion. Much of this complementarity will have been implicit earlier.

As we have seen, women are far better suited than men for physical closeness and intimacy, as when dealing with babies and children. Women are softer, smoother, smell sweeter, and have a friendlier voice, while men are physically rougher, hairier, smellier, and have a lower and scarier voice. Men are less sensitive to temperature, smells, sounds, tastes, and to social communication of emotions. These are all weaknesses when one is dealing with babies, children, and even many adults, but they are all strengths when one is working in a harsh physical environment. Furthermore, in politics, in war, and in business, it often doesn't pay to be too sensitive to criticism, or your own feelings will hamper your activity; too much sensitivity for the feelings of others may get in the way of necessary decisions.

Complementarity also shows in men's and women's very bodies. Men's hands and feet are bigger than women's. Again, this is both a strength and a liability. Greater strength and big hands are fine for heavy rough work, for building, for working with machinery, for fighting, for many competitive sports, and so forth. Men's greater physical strength and capacity for rough work are typically accepted and appreciated by women. However, one common physical liability in men associated with this greater strength is their relative physical stiffness,

---

95. D. M. Greenberg, V. Warrier, C. Allison, and S. Baron-Cohen, "Testing the Empathizing-Systemizing Theory of Sex Differences and the Extreme Male Brain Theory of Autism in Half a Million People," *Proceedings of the National Academy of Sciences of the United States of America* 115, no. 48 (2018): 12,152–57.

which is complemented by the greater physical flexibility of girls and women, which, besides adding to their beauty, is an aid when coping with active, squirming children.[96]

Women have smaller fingers and better fine-muscle coordination. For small delicate responses, such as cleaning a baby who is soiled, or sick, or cut and bleeding, such fingers are more apt. Likewise, for weaving, fine sewing, needlepoint, and knitting, such fingers are more functional.[97] Thus, for humans to survive and thrive both the heavy, coarse, outside work of building houses and making machines and the inside work of helping, nurturing children, and building positive relationships are complementary and necessary.

Furthermore, when women feel protected from physical danger and possible outside enemies, they then can concentrate on their major concern of actively maintaining a social network of friends, having children, and raising a family. Children need an attentive interpersonal parent who is readily available and sensitive to their needs—that is, a woman—a mother. But they also need protection, and they need resources that must be assertively sought in the outside world as commonly provided by a man—a father.

In fact, the large amount of evidence of male and female difference interpreted within an evolutionary framework strongly implies complementarity.[98] That is, each sex specializes in certain necessary biological and social tasks so as to create an environment better suited for human survival. It seems obvious that the general specialization of women to nurture babies and children and adult relationships effectively in a less risk-taking manner and of men to deal effectively in a more risk-taking manner with ideas, the physical world, and organized social power make for a much better chance of human flourishing than what some kind of unisex average human could ever accomplish.

Evidence of complementarity is also clear in the sexually different long-term mating strategies of men and women.[99] There is wide acceptance of the interpretation that women focus on mate selection to

---

96. Geary, *Male, Female*, 290.
97. Ellis et al., *Sex Differences*, 238.
98. See Buss, *Evolutionary Psychology*, and Geary, *Male, Female*.
99. Buss, *Evolutionary Psychology*.

provide for the welfare of their children and men obtain mates through social power, often based on money or physical prowess, and through status-striving in political and business structures, activities that normally result in the acquisition of resources. In other words, men compete with men in such a way as to provide the resources women need, while women compete with women, through their beauty and interpersonal gifts, for the men with resources.

In table 5-3 I propose a positive summary of psychological characteristics that underlie and support a Complementary Model. Note that masculine and feminine strengths tend to complement or balance each other. Thus, taken together, they are implicitly synergistic. Some of the many studies now identifying differences in male and female personality also note typical negative traits associated with each sex.[100] These traits balance and thus complement each other.

In understanding table 5-3, always keep in mind that these are based on averages, and there is always overlap between the populations of men and women.[101]

Synergistic Effects

As just noted, male and female differences when working in a complementary way are also often synergistic. By "synergy" is meant the capacity of male and female differences to bring about something greater than either sex could alone. Synergy is certainly implied in much com-

---

100. See, for instance, J. T. Spence, R. L. Helmreich, and C. K. Holahan, "Negative and Positive Components of Psychological Masculinity and Femininity and Their Relationships to Self-Reports of Neurotic and Acting Out Behaviors," *Journal of Personality and Social Psychology* 37, no. 10 (1979): 1673–82. Other relevant studies include P. Costa, Antonio Terracciano, and Robert R. McCrae, "Gender Differences in Personality Traits across Cultures: Robust and Surprising Findings," *Journal of Personality and Social Psychology* 81 (2001): 322–28; Alan Feingold, "Gender Differences in Personality: A Meta-Analysis," *Psychological Bulletin* 116 (1994): 429–56; B. Gentile et al., "Gender Differences in Domain-Specific Self-Esteem: A Meta-Analysis," *Review of General Psychology* 13 (2009): 34–45; D. P. Schmitt et al., "Why Can't a Man Be More Like a Woman? Sex Differences in Big Five Personality Traits across 55 Cultures," *Journal of Personality and Social Psychology* 94 (2008): 168–82; and John E. Williams and Deborah I. Best, *Measuring Sex Stereotypes: A Multination Study* (Thousand Oaks, Calif.: Sage, 1990).

101. S. H. Louden and L. J. Francis, "The Personality Profile of Roman Catholic Parochial Secular Priests in England and Wales," *Review of Religious Research* 41 (1999): 65–79.

TABLE 5-3

Proposed Masculine and Feminine Psychological Strengths and Weaknesses

		Masculine	Feminine
1	positive	**assertive**	**nurturing**
	negative	angry/dominating	controlling/smothering
2	positive	**risk-taking**	**careful/cautious**
	negative	impetuous/rash	timid/retiring
3	positive	**logical**	**intuitive**
	negative	rigid	irrational
4	positive	**calm**	**emotional responsiveness**
	negative	machine-like	overly emotional
5	positive	**abstract**	**concrete/practical**
	negative	impractical	too literal
6	positive	**objective/problem solving**	**subjective/empathetic**
	negative	cold/heartless	overly identified/merged
7	positive	**systematic**	**open minded**
	negative	Closed-minded	chaotic
8	positive	**focus on external things**	**focus on persons**
	negative	indifference to persons	relationships everything
9	positive	**mental toughness**	**sensitive to others**
	negative	insensitive/clueless	easily hurt/cries often
10	positive	**skeptical**	**trusting**
	negative	too doubting	credulous

plementarity and, as noted, even in the evolutionary interpretation of sex differences. Synergy is, of course, best illustrated by the creation of a family and its generational history but is also clear at times of family crisis. For example, we have all seen in movies or read in books this sort of scene: a snowstorm arrives at the same time that a child gets sick and medicine is needed. In the storm a tree hits the house or blocks the driveway. The father gets out his chain saw and takes the tree off the house or frees the driveway. He then drives for medicine or needed supplies. The mother guides the children to a safe room, comforts them, prepares food, and distracts the children by reading them stories. In much smaller crises, less dramatic but similarly differential responses occur. As a general rule, the father is a "mister outside" and the mother is a "missus inside."

Conclusion

A complementary model allows a fuller understanding of how, *taken together*, *men and women*, in their strengths, demonstrate a more complete image of God than does either sex alone. The best way to describe the effects of complementary interaction is with the word "synergy."[102] The interaction creates much more than what is provided by either the man or woman alone. For example, if a man has ten units of male goodness and a woman has ten units of female goodness, when taken separately they add up to twenty units of goodness. But when men and women are working together synergistically, their interaction can result in ten times ten, or one hundred units of goodness! Together they create a child, a family, and much more—an entire culture.[103]

---

102. Again, thanks to Sr. Mary Prudence Allen.
103. See also E. R. Schiltz, "The Promise and the Threat of the 'Three' in Integral Complementarity," in *Promise and Challenge: Catholic Women Reflect on Feminism, Complementarity, and the Church*, ed. M. R. Hasson (Huntington, Ind.: Our Sunday Visitor, 2015), 53–83.

BIBLIOGRAPHY

Alberti, Leon Battista. *I Libri della Famiglia*. Turin: Einaudi, 1994.
Allen, Sr. Prudence, RSM. "A Woman and a Man as Prime Analogical Beings." *American Catholic Philosophical Quarterly* 64, no. 4 (1992): 456–82.
———. "Metaphysics of Form, Matter, and Gender." *Lonergan Workshop* 12 (1996): 1–26.
———. *The Concept of Woman*. Vols. 1–3. Grand Rapids, Mich.: Eerdmans, 1997, 2002, 2017.
———. "Man-Woman Complementarity: The Catholic Inspiration." *Logos: A Journal of Catholic Thought and Culture* 9, no. 3 (Summer 2006): 87–108.
———. "Catholic Marriage and Feminism." In *The Church, Marriage, and the Family: Proceedings of the 27th Annual Fellowship of Catholic Scholars Convention*, edited by Kenneth D. Whitehead, 95–144. South Bend, Ind.: St. Augustine's Press, 2007.
———. "*Mulieris Dignitatem* Twenty Years Later: An Overview of the Document and Challenges." *Ave Maria Law Review* 8, no. 1 (Fall 2009): 13–47.
———. "Gender Reality." *Solidarity: The Journal of Catholic Social Thought and Secular Ethics* 4, no. 1 (2014): 1–35.
———. "Four Principles of Complementarity: A Philosophical Perspective." In *Not Just Good, But Beautiful: The Complementary Relationship Between Man and Woman*, edited by Steven Lopes and Helen Alvaré, 49–59. Walden, N.Y.: Plough, 2014.
American Psychiatric Association. *Diagnostic and Statistical Manual of Mental Disorders*. 5th ed. Arlington, Va.: American Psychiatric Association, 2013.
Andreano, J. M., and L. Cahill. "Sex Influences on the Neurobiology of Learning and Memory." *Learning and Memory* 16, no. 4 (2009): 248–66.
Aquinas, Thomas. *Commentary on the Letters of Saint Paul to the Corinthians*. Edited by J. Mortensen and E. Alarcón. Translated by F. R. Larcher, OP, et al. Lander, Wyo.: Aquinas Institute for the Study of Sacred Doctrine, 2012.
———. *De Ente et Essentia*. Translated by Armand Maurer. Toronto: Pontifical Institute of Mediaeval Studies, 1963.
———. *Summa contra Gentiles*. Book 2. Translated by J. F. Anderson. New York: Doubleday, 1956.
———. *Summa Theologiae*. In *Basic Writings of Saint Thomas Aquinas*, vol. 1, reprint. Translated by Anton Pegis. Indianapolis: Hackett, 1997.
Archer, John. "Sex Differences in Aggression in Real-World Settings: A Meta-Analytic Review." *Review of General Psychology* 8, no. 4 (2004): 291–322.
Aristotle. *Generation of Animals*. Edited and translated by A. L. Peck. Cambridge, Mass.: Harvard University Press, 1943.

Aristotle. *Metaphysics*. Edited by W. D. Ross. Oxford: Clarendon, 1924.
Ashley, Benedict. *Theologies of the Body: Humanist and Christian*. 2nd ed. Braintree, Mass.: Pope John Center, 1996.
Atkinson, Joseph. *Biblical and Theological Foundations of the Family*. Washington D.C.: The Catholic University of America Press, 2014.
Augustine. *The City of God*. Books XVII–XXII. Translated by Gerald G. Walsh, SJ, and Daniel J. Honan. Fathers of the Church 24. Washington, D.C.: The Catholic University of America Press, 1954.
Bachiochi, Erika. "Embodied Caregiving." *First Things* 266 (October 2016): 39–44.
Barnes, Bernadine. *Michelangelo's Last Judgment: The Renaissance Response*. Berkeley: University of California Press, 1998.
Baron-Cohen, Simon. *The Essential Difference: Male and Female Brains and the Truth about Autism*. New York: Basic Books, 2003.
Bartley, E. J., and R. B. Fillingim. "Sex Differences in Pain: A Brief Review of Clinical and Experimental Finding." *British Journal of Anaesthesia* 111, no. 1 (2013): 52–58.
Bartz, J. A., J. Zaki, N. Bolger, E. Hollander, N. N. Ludwig, A. Kolevzon, and K. N. Ochsner. "Oxytocin Selectively Improves Empathic Accuracy." *Psychological Science* 21, no. 10 (2010): 1426–28.
Baxandall, Michael. *Painting and Experience in Fifteenth-Century Italy*. Oxford: Oxford University Press, 1988.
Beach, Frank A. "Alternative Interpretations of the Development of G-I/R." In Reinisch, Rosenblum, and Sanders, *Masculinity/Femininity: Basic Perspectives*, 29–34.
Beauchine, T. P., S. P. Hinshaw, and J. A Bridge. "Nonsuicidal Self-Injury and Suicidal Behaviors in Girls: The Case for Targeted Prevention in Preadolescence." *Clinical Psychological Science* 7, no. 4 (2019): 643–67.
Belluck, Pam. "Oxytocin Found to Stimulate Social Brain Regions in Children with Autism." *New York Times*, December 2, 2013: A18. https://www.nytimes.com/2013/12/03/health/oxytocin-found-to-stimulate-brain-in-children-with-autism.html.
Benedict XVI. *Regina Caeli, Easter Monday*. April 9, 2012. http://www.vatican.va/content/benedict-xvi/en/angelus/2012/documents/hf_ben-xvi_reg_20120409_easter-monday.html.
Benenson, Joyce F. "Greater Preference among Females Than Males for Dyadic Interaction in Early Childhood." *Child Development* 64, no. 2 (1993): 544–55.
Bennison, Joyce F., Henry Markovits, Brittney Hultgren, Tuyet Nguyen, Grace Bullock, and Richard Wrangham. "Social Exclusion: More Important to Human Female than Males." *PLOS One* 8 (February 6, 2013). Essay e55851. http://doi:10.1371/journal.pone.0055851.
Berenbaum, S. A., and E. Snyder. "Early Hormonal Influences on Child Sex Typed Activity and Playmate Preferences: Implications for the Development of Sexual Orientation." *Developmental Psychology* 31, no. 1 (1995): 31–42.
Blankenhorn, David. *Fatherless America: Confronting Our Most Urgent Social Problem*. New York: HarperCollins, 1995.

Bibliography | 219

Boccaccio, Giovanni. "De Mulieribus Claris." In *Letteratura Italiana Storia e Testi*, edited by Pier Giorgio Ricci. Vol. 9. Milan: R. Ricciardi, 1965.
Botterweck, G. Johannes, Helmer Ringren, and Heinz-Josef Fabry, eds. *Theological Dictionary of the Old Testament*. Vol. 12. Grand Rapids, Mich.: Eerdmans, 2003.
Bouyer, Louis. "Woman and God." In *Women in the Church*, 29–39. San Francisco, Calif.: Ignatius Press, 1979.
Brizendine, Louann. *The Female Brain*. New York: Broadway Books, 2006.
———. *The Male Brain*. New York: Broadway Books, 2010.
Budziszewski, J. *On the Meaning of Sex*. Wilmington, Del.: ISI, 2012.
Burggraf, Jutta. "Gender." In *Lexicon: Ambiguous and Debatable Terms Regarding Family Life and Ethical Questions*, edited by Pontifical Council for the Family, 399–408. Front Royal, Va.: Human Life International, 2006.
Buss, A. H., and N. W. Portnoy. "Pain Tolerance and Group Identification." *Journal of Personality and Social Psychology* 6, no. 1 (1967): 106–8.
Buss, David. *Evolutionary Psychology: The New Science of the Mind*. 5th ed. London: Routledge, 2015.
Butler, Judith. *Gender Trouble: Feminism and the Subversion of Identity*. New York: Routledge, 1990.
———. *Undoing Gender*. New York: Routledge, 2004.
Butler, Sarah. "Catholic Women and Equality: Women in the Code of Canon Law." In *Feminism, Law, and Religion*, edited by Marie A. Failinger, Elizabeth R. Schiltz, and Susan Stabile, 345–70. Burlington, Vt.: Ashgate, 2013.
Cahill, Larry. "His Brain, Her Brain." *Scientific American* 292, no. 5 (2005): 40–47.
———. "Why Sex Matters for Neuroscience." *Nature Reviews: Neuroscience* 7 (2006): 477–84.
Campbell, Anne. *A Mind of Her Own: The Evolutionary Psychology of Women*. 2nd ed. Oxford: Oxford University Press, 2013.
Campbell, Antony F., and Mark A. O'Brien. *Sources of the Pentateuch*. Minneapolis: Fortress, 1993.
Carron, A. V., and D. A. Bailey. "Strength Development in Boys from 10 through 16 Years." *Monographs of the Society for Research in Child Development* 39, no. 4, serial no. 157 (1974).
Center for Applications of Psychological Types. "Estimated Frequencies of the Types in the United States Population." http://www.capt.org/mbti-assessment/estimated-frequencies.htm.
Charness, Gary, and Uri Gneezy. "Strong Evidence for Gender Differences in Risk Taking." *Journal of Economic Behavior and Organization* 8, no. 1 (2012): 50–58.
Childs, Brevard S. *Myth and Reality in the Old Testament*. Naperville, Ill.: Allenson, 1960.
———. *Old Testament Theology in a Canonical Context*. Philadelphia: Fortress, 1985.
Christen, Yves, and Nicholas Davidson. *Sex Differences: Modern Biology and the Unisex Fallacy*. New Brunswick, N.J.: Transaction, 1991.
Chrysostom, St. John. *Catechesis* 3.13–19. In *Jean Chrysostome: Huit Catéchèses Baptismales Inédites*, edited by A. Wenger, 174–77. Sources Chrétiennes 50. Paris: Cerf,

2005. English translation: *Baptismal Instructions*. Translated by Paul W. Harkins, SJ. Ancient Christian Writers 31. Westminster, Md.: Newman Press, 1963.

Clarke, W. Norris, SJ. *The One and the Many: A Contemporary Thomistic Metaphysics*. Notre Dame, Ind.: University of Notre Dame Press, 2001.

Colalucci, Gianluigi. "Tecniche di restauro" [The Technique of the Sistine Ceiling Frescos]. Chapter 9 in *La Cappella Sistina. I Primi Restauri: La Scoperta del Colore*, edited by Marcella Boroli. Novara, Italy: Istituto Geografico De Agostini, 1986.

Colapinto, John. *As Nature Made Him: The Boy Who Was Raised as a Girl*. New York: Harper Perennial, 2000.

Collaer, M. L., and M. Hines. "Human Behavioral Sex Differences: A Role for Gonadal Hormones during Early Development?" *Psychological Bulletin* 118 (July 1995): 55–107.

Compendium of the Social Doctrine of the Church. Vatican City: Libreria Ed. Vaticana, 2004.

Condivi, Ascanio. *The Life of Michelangelo*. University Park: Pennsylvania State University Press, 1999.

Congregation for the Doctrine of the Faith. *Letter to the Bishops on the Collaboration of Men and Women in the Church and in the World*. By Joseph Cardinal Ratzinger, Prefect. July 31, 2004.

Connellen, Jennifer, Simon Baron-Cohen, Sally Wheelwright, Anna Batki, and Jag Ahluwalia. "Sex Differences in Human Neonatal Social Perception." *Infant Behavior and Development* 23, no. 1 (2000): 113–18.,

Costa, P. T., Antonio Terracciano, and Robert R. McCrae. "Gender Differences in Personality Traits across Cultures: Robust and Surprising Findings." *Journal of Personality and Social Psychology* 81, no. 2 (2001): 322–31.

Cozolino, Louis. *The Neuroscience of Human Relationships: Attachment and the Developing Social Brain*. 2nd ed. New York: Norton, 2014.

Crews, David. "Functional Associations in Behavioral Endocrinology." In Reinisch, Rosenblum, and Sanders, *Masculinity/Femininity: Basic Perspectives*, 83–105.

Daly, Martin, and Margo Wilson. *Sex, Evolution and Behavior*. Boston: Willard Grant, 1983.

de Fraine, Jean. *Adam and the Family of Man*. Staten Island, N.Y.: Alba House, 1965.

De Vries, Geert J., and Nancy G. Forger. "Sex Differences in the Brain: A Whole Body Perspective." *Biology of Sex Differences* 6, no. 1 (August 15, 2015). https://www.ncbi.nim.nih.gov/pmc/articles/PMC4536872/.

Dobbs, Darrell. "Family Matters: Aristotle's Appreciation of Women and the Plural Structure of Society." *American Political Science Review* 90, no. 1 (1996): 74–89.

Dozeman, Thomas B., and Konrad Schmid, eds. *A Farewell to the Yahwist?: The Composition of the Pentateuch in Recent European Interpretation*. Symposium Series 34. Atlanta: Society of Biblical Literature, 2006.

Durante, K. M., A. Rae, and V. Griskevicius. "The Fluctuating Female Vote: Politics, Religion, and the Ovulatory Cycle." *Psychological Science* 24, no. 6 (201): 1007–16.

Eaton, W. O., and L. R. Enns. "Sex Differences in Human Motor Activity Level." *Psychological Bulletin* 100, no. 1 (1986): 19–28.

Eberstadt, Mary. *Adam and Eve after the Pill: Paradoxes of the Sexual Revolution*. San Francisco: Ignatius Press, 2012.

Eberstadt, Nicholas. *America's Invisible Crisis: Men without Work*. West Conshohocken, Pa.: Templeton, 2016.

Eder, D., and M. T. Hallinan. "Sex Differences in Children's Friendships." *American Sociological Review* 43, no. 2 (1978): 237–50.

Eibl-Eibesfeldt, Irenäus. *Human Ethology*. New York: Aldine de Gruyter, 1989.

Eisenberg, N., and R. Lennon. "Sex Difference in Empathy and Related Capacities." *Psychological Bulletin* 94, no. 1 (1983): 100–131.

Eisenbruch, A. B., Z. L. Simmons, and J. R. Roney. "Lady in Red: Hormonal Predictors of Women's Clothing Choices." *Psychological Science* 26, no. 8 (2015): 1332–38.

Ellis, B. J. "The Evolution of Sexual Attraction: Evaluative Mechanisms in Women." In *The Adapted Mind*, edited by J. Barkow, L. Cosmides, and J. Tooby, 164–88. New York: Oxford University Press, 1992.

Ellis, L., S. Hershberger, E. Field, S. Wersinger, S. Pellis, D. Geary, C. Palmer, K. Hoyengs, A. Hetsroni, and K. Karadi. *Sex Differences: Summarizing More Than a Century of Scientific Research*. New York: Psychology Press, Taylor and Francis Group, 2008.

Failinger, Marie A., Elizabeth R. Schiltz, and Susan Stabile, eds. *Feminism, Law, and Religion*. Burlington, Vt.: Ashgate, 2013.

Feingold, Alan. "Gender Differences in Personality: A Meta-Analysis." *Psychological Bulletin* 116, no. 3 (1994): 429–56.

Finley, John. "The Metaphysics of Gender: A Thomistic Approach." *Thomist* 79, no. 4 (2015): 585–614.

Fortin, Timothy. *Fatherhood and the Perfection of Masculinity*. Rome: Pontificia Universitas Sanctae Crucis, 2008.

Fossati, A., R. F. Krueger, K. E. Markon, S. Borroni, C. Maffei, and A. Somma. "The DSM-5 Alternative Model of Personality Disorders from the Perspective of Adult Attachment." *Journal of Nervous and Mental Disease* 203, no. 4 (2015): 252–58.

Foucault, Michel. *The Order of Things: An Archaeology of the Human Sciences*. Edited by R. D. Laing. New York: Vintage, 1970.

———. *Herculine Barbin: Being the Recently Discovered Memoirs of a Nineteenth-Century French Hermaphrodite*. Translated by Richard McDougall. Brighton, UK: The Harvester Press, 1980.

———. *The History of Sexuality*. Vol. 1, *An Introduction*. New York: Vintage, 1980.

Frick, A., W. Mohring, and N. S. Newcombe. "Development of Mental Transformation Abilities." *Trends in Cognitive Sciences* 18 (Oct. 2014): 536–42.

Geary, D. C. *Male, Female: The Evolution of Sex Differences*. 2nd ed. Washington, D.C.: American Psychological Association, 2010.

Gebhard, Paul H., and Alan B. Johnson. *The Kinsey Data: Marginal Tabulations of the 1938–1963 Interviews Conducted by the Institute for Sex Research*. Philadelphia: W. B. Saunders, 1979.

Geddes, Donald Porter, ed. *An Analysis of the Kinsey Reports on Sexual Behavior in the Human Male and Female*. New York: Mentor, 1954.

Gee, D. G., L. Gabard-Durnam, E. H. Telzer, K. L. Humphreys, B. Goff, M. Shapiro, J. Flannery, D. S. Lumian, D. S. Fareri, C. Calders, and N. Tottenham. "Maternal Buffering of Human Amygdala-Prefrontal Circuitry during Childhood but not during Adolescence." *Psychological Science* 25, no. 11 (2014): 2067–78.

Gentile, B., S. Grabe, B. Dolan-Pascoe, J. M. Twenge, B. E. Wells, and A. Maitino. "Gender Differences in Domain-Specific Self-Esteem: A Meta-Analysis." *Review of General Psychology* 13, no. 1 (2009): 34–45.

George, Robert P. *The Clash of Orthodoxies*. Wilmington, Del.: ISI, 2001.

Glendon, Mary Ann. "The Pope's New Feminism." *Crisis* 15, no. 3 (March 1997): 28–31.

———. "What Happened at Beijing." In *Traditions in Turmoil*, 301–13. Ann Arbor, Mich.: Sapientia Press of Ave Maria, 2006.

Gormally, Luke. *Euthanasia, Clinical Practice and the Law*. London: Linacre Center, 1994.

Geary, D. C. *Male, Female: The Evolution of Sex Differences*. 2nd ed. Washington, D.C.: American Psychological Association Press, 2010.

Grebe, N. M., S. W. Gangestad, C. E. Garver-Apgar, and R. Thornhill. "Women's Luteal-Phase Sexual Proceptivity and the Functions of Extended Sexuality." *Psychological Science* 24, no. 10 (2013): 2106–10.

Greenberg, D. M., V. Warrier, C. Allison, and S. Baron-Cohen. "Testing the Empathizing-Systemizing Theory of Sex Differences and the Extreme Male Brain Theory of Autism in Half a Million People." *Proceedings of the National Academy of Sciences of the United States of America* 115, no. 48 (2018): 12,152–57.

Greenspan, Joel D., et al. "Studying Sex and Gender Differences in Pain and Analgesia: A Consensus Report." *Pain* 132, Supplement 1 (2007): S26–45. http://doi.org/10.1016/j.pain.2007.10.014.

Grenz, Stanley. *A Primer on Postmodernism*. Grand Rapids, Mich.: Eerdmans, 1996.

Griffin, Carter. *Why Celibacy?: Reclaiming the Fatherhood of the Priest*. Steubenville, Ohio: Emmaus Road, 2019.

Gurian, Michael. *Boys and Girls Learn Differently: A Guide for Teachers and Parents*. Rev. 10th ed. San Francisco, Calif.: Jossey-Bass, 2011.

———. *The Minds of Girls: A New Path for Raising Healthy, Resilient and Successful Women*. Spokane, Wash.: Gurian Institute Press, 2018.

Hahn, Scott, and Curtis Mitch, eds. *The Ignatius Catholic Study Bible*. San Francisco: Ignatius Press, 2010.

Harris, C. R., M. Jenkins, and D. Glaser. "Gender Differences in Risk Assessment: Why Do Women Take Fewer Risks than Men?" *Judgment and Decision Making* 1, no. 1 (2006): 48–63.

Haviland, Jeanette Jones, and Carol Zander Malatesta. "The Development of Sex Differences in Nonverbal Signals: Fallacies, Facts and Fantasies." In *Gender and Nonverbal Behavior*, edited by Clara Mayo and Nancy M. Henley, 183–208. New York: Springer-Verlag, 1981.

Hegarty, M., and D. Waller. "Individual Differences in Spatial Abilities." In *The Cambridge Handbook of Visuospatial Thinking*, edited by P. Shah and A. Miyake, 121–69. Cambridge: Cambridge University Press, 2005.

Herlitz, A., and J. Loven. "Sex Differences and the Own-Gender Bias in Face Recognition: A Meta-Analytic Review." *Visual Cognition* 21, no. 9–10 (2013): 1306–36.
Herlitz, A., and J. Rehnman. "Sex Differences in Episodic Memory." *Current Directions in Psychological Science* 17, no. 1 (2008): 52–56.
"Hic Mulier." In *Half Humankind: Contexts and Texts of the Controversy about Women in England, 1540–1640*, edited by Katherine Usher Henderson and Barbara F. McManus, 264–89. Urbana: University of Illinois Press, 1985.
Hoekzema, E., E. Barba-Muller, C. Pozzobon, M. Picado, F. Lucco, D. Garcia-Garcia, J. C. Soliva, A. Tobena, M. Desco, E. Crone, A. Ballesteros, S. Carmona, and O. Vilarra. "Pregnancy Leads to Long-Lasting Changes in Human Brain Structure." *Nature Neuroscience* 20 (2017): 287–96. http://doi.org/10.1038/nn.4458.
Hoffman, M. L. "Sex Differences in Empathy and Related Behaviors." *Psychological Bulletin* 84, no. 4 (1977): 712–22.
———. *Empathy and Moral Development: Implications for Caring and Justice*. Cambridge: Cambridge University Press, 2000.
Hoyenga, Katharine Blick, and Kermit T. Hoyenga. *The Question of Sex Differences: Psychological, Cultural, and Biological Issues*. Boston: Little, Brown, 1979.
Hu, Y-H., and N. Goldman. "Mortality Differentials by Marital Status: An International Comparison." *Demography* 27, no. 2 (May 1990): 233–50.
Hymowitz, Kay S. *Manning Up: How the Rise of Women Has Turned Men into Boys*. New York: Basic, 2012.
Ingalhalikar, M., A. Smith, D. Parker, T. D. Satterthwaite, M. A. Elliott, K. Ruparel, H. Hakonarson, R. E. Gur, R. C. Gur, and R. Verma. "Sex Differences in the Structural Connectome of the Human Brain." *Proceedings of the National Academy of Sciences of the United States of America* 111, no. 2 (2014): 823–28.
Insel, T. R. "Oxytocin: A Neuropeptide for Affiliation." *Psychoneuroendocrinology* 17, no. 1 (1992): 3–35.
Insel, T. R., and L. J. Young. "The Neurobiology of Attachment." *National Review of Neuroscience* 2, no. 2 (2001): 129–36.
Irenaeus of Lyons. *Against the Heresies*. Vol. 3, *Book 3*. Ancient Christian Writers 64. Translated by Dominic J. Unger. New York: Newman Press, 2012.
Jardine, Rosemary, and N. G. Martin. "Spatial Ability and Throwing Accuracy." *Behavior Genetics* 13, no. 4 (July 1983): 331–40.
Jerome. "Epistle 22 (*To Eustochium*)." In *The Letters of Saint Jerome*, vol. 1, *Letters 1–22*. Ancient Christian Writers 33. Translated by Charles Christopher Mierow. New York: Newman Press, 1963.
John XXIII. *Pacem in Terris*. Encyclical Letter. April 11, 1963.
John Paul II. *Laborem Exercens*. Encyclical Letter. September 14, 1981.
———. *The Original Unity of Man and Woman*. Boston: Daughters of St. Paul, 1981.
———. *Mulieris Dignitatem*. Apostolic Letter. August 15, 1988. Boston: St. Paul Books and Media, 1988.
———. *Redemptoris Custos (Guardian of the Redeemer)*. Apostolic Exhortation. August 15, 1989. Boston: St. Paul Books and Media, 1989.
———. *Homily at Unveiling of Restored Sistine Chapel Frescos*. April 8, 1994.

———. *Evangelium Vitae: The Gospel of Life*. Encyclical Letter. March 25, 1995. Boston: Pauline Books and Media, 1995.

———. *Letter to Women*. June 29, 1995.

———. *Gift and Mystery: On the Fiftieth Anniversary of My Priestly Ordination*. New York: Doubleday, 1996.

———. *Christifidelis Laici*. Apostolic Exhortation. December 30, 1998.

———. *Fides et Ratio*. Encyclical Letter. September 14, 1998.

———. *The Poetry of John Paul II: Roman Triptych, Meditations*. Translated by Jerzy Peterkiewicz. Washington, D.C.: USCCB, 2003.

———. *Rise, Let Us Be on Our Way*. New York: Warner, 2004.

———. *Man and Woman He Created Them: A Theology of the Body*. Translated by Michael Waldstein. Boston, Mass.: Pauline Books and Media, 2006.

Johnson, Elizabeth A. "Imaging God, Embodying Christ: Women as a Sign of the Times." In *The Church Women Want*, edited by Elizabeth A. Johnson, 45–59. New York: Crossroad, 2002.

Jordan-Young, Rebecca. *Brainstorm*. Cambridge, Mass.: Harvard University Press. 2010.

Kautzky-Willer, A. J. Harrieter, and G. Pacini. "Sex and Gender Differences in Risk, Pathophysiology and Complications of Type 2 Diabetes Mellitus." *Endocrine Reviews* 37, no. 3 (June 2016): 278–316.

Kell, H. J., D. Lubinski, C. P. Benbow, and J. H. Steiger. "Creativity and Technical Innovation: Spatial Ability's Unique Role." *Psychological Science* 24, no. 9 (2013): 1831–36.

Kelley, David. *The Art of Reasoning*. New York: W. W. Norton, 1988.

Kessler, Suzanne J., and Wendy McKenna. *Gender: An Ethnomethodological Approach*. New York: John Wiley and Sons, 1978.

Kimura, Doreen. "Sex Difference in the Brain." *Scientific American* 267, no. 3 (1992): 119–25.

———. *Sex and Cognition*. Cambridge, Mass.: MIT Press, 1999.

Kinsey, Alfred C., Wardell B. Pomeroy, and Clyde E. Martin. *Sexual Behavior in the Human Male*. Philadelphia: W. B. Saunders, 1948.

Kinsey, Alfred C., Wardell B. Pomeroy, Clyde E. Martin, and Paul H. Gebhard. *Sexual Behavior in the Human Female*. Philadelphia: W. B. Saunders, 1953.

Kittay, E. F. *Love's Labor: Essays on Women, Equality, and Dependency*. New York: Routledge, 1999.

Klein, K. K., and W. B. Wilcox. *Mother Bodies, Father Bodies: How Parenthood Changes Us from the Inside Out*. New York: Institute for American Values, 2014.

Konner, Melvin. *Women After All: Sex, Evolution, and the End of Male Supremacy*. New York: W. W. Norton, 2015.

Krapiec, Mieczylaw A. *I-Man*. New Britain, Conn.: Mariel, 1983.

Krems, J. A., S. L. Neuberg, G. Filip-Crawford, and D. T. Kenrick. "Is She Angry? (Sexually Desirable) Women 'See' Anger on Female Faces." *Psychological Science* 26, no. 11 (2015): 1655–63.

Kring, A. M. "Gender and Anger." In *Gender and Emotion: Social Psychological Perspectives. Studies in Emotion and Social Interaction*, edited by A. H. Fischer, 211–31. New York: Cambridge University Press, 2000.

Kuukasjärvi, S., C. J. P. Eriksson, E. Koskela, T. Mappes, K. Nissinen, and M. J. Rantala. "Attractiveness of Women's Body Odors over the Menstrual Cycle: The Role of Oral Contraceptives and Receiver Sex." *Behavioral Ecology* 15, no. 4 (July 2004): 579–84.

Kwang, T., E. Crockett, D. T. Sanchez, and W. B. Swann Jr. "Men Seek Social Standing, Women Seek Companionship: Sex Differences in Deriving Self-Worth from Relationships." *Psychological Science* 24, no. 7 (2013): 1142–50.

Lactantius. *Divine Institutes: Books I–VII*. Translated by Sister Mary Francis McDonald, OP. Fathers of the Church 49. Washington, D.C.: The Catholic University of America Press, 1964.

Landgraf, R. "Intracerebrally Released Vasopressin and Oxytocin: Measurement, Mechanisms, and Behavioral Consequences." *Journal of Neuroendocrinology* 7 (1995): 243–53.

Langman, Peter. *School Shooters: Understanding High School, College and Adult Perpetrators*. Lanham, Md.: Rowman and Littlefield, 2015.

Lauer, J. E., and S. F. Lourenco. "Spatial Processing in Infancy Predicts Both Spatial and Mathematical Aptitude in Childhood." *Psychological Science* 27, no. 10 (2016): 1291–98.

Laureates, Teresa de. *Technologies of Gender*. Bloomington: Indiana University Press, 1987.

Lev, Elizabeth. "Reading Theological Context: A Marian Interpretation of Michelangelo's Roman Pietà." In *Revisioning: Critical Methods of Seeing Christianity in the History of Art*, edited by James Romaine and Linda Stratford, 207–22. Eugene, Ore.: Cascade, 2013.

Lev, Elizabeth, and Jose Granados. *A Body for Glory*. Vatican City: Edizioni Musei Vaticani, 2014.

Lever, J. "Sex Differences in the Complexity of Children's Play and Games." *American Sociological Review* 43, no. 4 (1978): 471–83.

Lewis, C. S. *Perelandra: A Novel*. New York: Macmillan, 1944.

Lin, P. Y., N. S. Grewal, C. Morin, W. D. Johnson, and P. J. Zak. "Oxytocin Increases the Influence of Public Service Advertisements." *PLOS One* 8, no. 2 (2013): 1–11.

Linn, M. C., and A. C. Petersen. "Emergence and Characterization of Sex Differences in Spatial Ability: A Meta-Analysis." *Child Development* 56, no. 6 (1985): 1479–98.

Lipien, Ted. *Wojtyła's Women: How They Shaped the Life of Pope John Paul II and Changed the Catholic Church*. Winchester, UK: O Books, 2008.

Llamas, Marta. "Cuerpo: Diferencia sexual y género." In Dale O'Leary, *The Gender Agenda: Redefining Equality*. Lafayette, La.: Vital Issues, 1997.

Lonergan, Bernard. "Finality, Love, Marriage." *Theological Studies* 4, no. 4 (1943): 477–510. Reprinted in *Collected Works of Bernard Lonergan*, edited by Frederick E. Crowe and Robert M. Doran, 17–26. Toronto: University of Toronto Press, 1988. Originally published in 1967.

Lopes, Steven, and Helen Alvaré. *Not Just Good, but Beautiful: The Complementary Relationship between Man and Woman*. Walden, N.Y.: Plough, 2015.

Louden, S. H., and L. J. Francis. "The Personality Profile of Roman Catholic Parochial Secular Priests in England and Wales." *Review of Religious Research* 41, no. 1 (1999): 65–79.

Lueptow, L. B., and L. Garovich-Szabo. "Social Change and the Persistence of Sex Typing: 1974–1997." *Social Forces* 80, no. 1 (2001): 1–36.

Lutchmaya, Svetlana, and Simon Baron-Cohen. "Human Sex Differences in Social and Non-Social Looking Preferences, at 12 Months of Age." *Infant Behavior and Development* 25, no. 3 (2002): 319–25.

Maas, A. H. E. M., and Y. E. A. Appelman. "Gender Differences in Coronary Heart Disease." *Netherlands Heart Journal* 18, no. 12 (2010): 596–602.

MacDonald, Heather. "Gender Is a Construct—Except When It's Not." *City Journal*, August 17, 2018. https://www.city-journal.org/html/gender-construct-16117.html.

Macrae, C. N., K. A. Alnwick, A. B. Milne, and A. M. Schloerscheidt. "Person Perception across the Menstrual Cycle: Hormonal Influences on Social-Cognitive Functioning." *Psychological Science* 13, no. 6 (November 2002): 532–36.

Maeder, Edward. "The Costumes Worn by the Ancestors of Christ." Chapter 6 in *The Sistine Chapel: A Glorious Restoration*, edited by Pierluigi De Vecchi. New York: Abradale, 1999.

Mancinelli, Fabrizio, and Anna Maria De Strobel, eds. *Michelangelo: Le Lunette e le Vele della Cappella Sistina; Liber Generationuis Jesu Christi*. Rome: Leonardo-De Luca, 1992.

Marcel, Gabriel. *Homo Viator: Introduction to a Metaphysic of Hope*. Translated by Emma Craufurd. New York: Harper Torchbooks, 1962.

———. *Metaphysical Journal 1943*. In *Presence and Immortality*. Pittsburgh, Pa.: Duquesne University Press, 1967.

———. *Creative Fidelity*. Translated by Robert Rosthal. New York: Fordham University Press, 2002.

Maritain, Jacques. Chapter 5, "Thomist Study Circles and Their Annual Retreats (1919–1939)." In *Notebooks*, translated by Joseph W. Evans, 134–35. Albany, N.Y.: Magi, 1984.

Martin, Biddy. "Feminism, Criticism, and Foucault." *Feminism and Foucault: Reflections on Resistance*, edited by Irene Diamond and Lee Quinby, 3–20. Boston: Northeastern University Press, 1988.

Martin, Francis. *The Feminist Question: Feminist Theology in the Light of Christian Tradition*. Grand Rapids, Mich.: Eerdmans, 1994.

Mayer, L. S., and P. R. McHugh. "Sexuality and Gender: Findings from the Biological, Psychological, and Social Sciences." *New Atlantis* 50 (Fall 2016): 1–143.

McCarthy, M. H. "'Headship': Making the Case for Fruitful Equality in a World of Indifferent Sameness and Unbridgeable Difference." *Religions* 11, no. 6 (2020): 295.

McCarthy, Margaret M., Arthur P. Arnold, Gregory F. Ball, Jeffry D. Blaustein, and Geert J. DeVries. "Sex Differences in the Brain: The Not So Inconvenient Truth." *Journal of Neuroscience* 32, no. 7 (2012): 2241–47.

McClure, E. B. "A Meta-Analytic Review of Sex Differences in Facial Expression Processing and Their Development in Infants, Children and Adolescents." *Psychological Bulletin* 126, no. 3 (2000): 424–53.

McCrae, Robert R., and Oliver P. John. "An Introduction to the Five-Factor Model and Its Applications." *Journal of Personality* 60, no. 2 (1992): 175–215.

McGuinness, D., and K. H. Pribram. "The Origins of Sensory Bias in the Development of Gender Differences in Perception and Cognition." In *Cognitive Growth and Development: Essays in Memory of Herbert G. Birch*, edited by M. Bortner, 3–56. New York: Brunner/Mazel, 1979.

McHugh, Paul. "Surgical Sex." *First Things* 147 (November 2004): 34–38.

McLanahan, Sara. "Family Structure and the Reproduction of Poverty." *American Journal of Sociology* 90, no. 4 (January 1985): 873–901.

Mead, Margaret. *Male and Female: A Study of the Sexes in a Changing World*. New York: William Morrow, 1949.

———. *Blackberry Winter: My Earlier Years*. New York: Touchstone, 1972.

Meeker, Meg. *Boys Should Be Boys: 7 Secrets to Raising Healthy Sons*. New York: Ballantine, 2009.

Meshberger, Frank Lynn. "An Interpretation of Michelangelo's Creation of Adam Based on Neuroanatomy." *JAMA* 264, no. 14 (October 10, 1990): 1837–41.

Michaelangelo. *Complete Poems and Selected Letters of Michelangelo*. Translated by Creighton Gilbert. Edited by Robert N. Linscott. Princeton, N.J.: Princeton University Press, 1980.

Miller, G., J. M. Tybur, and B. D. Jordan. "Ovulatory Cycle Effects on Tip Earnings by Lap Dancers: Economic Evidence for Human Estrus." *Evolution and Human Behavior* 28, no. 6 (2007): 375–81.

Miller, James. *The Passion of Michel Foucault*. New York: Simon and Schuster, 1993.

Millett, Kate. *Sexual Politics*. Garden City, N.Y.: Doubleday, 1970.

Moir, Anne, and David Jessel. *Brain Sex: The Real Difference between Men and Women*. New York: Delta, 1991.

Money, John. "Hermaphroditism, Gender and Precocity in Hyperandrenocorticism: Psychological Findings." *Bulletin of Johns Hopkins Hospital* 96, no. 6 (1955): 253–64.

———. *Sex Research, New Developments*. New York: Holt, 1965.

———. "Pornography in the Home." In *Contemporary Sexual Behavior*, edited by Joseph Zubin and John Money, 409–40. Baltimore, Md.: Johns Hopkins University Press, 1973.

———. *Love and Love Sickness: The Science of Sex, Gender Difference and Pair-Bonding*. Baltimore: Johns Hopkins University Press, 1980.

———. Interview. *Paidika: The Journal of Paedophilia* 2, no. 3 (Spring 1991): 2–13.

Money, John, and Anke A. Ehrhardt. *Man and Woman, Boy and Girl: Gender Identity from Conception to Maturity*. Northvale, N.J.: Jason Aronson, 1996.

Money, John, Joam G. Hampson, and John L. Hampson. "An Examination of Some Basic Sexual Concepts: The Evidence of Human Hermaphroditism." *Bulletin of Johns Hopkins Hospital* 97, no. 4 (1955): 301–19.

———. "Imprinting and the Establishment of Gender Role." *Archives of Neurology and Psychiatry* 77, no. 3 (1957): 333–36.

Money, John, and Patricia Tucker. *Sexual Signatures: On Being a Man or a Woman*. Boston: Little, Brown, 1975.

Mooney, Carol Garhart. *Theories of Attachment: An Introduction to Bowlby, Ainsworth, Gerber, Brazelton, Kennell, and Klause*. St. Paul, Minn.: Redleaf, 2010.

Moore, D. S., and S. P. Johnson. "Mental Rotation in Human Infants: A Sex Difference." *Psychological Science* 19, no. 11 (2008): 1063–66.

Mounier, Emmanuel. "La femme aussi est une personne" [Woman Is Also a Person]. *Esprit* (June 1936): 292–97.

———. *A Personalist Manifesto*. London: Longmans, Green, 1938.

———. *Personalism*. Translated by the Monks of St. Johns Abbey. Notre Dame, Ind.: University of Notre Dame Press, 1952.

National Center for Fathering. "The Consequences of Fatherlessness." http://fathers.com/statistics-and-research/the-consequences-of-fatherlessness/.

NCCB/USCC. *John Paul II on the Genius of Women*. Washington, D.C.: United States Catholic Conference, 1997.

Newman, John Henry. "A Letter Addressed to the Rev. E. B. Pusey, D.D., on Occasion of His Eirenicon." In *Certain Difficulties Felt by Anglicans in Catholic Teaching*. Vol. 2. Pittsburgh: The National Institute for Newman Studies, 2007.

O'Leary, Dale. *The Gender Agenda: Redefining Equality*. Lafayette, La.: Vital Issues, 1997.

———. "Don't Say Gender When You Mean Sex." Pontifical Council on the Laity Online Library: *Women* (January–February 2012).

———. "A Woman's Perspective on Mainstreaming a Gender Perspective." May 2011. Pontifical Council on the Laity Online Library: *Women* (January–February 2012). http://www.laici.va/content/laici/en/sezioni/donna.html.

Oliver, M. B., and J. S. Hyde. "Gender Differences in Sexuality: A Meta-Analysis." *Psychological Bulletin*, 114, no. 1 (1993): 29–51.

Onions, Charles Talbut, ed. *The Oxford Dictionary of English Etymology*. Oxford: Clarendon, 1966.

Panksepp, J. "Oxytocin Effects on Emotional Processes: Separation Distress, Social Bonding, and Relationships to Psychiatric Disorders." *Annals of the New York Academy of Sciences* 652 (1992): 243–52.

Paul VI. *Closing of the Second Vatican Council: Address to Women*. Speech. December 8, 1965.

———. "Discourse à La Commission d' étude sur la Femme dans las Société et dans l'Eglise." Speech. January 31, 1976.

———. "Discorso Alle Partecipanti al Congresso Nazionale Del Centro Italiano Femminile." Speech. December 6, 1976.

Pearlstein, Mitch. *From Family Collapse to America's Decline: The Educational, Economic, and Social Costs of Family Fragmentation*. Lanham, Md.: Rowman and Littlefield, 2011.

———. *Broken Bonds: What Family Fragmentation Means for America's Future*. Lanham, Md.: Rowman and Littlefield, 2014.

Pedersen, Johannes. *Israel: Its Life and Culture*. London: Oxford University Press, 1959.

Peeters, Marguerite A. "Current Proposals and the State of the Debate." In *Men and Women: Diversity and Mutual Complementarity*, by the Pontifical Council for the Laity, 73–98. Vatican City: Libreria Editrice Vaticana, 2006.

———. *The Globalization of the Western Cultural Revolution: Key Concepts, Operational Mechanisms*. Translated by Benedict Kobus. Brussels: Institute for Intercultural Dialogue Dynamics [ASBL], 2007.

———. "Gender: An Anthropological Deconstruction and a Challenge for Faith." In *Woman and Man: The Humanum in Its Entirety*, edited by Pontifical Council for the Laity. Vatican City: Libreria Editrice Vaticana, 2010.

———. "The New Global Ethic: Challenges for the Church." Pontifical Council on the Laity Online Library: *Women* (January–February 2012).

Peplau, L. "Human Sexuality: How Do Men and Women Differ?" *Current Directions in Psychological Science* 12, no. 2 (2003): 37–40.

Pettit, Becky. *Invisible Men: Mass Incarceration and the Myth of Black Progress*. New York: Russell Sage Foundation, 2012.

Pfeiffer, Heinrich. *The Sistine Chapel: A New Vision*. New York: Abbeville, 2007.

Pheasant, S. T. "Sex Differences in Strength—Some Observations on Their Variability." *Applied Ergonomics* 14, no. 3 (1983): 205–11.

Pillemer, D. B., P. Wink, T. E. DiDonato, and R. L. Sanborn. "Gender Differences in Autobiographical Memory Styles of Older Adults." *Memory* 11, no. 6 (November 2003): 525–32.

Pintzka, Carl W. S., Hallvard R. Evensmoen, Hanne Lehn, and Asta K. Håberg. "Changes in Spatial Cognition and Brain Activity after a Single Dose of Testosterone in Healthy Women." *Behavioral Brain Research* 298, part B (February 1, 2016): 78–90.

Pius XII. *Women's Duties in Social and Political Life: Address of His Holiness Pope Pius XII to Members of Various Catholic Women's Associations* [Questa Grande Vostra Aduntana], October 21, 1945. London: Catholic Truth Society, 1955.

Pomeroy, Wardell D. *Dr. Kinsey and the Institute for Sex Research*. New York: Harper and Row, 1972.

Pontifical Council for the Family, ed. *Lexicon: Ambiguous and Debatable Terms regarding Family Life and Ethical Questions*. Front Royal, Va.: Human Life International, 2006.

Pontifical Council for the Laity. "Safeguarding the Human Being, Created as Man and Woman." September–October 2013. http://www.laicos.va/content/laici/en/sezioni/donna/salvaguardar-al-ser-humano—creado-varon-y-mujer.html.

Popenoe, David. *Life without Father*. Cambridge, Mass.: Harvard University Press, 1996.

Pruett, Kyle. *Fatherneed: Why Father Care Is as Essential as Mother Care for Your Child*. New York: Broadway, 2000.

Quinn, P. C., and L. S. Liben. "A Sex Difference in Mental Rotation in Young Infants." *Psychological Science* 19, no. 11 (2008): 1067–70.

Raeburn, P. *Do Fathers Matter? What Science Is Telling Us about the Parent We've Overlooked*. New York: Scientific American and Farrar, Straus and Giroux, 2014.

Reidel, R., and A. Javor. "The Biology of Trust: Integrating Evidence from Genetics, Endocrinology, and Functional Brain Imaging." *Journal of Neuroscience, Psychology and Economics* 5, no. 2 (2012): 63–91.

Reinisch, June M., Leonard A. Rosenblum, and Stephanie A. Sanders, eds. *Masculinity/Femininity: Basic Perspectives*. Kinsey Institute Series. Oxford: Oxford University Press, 1987.

Reisman, Judith A. *Kinsey: Crimes and Consequences; The Red Queen and the Grand Scheme*. Arlington, Va.: Institute for Media Education, 1998.

Reisman, Judith A., Mary E. McAlister, and Paul E. Rondeau. "Global Sex Deviance Advocacy: The Trojan Horse to Destroy the Family and Civil Society; A Report on UNESCO and International Planned Parenthood Federation." *Ave Maria International Law Journal* 1, no. 2 (Spring 2012): 231–63.

Revoredo, Oscar Alzamore. "An Ideology of Gender: Dangers and Scope." In Pontifical Council for the Family, *Lexicon*, 465–82.

Rhoades, Steven E. *Taking Sex Differences Seriously*. San Francisco: Encounter, 2004.

Rohner, R. P., and R. A. Veneziano. "The Importance of Father Love: History and Contemporary Evidence." *Review of General Psychology* 5, no. 4 (2001): 382–405.

Rose, A. J., and K. D. Rudolph. "A Review of Sex Differences in Peer Relationship Processes: Potential Trade-Offs for the Emotional and Behavioral Development of Girls and Boys." *Psychological Bulletin* 132, no. 1 (2006): 98–131.

Round, J. M., D. A. Jones, J. W. Honour, and A. M. Nevill. "Hormonal Factors in the Development of Differences in Strength between Boys and Girls during Adolescence: A Longitudinal Study." *Annals of Human Biology* 26 (1999): 49–62.

Rubin, Gayle. "The Traffic in Women: Notes on the 'Political Economy' of Sex." In *Toward an Anthropology of Women*, edited by Rayna R. Reiter, 157–210. New York: Monthly Review, 1975.

———. "The Valley of the Kings: Leathermen in San Francisco 1960–1990." Ph.D. diss. University of Michigan, 1994.

Ruigrok, A. N. V., G. Salimi-Khorshidi, M-C. Lai, S. Baron-Cohen, M. V. Lombardo, R. J. Tait, and J. Suckling. "A Meta-Analysis of Sex Differences in Human Brain Structure." *Neuroscience and Biobehavior Reviews* 39, no. 100 (2014): 34–50.

Sandberg, D. E., and H. F. L. Meyer-Bahlburg. "Variability in Middle Childhood Play Behavior: Effects of Gender, Age, and Family Background." *Archives of Sexual Behavior* 23, no. 6 (1994): 645–63.

Savage, Deborah. "The Metaphysics of Creation as the Foundation of Environmental Stewardship and Economic Prosperity." *Nova et Vetera* (English ed.) 12 (Winter 2010): 233–52.

———. "The Centrality of Lived Experience in Wojtyła's Account of the Person." *Roczniki Filozoficzne* [Philosophical Annals] 61, no. 4 (January 2014): 19–51.

———. "The Nature of Woman in Relation to Man: Genesis 1 and 2 through the Lens of the Metaphysical Anthropology of Thomas Aquinas." *Logos: A Journal of Catholic Thought and Culture* 18, no. 1 (Winter 2015): 71–93.

———. "The Genius of Man." In *Promise and Challenge: Catholic Women Reflect on Feminism, Complementarity, and the Church*, edited by Mary Hasson, 129–54. Huntington, Ind.: Our Sunday Visitor, 2015.

———. "Adam's Gift: Man in the Order of Creation." *Humanum: Issues in Family, Culture, and Science* (2016). http://humanumreview.com/articles/adams-gift-man-in-the-order-of-creation.

———. "Man, Woman, and the Mission of the Laity." *Church Life Journal*, October 24, 2016. https://churchlifejournal.nd.edu/articles/man-woman-and-the-mission-of-the-laity.

Sax, Leonard. *Boys Adrift: The Five Factors Driving the Growing Epidemic of Unmotivated Boys and Underachieving Young Men*. New York: Basic Books, 2007.

Schiltz, E. R. "The Promise and the Threat of the 'Three' in Integral Complementarity." In *Promise and Challenge: Catholic Women Reflect on Feminism, Complementarity, and the Church*, edited by M. R. Hasson, 53–83. Huntington, Ind.: Our Sunday Visitor, 2015.
Schiltz, Lisa. "A Contemporary Catholic Theory of Complementarity." In Failinger, Schiltz, and Stabile, *Feminism, Law, and Religion*, 3–24.
Schmitt, D. P., A. Realo, M. Voracek, and J. Allik. "Why Can't a Man Be More Like a Woman? Sex Differences in Big Five Personality Traits across 55 Cultures." *Journal of Personality and Social Psychology* 94, no. 1 (2008): 168–82.
Schultz, J. F., and C. Thoni. "Overconfidence and Career Choice." *PLOS One* 11, no. 1 (2016), essay e0145126. http://doi.org/10.1371/journal.pone.0145126.
Schumacher, Michelle M., ed. *Women in Christ: Towards a New Feminism*. Grand Rapids, Mich.: Eerdmans, 2004.
Scola, Angelo Cardinal. *The Nuptial Mystery*. Grand Rapids, Mich.: Eerdmans, 2005.
Shea, D. L., D. Lubinski, and C. P. Benbow. "Importance of Assessing Spatial Ability in Intellectually Talented Young Adolescents: A 20-Year Longitudinal Study." *Journal of Educational Psychology* 93, no. 3 (2001): 604–14.
Simner, Marvin. "Newborn's Response to the Cry of Another Infant." *Developmental Psychology* 5, no. 1 (1971): 136–50, http://dx.doi.org/10.1037/h0031066.
Skowronski, John J., Andrew L. Betz, Charles P. Thompson, and Laura Shannon. "Social Memory in Everyday Life: Recall of Self-Events and Other-Events." *Journal of Personality and Social Psychology* 60, no. 6 (1991): 831–43.
Smith, Christopher H. (R.-N.J). Keynote Address: "Pro-Family Prospects in the Congress." Chapter 1 in *The Church, Marriage and the Family*, edited by Kenneth D. Whitehead. Notre Dame, Ind.: St. Augustine's Press, 2007.
Smuts, Barbara. "The Evolutionary Origins of Patriarchy." *Human Nature* 6, no. 1 (1995): 1–32.
Sokolowski, Msgr. Robert. "What Is Phenomenology? An Introduction for the Uninitiated." *Crisis* 12, no. 4 (April 1994): 26–29.
———. *Introduction to Phenomenology*. Cambridge: Cambridge University Press, 2000.
———. *Phenomenology of the Human Person*. Cambridge: Cambridge University Press, 2008.
Sommers, Christina Hoff. *The War against Boys: How Misguided Feminism Is Harming Our Young Men*. New York: Simon and Schuster, 2000.
Spaemann, Robert. *Persons: The Difference between "Someone" and "Something."* Translated by Oliver O'Donovan. New York: Oxford University Press, 2006.
Spence, J. T., R. L. Helmreich, and C. K. Holahan. "Negative and Positive Components of Psychological Masculinity and Femininity and Their Relationships to Self-Reports of Neurotic and Acting Out Behaviors." *Journal of Personality and Social Psychology* 37, no. 10 (1979): 1673–82.
Stefaniak, Regina. *Mysterium Magnum: Michelangelo's Tondo Doni*. Boston: Brill, 2008.
Stein, Edith. *Self-Portrait in Letters: 1916–1942*. Washington, D.C.: ICS, 1993.
———. *Essays on Woman*. 2nd ed. Translated by Freda Mary Oben. Volume 2 of *Collected Works of Edith Stein*, edited by Lucy Gelber and Romaeus Leuven. Washington, D.C.: ICS, 1996.

———. *Finite and Eternal Being*. Washington D.C.: ICS, 2002.
Stoller, Robert J. *Sex and Gender*. New York: Science House, 1968.Strawson, Peter F. *Individuals*. London: Metheun, 1961.
Tannen, Deborah. *You Just Don't Understand: Women and Men in Conversation*. New York: Ballantine, 1990.
Taylor, S. F. "Tend and Befriend: Biobehavioral Bases of Affiliation Under Stress." *Current Directions in Psychological Science* 15, no. 6 (2006): 273–77.
Theological Dictionary of the Old Testament. Vol. 12. Edited by G. Johannes Botterweck, Helmer Ringren, and Heinz-Josef Fabry. Grand Rapids, Mich.: Eerdmans, 2003.
Thomas, J. R., and K. E. French. "Gender Differences across Age in Motor Performance: A Meta-Analysis." *Psychological Bulletin* 98, no. 2 (1985): 260–82.
Trilling, Lionel. "The Kinsey Report." In *An Analysis of the Kinsey Reports on Sexual Behavior in the Human Male and Female*, edited by Donald Porter Geddes, 213–29. New York: Mentor, 1954.
Tsai, Tyjen, and Paola Scommegna. "U.S. Has World's Highest Incarceration Rate." Population Reference Bureau website. Last updated October 24, 2014. https://www.prb.org/us-incarceration/.
Tunç, B., B. Solmaz, D. Parker, T. D. Satterthwhaite, M. A. Elliott, M. E. Calkins, K. Ruparel, R. E. Gur, R. C. Gur, and R. Verma. "Establishing a Link between Sex-Related Differences in the Structural Connectome and Behaviour." *Philosophical Transactions of the Royal Society B: Biological Sciences* 371 (Feb. 2016): 16–88.
United Nations Office on Drugs and Crime. *Global Report on Trafficking in Person* (2014). http://www.unodc.org/documents/data-and-analysis/glotip/GLOTIP_2014_full_report.pdf.
Vaillancourt, T., and A. Sharma. "Intolerance of Sexy Peers: Intrasexual Competition among Women." *Aggressive Behavior* 37, no. 6 (2011): 569–77.
Vasari, Giorgio. *Lives of the Artists*. Vol. 1. Translated by George Bull. London: Penguin, 1987.
Virgil. *Aenead*. Book VI. Translated by Seamus Heaney. New York: Farrar, Straus and Giroux, 2016.
———. *Eclogue*. Translated by David Ferry. New York: Farrar, Straus and Giroux, 1999.
Vitz, P. C., and M. McCall. "The Importance of the Father for the Family: Research and Theory." Unpublished paper. Arlington, Va.: Divine Mercy University, 2016.
von Hildebrand, Alice. *The Privilege of Being a Woman*. Ann Arbor, Mich.: Sapientia Press of Ave Maria, 2002.
von Hildebrand, Dietrich. *Marriage: The Mystery of Faithful Love*. Manchester, N.H.: Sophia Institute Press, 1991.
———. *Man and Woman: Love and the Meaning of Intimacy*. Manchester, N.H.: Sophia Press, 1992.
———. *The Nature of Love*. South Bend, Ind.: St. Augustine's Press, 2009.
Voyer, D., S. Voyer, and M. P. Bryden. "Magnitude of Sex Differences in Spatial Abilities: A Meta-Analysis and Consideration of Critical Variables." *Psychological Bulletin* 117, no. 2 (1995): 250–70.
Vuoksimaa, E., J. Kaprio, W. S. Kremen, L. Hokkanen, R. J. Viken, A. Tuulio-

Henriksson, and R. J. Rose. "Having a Male Co-Twin Masculinizes Mental Rotation Performance in Females." *Psychological Science* 21, no. 8 (2010): 1069–71.

Wai, Jonathan, David Lubinski, and Camilla P. Benbow. "Spatial Ability for STEM Domains: Aligning Over 50 Years of Cumulative Psychological Knowledge Solidifies Its Importance." *Journal of Educational Psychology* 101, no. 4 (2009): 817–35.

Watson, Neil V., and Doreen Kimura. "Nontrivial Sex Differences in Throwing and Intercepting: Relation to Psychometrically Defined Spatial Functions." *Personality and Individual Differences* 12, no. 5 (1991): 375–85.

Whiting, B. B., and C. P. Edwards. "A Cross-Cultural Analysis of Sex Differences in the Behavior of Children Aged Three through Eleven." *Journal of Social Psychology* 91, no. 2 (1973): 171–88.

———. *Children of Different Worlds: The Formation of Social Behavior*. Cambridge, Mass.: Harvard University Press, 1988.

Williams, John E., and Deborah L. Best. *Measuring Sex Stereotypes: A Multination Study*. Thousand Oaks, Calif.: Sage, 1990.

Wippel, John F. *The Metaphysical Thought of Thomas Aquinas: From Finite Being to Uncreated Being*. Washington, D.C.: The Catholic University of America Press, 2000.

Wittig, Monique. "The Straight Mind." *Feminist Issues* 1 (Summer 1980): 108–11.

Wojtyła, Karol. *The Acting Person*. Translated by Andrzej Potocki. Dordrecht: D. Reidel, 1979.

———. *Love and Responsibility*. San Francisco: Ignatius Press, 1981.

———. *Person and Community*. Edited by Andrew Woznicki. Translated by Theresa Sandok. New York: Peter Lang, 1993.

Wolfe, Linda. *Kinsey: Public and Private*. New York: New Market, 2004.

Yeo, Ronald A., Sephira G. Ryman, Melissa E. Thompson, Martijn P. van den Heuval, Marcel A. deReus, Jessica Pommy, and Rex E. Jung. "Cognitive Specialization for Verbal vs. Spatial Ability in Men and Women: Neural and Behavioral Correlates." *Personality and Individual Differences* 102 (November 2016): 260–67.

Zahn-Waxler, C., M. Radke-Yarrow, E. Wagner, and M. Chapman. "Development of Concern for Others." *Developmental Psychology* 28, no. 1 (1992): 126–36.

CONTRIBUTORS

J. BUDZISZEWSKI is a professor of government and philosophy at the University of Texas, Austin, specializing in topics related to natural law. He is the author of numerous books, including *On the Meaning of Sex*; *What We Can't Not Know: A Guide*; and several commentaries on the work of Thomas Aquinas, most recently, *Commentary on Thomas Aquinas's Treatise on Divine Law*.

SR. MARY PRUDENCE ALLEN, RSM, is a member of the Religious Sisters of Mercy of Alma, Michigan. She was named Distinguished Professor Emeritus by Concordia University, Montreal, in 1996; and the Charles J. Chaput Endowed Chair of Philosophy, St. John Vianney Theological Seminary, Denver, in 2011; and more recently served on the International Theological Commission. She is the author of many publications on gender issues in the history of philosophy, including a three-volume work, *The Concept of Woman*.

ELIZABETH LEV studied art history at University of Chicago as an undergraduate and received her graduate degree from the University of Bologna. She teaches for Duquesne University's Italian Campus and is the author of four books, including *How Catholic Art Saved the Faith*. She is currently working on *Michelangelo's Women,* an analysis of the Florentine artist's portrayal of women in his sculpture, painting, and poetry.

DEBORAH SAVAGE is clinical professor of philosophy and theology at St. Paul Seminary School of Divinity, University of St. Thomas, St. Paul, Minnesota. Her recent publications include "Redeeming Woman: A Response to the Second Sex Issue from the Catholic Exegetical Tradition" (*Religions Journal*); and "The Therapeutic and Pastoral Implications of Pope St. John Paul II's Account of the Person" (*Journal of Christian Bioethics*).

PAUL C. VITZ is senior scholar and professor at the Institute for the Psychological Sciences, Divine Mercy University, Sterling, Virginia, and professor emeritus of psychology at New York University. His research focuses on the integration of Christian theology, especially Catholic anthropology, with psychology and breaks from secularism and postmodern relativism. A prolific author and editor in various media, he most recently published *A Catholic Christian Meta-Model of the Person: Integration with Psychology and Mental Health Practice*.

INDEX

abortion, 58, 64, 67, 83
Abzug, Bella, 64
action: and contemplation, 6, 34, 110, 148, 150; divine, 73, 95, 129, 136; feminine, 34, 83, 87, 151–52, 154–55, 167–70, 173, 212; human, 14, 17, 22, 72, 80–81, 84, 110, 112, 118, 125; masculine, 116, 125, 148–50, 154–55, 157, 167, 189, 193, 199
Adam: and creation, 97–104, 107–9, 136–40; and the fall, 112, 121–24, 143; and generation, 71–72, 160; and masculinity, 114–18; prefiguring Christ, 172–73, 178
aggression, 3, 155, 182, 196, 197, 206–7; channelling, 32–33, 202
Alberti, Leon Battista, 166–67, 169, 171
Alexander VI, 146
Ambrose, 141
angelism, 16
anthropology, 42; Christian, 93; and gender ideology, 56; Hebraic, 71–72, 94, 96–99, 102; modern, 41–42, 59–60; and phenomenology, 76; Thomistic, 36, 38, 75–76, 88, 94, 101–2, 104. *See also* nature, human
Aquinas. *See* Thomas Aquinas
Aristotle: biology of, 72, 80, 106n48; metaphysics of, 36, 38, 74–76, 97n28; and soul, 14
assertiveness, 20–22, 212, 214
Augustine 124, 148
Augustinian order, 135–36
autism, 205, 209–10

baptism, 74, 166, 178
Barbin, Alexina-Herculine, 44
Baron-Cohen, Simon, 196, 203, 209–10
Beach, Frank A., 45

Berdjaev, Nicholai, 79
Bernard of Clairvaux, 175
Bernadus Silvestris, 37
binary distinction, 36, 73–74, 85, 88, 184–85; creation of, 90, 95; exceptions to, 86, 184–85; rejection of, 58, 60, 63. *See also* gender realities
body: in art, 135, 143; of Christ, 175; and mind, 14, 16, 24; and motherhood, 27, 29, 198; and personhood, 25, 77; rejection of, 40; sacramental meaning of, 89, 96; and sex difference, 77–78, 85–86, 185, 195–96; and sex/gender, 24–25, 37, 60–61. *See also* unity, body and soul
Bocaccio, 170
Bohr, Niels, 80
Botticelli, 163, 168
brain. *See* body; mind; neuroscience
Brizendine, Louann, 194–95
Burggraf, Jutta, 69–70
Buss, David, 195
Butler, Judith, 62

Cahill, Larry, 11–13
Campbell, Anne, 182
Cárdenas, Maria Eugenia, 71
choices, 28, 126, 130, 203, 207
children: bearing, 11, 16, 26–27, 122; and career, 28; and family, 16, 29, 31, 79–80, 86, 114, 166–67, 201–2, 212; as fulfillment of complementarity, 79; and gender ideology, 68; generation of, 160, 181, 187; mistreatment of, 23, 26, 50–53; raising of, 7, 23, 26, 31–32; and sex difference, 188–93; and sex reassignment, 43–44, 49–51, 54; and sexuality, 46–48, 50, 51, 55

237

Chrysostom, John, 178
Church, Catholic: attacks on, 55; as Bride, 86, 179–80; and complementarity, 1, 4–5, 6, 72–74, 146; and gender ideology, 63–71; on marriage, 6, 79–86, 130; sex abuse scandal, 53, 56; and women, 90–92, 173–74
civilization, 42, 146; and complementarity, 126, 131, 215; creation of, 5, 32, 117–18; of love, 55. *See also* culture
Colapinto, John, 49
color: for emphasis, 139, 171; figurative, 9, 157, 168; technique, 162; use of, 145, 151, 155, 163–64, 177
complementarity, 11, 75–82, 186–87, 211–13; and civilization, 126, 131, 215; and dignity, 80, 133, 172, 183–84; and the fall, 131, 143–44; and generation, 161, 184; as mission, 93, 130; in parenting, 23, 27–28, 30–32, 171, 201, 212–15; polaric, 14–15; principles of, 133, 172, 183–84; in the Sistine Chapel, 154–57, 161, 166–67, 170, 172, 179, 181. *See also* original sin; procreation; synergy
Conrad-Martius, Hedwig, 78, 81
contemplation: and action, 6, 34, 110, 148, 150; in men, 147, 151, 172; in women, 148, 150, 153, 174, 175. *See also* passivity
cooperation, 192; in salvation, 133, 172, 174; between the sexes, 133
Costa, Paul T., Jr., 19
Cozolino, Louis, 197
creation, 136; accounts of, 94–119, 132–33, 136–40; and complementarity, 85; new, 128; order of, 121–23, 173–74. *See also* Genesis
culture: and complementarity, 93–94, 215; cross-cultural surveys, 17, 58, 202–3; of death, 53–56; deconstruction of, 41; and gender ideology, 40–41, 54; revolution, 68; and sex difference, 10, 19, 22, 33, 37, 41–42, 61, 64, 182, 209; and sexuality, 59; and women, 79, 87, 91, 121, 125–26. *See also* civilization; gender roles

Daly, Mary, 74
Daniel, 147, 149–50
David, 154
de Beauvoir, Simone, 52, 74
deconstructionism: evils of, 114; and language, 41; and the person, 4, 36, 40–41, 60–62
de Laureates, Teresa, 61
De' Medici, Lorenzo, 135
Descartes, René, 38, 210; philosophy of, 4, 36, 38, 46, 60, 64
Diamond, Milton, 52–53
differences, sexual, 9–10, 27–28, 36, 87, 105–6, 182–83; in behavior, 12, 153, 157, 190–94, 206–7; in biology, 24, 185, 190–91, 195–96, 199–201, 204–5, 211; and complementarity, 22–23, 76–77, 133, 157, 186–87, 211–13; as created, 102–3; in development, 189–90; in emotion, 12, 17, 19–20, 188, 190, 194–95, 205–6, 210, 211, 214; and gift of self, 110, 125, 202; and individuals, 3, 19, 22, 37, 46, 58, 62, 75–76; overlap of, 3, 20–21, 184, 213; in parenting, 27–31, 166–67, 197–99, 201–2; in psychology, 206–11; rejection of, 61, 64–65; in relationship, 77–78, 82, 196–98; scientific evidence for, 2–8, 11–12, 49–51, 81, 199–201; and sexual desire, 13, 83, 122, 196; in sin, 83, 120; in strengths, 29–30, 110–11, 187–88, 203; in thinking, 17, 20, 191–94, 200–204. *See also* equality; gender reality; love; original sin
dignity: and complementarity, 80, 133, 172, 183–84; equal, 7, 13, 31, 76, 79–80, 87, 91, 101–3; human, 67, 76, 82, 84, 118; of women, 79, 90–91, 101, 106
Dionysius of Halicarnassus, 147
domination: vs. collaboration, 8; male, 59, 83, 126, 183, 214; and sex difference, 61; and sin, 120, 122
dualism, 38, 60
duality: of nature, 13–15; of path, 13–15, 28; and unity, 93

Ehrhardt, Anke, 45
emotion: and neuroscience, 198–99; sensitivity to, 19–20, 192, 194; and sex differences,

12, 17, 19–20, 188, 190, 194–95, 205–6, 210, 211, 214
empathy, 3, 188–89, 196, 198, 205, 210–11, 214
equality, 13, 80, 84, 102; and difference, 1, 11, 15, 74, 92–94, 105–6, 109, 183; of the sexes, 108–11, 120–21, 130; of substance, 104–5, 120; unisex, 64–65, 69. *See also* dignity
eroticism, 40, 41, 55, 67, 164–65, 195
Esolen, Anthony, 117
essence, 21–25, 75, 78, 99, 101, 105, 120; and accident, 11. *See also* substance
Esther, 156–57
Eve, 103, 108–9, 139–40, 170–71; and the fall, 120–23, 143; and Mary, 172–73
Ezekiel, 140–41, 148

fall, the, 85, 111–12, 119–26, 143–45, 184. *See also* original sin
family: and complementarity, 168, 211–15; depiction of, 159, 166–69; father's role in, 127–29; governance of, 30, 116, 124, 130; need for, 114. *See also* children; motherhood
fatherhood, 29–31, 80, 84, 130; and complementarity, 23, 27–28, 30–32, 171, 201, 212–15; depiction of, 166–67; importance of, 125, 201–2; lack of, 29, 113–14; and masculinity, 86. *See also* Joseph; men
femininity. *See* women
feminism, 8, 15; and gender ideology, 56–62, 126; and gender reality, 87; and men, 113; and womanhood, 28
flourishing, 112, 117, 118, 125, 212
Foucault, Michel, 40, 44, 53–54, 61
Fra Angelico, 180
Francis (pope), 1, 91
Franciscan order, 136
fresco, 145, 161–62
Freud, Sigmund, 33

Gaddi, Taddeo, 160
Geary, David C., 195
Genazzano, Mariano da, 135
gender: in the Bible, 71–73; as construct, 60–61, 64, 186; deconstruction of, 62; definition of, 64–65, 69–70, 182–83; formation of, 43, 52; and generation, 71–73; ontology of, 105; revolution, 67; and sex, 37–38, 71–73, 186; types of, 42, 45, 59, 60, 63–64
gender identity. *See* identity, gender
gender ideologies, 1, 4, 36, 66, 87, 186; critique of, 44–56; and culture, 40; and culture of death, 53–56; and feminism, 56–62, 126; flawed support for, 51–53; history of, 37–43; and language, 42, 60–61, 64–65, 69; mainstreaming of, 65, 67–68; and pseudo-science, 39, 44, 56; and schools, 58, 68
gender realities, 4, 22, 36, 74, 86, 160, 186; evidence for, 49–51, 95; and language, 69–71; roots of, 71–73. *See also* binary distinction; differences, sexual
gender roles: and complementarity, 77–78, 133; as construct, 41–42, 59, 63–64; in the family, 30, 116, 166–71; and gender identity, 45–46; universality of, 182–183. *See also* culture
generation, 71–73, 158, 160; of children, 160, 181, 187; and complementarity, 161, 184. *See also* procreation
Genesis, 5, 73, 95–112, 114–24, 183; and genealogies, 71–72, 160; and the Sistine Chapel, 132, 135–36. *See also* creation
genius, 5, 125; feminine, 29, 30, 83, 92, 111–12, 177; masculine, 30, 84, 113–19, 127–29; as supernatural, 129–30. *See also* Joseph
Ghirlandaio, Domenico, 134, 146, 164, 168
Giles of Viterbo, 136
Gilson, Étienne, 81
Glendon, Mary Anne, 65
grace, 82, 95, 129–30
Gurian, Michael, 188–94

Henry VIII, 177
hermaphroditism, 43, 44
heroes and heroines: lack of, 114; Mary as, 174–75; parents as, 32, 171; of the Sistine Chapel, 154–57, 181

homosexuality, 41, 49, 60, 132
hormones, 12, 185, 190, 194–95, 197–98, 206; and gender, 52, 63
Hoyenga, Katharine and Kermit, 58–59
hylomorphism, 36, 38, 40, 75–76, 81. *See also* unity, body and soul

identicalism, 15, 21
identity, 38, 78; and complementarity, 85, 93, 103, 152–53; as construct, 52, 64; deconstruction of, 60–62; personal, 22, 85–86, 99; sexual, 38–41, 44, 66, 82, 86–87, 189. *See also* person, human
identity, gender, 45–46, 61, 76–78, 82, 87; and feminism, 58; formation of, 52, 55, 56–57; and language, 60–61; and sex, 59–60, 82, 86; and the sexual act, 40–41; study of, 85
ideology, 16, 40; and abuse of power, 48–51; and human rights, 67; and pseudo-science, 48–53; and universities, 58. *See also* gender ideologies
individual, 21–22, 78, 82, 101–5; and community, 98–99, 200, 210; dignity of, 67, 76, 82; disregard for, 49; and gender, 38, 46, 58, 62; and sex difference, 3, 19, 22, 37, 86, 102. *See also* person, human
Ingarden, Roman, 78, 82–83
intercession, 139–40, 157, 171, 180
interpersonal skills, 3, 7, 111–12, 118, 157, 187–88, 196–97, 200
Isaiah, 148

Jeremiah, 146, 151–52
Jesus Christ, 73, 126–28, 133, 139, 177–78, 180–81; birth of, 142; the Bridegroom, 86; genealogy of, 72, 136, 158–60, 165–71; knowledge of, 36; and Mary, 172–81; prophecies of, 148; and redemption, 85–86, 139, 171, 178; and women, 106
Joel, 147, 150–51
John the Baptist, 176, 178
John Paul II, 1, 5–6, 87, 183; anthropology of, 82–85, 95–97, 101–6; on fatherhood, 86, 127–28; on gender, 65–66, 73–75; on masculinity and femininity, 85–87, 183; on the Sistine Chapel, 132–33, 180–81; on women, 89–92, 111, 121, 126, 177. *See also* theology
Johnson, Virginia E., 57–58
Joseph, 84, 127–29, 176
Judith, 154
Julius II, 134, 162

Kant, Immanuel, 46
Kessler, Suzanne, 58
Kimura, Doreen, 11
Kinsey, Alfred, 38–39, 43, 48–49, 51, 53, 74
Krapiec, M. A., 82, 84–85

Lactantius, 145, 148
Lewis, C. S., 37–38
light: creation of, 107, 136; and shadow, 143–44, 149–50, 162; theories of, 80; use of, 148, 177
Lippi, Filippino, 146, 163
Llamas, Marta, 63
Lonergan, Bernard, 75, 81–82
love: aspects of, 22, 29, 31; and communion, 85–87; development of, 83–84; as gift of self, 77–78, 87, 108, 110, 117–18, 129, 177; lack of, 26, 49; need for, 123, 197

macho. *See* polarity, gender
Marcel, Gabriel, 75, 79–80
Maritain, Jacques and Raissa, 75, 76, 79–86, 166–71, 196, 202; and the Church, 6, 130; rejection of, 15–16, 122–23; and sexuality, 39–40, 49
Martin, Biddy, 61–62
Marxism, 59–60, 186
Mary, Blessed Virgin: depictions of, 169–76; and the feminine genius, 92; Gate of Heaven, 141, 178; and motherhood, 92, 159, 169, 172, 175–77; New Eve, 139–40, 172–73, 176–77, 178; and the Sistine Chapel, 133, 171–80
masculinity. *See* men
Masters, William H., 57–58
materialism, 13–16, 25
McCrae, Robert R., 19
McHugh, Paul, 52, 54

McKenna, Wendy, 58
McKenty, Mary, 50–51
Mead, Margaret, 41–42, 74
Meeker, Meg, 113
men, 76, 86, 203–4, 206–7, 211–13; attacks on, 113–14; and body, 76–78; definition of, 22, 29, 105, 116–18; and heroism, 32–33; importance of, 118–19, 125, 202; rejection of, 61. *See also* action; contemplation; fatherhood
Michelangelo, 134–36, 166; and Mary, 172; technique, 150, 161–62, 165–67; use of color, 145, 151, 155, 163–64
Miller, James, 53n53
Millett, Kate, 56–57
mind: and body, 14–16, 24; and brain, 15–16; and gender identity, 46; and soul, 14. *See also* soul; unity, body and soul
Money, John, 42–43, 44, 50–52, 57, 74; and pornography, 47–48, 54–55
Moses, 156–57
motherhood, 72, 130; and complementarity, 23, 27–28, 30–32, 171, 201, 212–15; depiction of, 158–60, 163–71; failure of, 23, 26; and femininity, 86, 111; and gender ideology, 67, 69; and generation, 160; and Mary, 92, 159, 169, 172, 175–77; physical aspects of, 27, 77, 83, 169–70, 197–99; potentiality for, 11, 25–26, 29, 111, 170; single, 32, 123; types of, 26–27, 29, 86. *See also* women
Mounier, Emmanuel, 75, 79, 80, 82

natural kinds, 21–22. *See also* binary distinction
nature, human, 13, 22, 33; and complementarity, 85, 92, 104; deconstruction of, 41, 61–62; as male and female, 98. *See also* anthropology; gender reality
need, mutual, 15, 31–32
neo-Platonism, 36–38
neo-Thomism, 80
neuroscience: amygdala, 12, 199; corpus callosum, 2, 7, 189, 199, 204–5, 206; limbic system, 12, 189, 206; and sex difference, 2–3, 11–12, 199–201, 204–6; and the soul, 25
Nicholas of Cusa, 37, 143

obedience, 121–22, 124, 139, 172–73, 175, 178–80
O'Leary, Dale, 63, 65
original sin, 94, 130–31; in men and women, 83, 112, 119–25. *See also* fall, the

parenting. *See* complementarity; fatherhood; motherhood
passivity: feminine, 34, 80, 143, 170; human, 136. *See also* contemplation
patriarchs, 162–63
Paul, 30
Paul III, 177
Paul IV, 90
pedophilia, 42, 50, 51, 53, 55
Peeters, Marguerite A., 67–69
person, human: abuse of, 49; and body, 14, 25, 77; and community, 85, 98–99; deconstruction of, 4, 36, 40–41, 60–62; definition of, 13, 21–22, 36, 38, 81, 84, 98, 101; as image of God, 85, 95, 97, 99–100, 103, 170, 183, 215; importance of, 118, 121, 125; as man or woman, 74, 76–77, 86–88, 93, 102, 105, 186; as subject (not object), 49, 61–62, 95–96, 102–3, 108, 124. *See also* dignity; identity; individual
personalism, 78–79, 90, 99–100
personality: corporate, 98–99, 102; and sex difference, 7, 12, 17–21, 182, 208–9, 213–14
Perugino, 168, 171, 177
Peter, 159
phenomenology, 76–78
Pinturicchio, Bernardino, 146
polarity, gender, 93, 143–44, 183
Półtawska, Wanda, 83
Pomeroy, Wardell, 39–40, 48
pornography, 47–48, 54–56, 196
priesthood, 86, 168
procreation, 93, 126; and complementarity, 133, 184, 215. *See also* generation
prophetesses. *See* sibyls

prophets, 145–153, 170
psychology: and ideology, 40; and sex difference, 2, 7, 17–20, 60, 77–78, 81, 206–11; surveys, 17–20, 23, 48–49, 202–3

Reimer, David (Bruce/Brenda) and Brian, 49–51, 54
Reisman, Judith, 47, 51
relationship, 111–12; and complementarity, 6, 76–77, 79, 81, 92–93, 126, 131; disordered, 112, 113, 122–24, 184; with God, 116–17, 121, 172; human, 84, 87, 89, 99; and the sex act, 20, 39–40; and sex differences, 3, 7, 28, 77–78, 82, 111–12, 194–98, 208–12
relativism, 42
Revoredo, Oscar Alzamore, 70
Rosselli, Cosimo, 168
Rossi, Alice, 57–58
Rubin, Gayle, 59

Sartre, Jean-Paul, 74
Savonarola, Girolamo, 135
sculptor, 134–35, 145, 154, 172, 175, 179
self-gift, 87, 108, 110, 117–18, 125, 129, 202. *See also* love
sexes: definition of, 24–25, 32; and gender, 37–38, 40, 59–60, 86; reversibility of, 47. *See also* differences, sexual; gender reality; men; women
sex reassignment surgery, 49–54
sexual act: and complementarity, 82; and gender, 37–38, 72; as identity, 40–41; and relationship, 20, 39–40, 49. *See also* generation; procreation
sexuality: as changeable, 45; development of, 46–48; and gender differences, 196–97; as identity, 40. *See also* differences, sexual
sibyls, 145–47, 153, 170; Cumean, 141–42, 147–48; Delphic, 150–51; Eritrean, 148; Hebrew/Persian, 148–49; Libyan, 151–52; Mary as, 174
Signorelli, Luca, 168
sin, 83, 119–24, 130–31; as disorder, 16, 111–12, 122–24. *See also* original sin
Sistine Chapel, 159, 170; and the Blessed Virgin Mary, 133, 171–80; and complementarity, 5–6, 132–34, 180–81; and conclave, 132, 168; history of, 134, 145, 167
Sixtus IV, 133, 174
Sokolowski, Robert, 82
soul: commensurate to body, 75–76, 104–5; definition of, 14, 25, 75, 99; and grace, 173; and personality, 98–99; rational, 101, 102, 120; redemption of, 177–80; as substantial form, 104–5, 120. *See also* unity, body and soul
statistics, 20–21, 49, 65, 184–85
Stein, Edith, 27, 75, 77–78, 81, 86
Stoller, Robert, 57
stress, 12, 19–20, 193, 194–95, 200
substance, 62, 81, 101–2. *See also* essence
synergy, 7, 72, 76, 79–80, 184, 213–15. *See also* complementarity

Teresa Benedicta of the Cross. *See* Stein, Edith
Terraccino, Antonio, 19
theology: in art, 135; of the body, 5–6, 89, 94–95, 133, 183; and complementarity, 1–2, 5–6, 93–94, 126; and gender ideology, 44; informed by science, 81–82; of women, 1, 91. *See also* John Paul II
Thomas Aquinas, 35–36, 75–76, 116; anthropology of, 94, 96, 101, 104–5, 120
Tree of Jesse, 159–60
trompe l'oeil, 154, 158

unity, body and soul, 4, 13, 25, 36, 75–76, 81, 101; and complementarity, 76; and creation, 96, 99; rejection of, 13–16, 38, 40; and sex, 105. *See also* body; hylomorphism; soul

Vasari, Giorgio, 151
Virgil, 142, 147
virtues: desire for, 29; feminine, 113, 179–211; male and female inflections of, 23, 27, 29–30; masculine, 32–33, 118; in relationship, 82, 166
vocation, 76, 85–88, 93; and complementarity, 126, 130; of women, 90–91

von Hildebrand, Alice, 26
von Hildebrand, Dietrich, 75, 76, 80–81

will, the: and family, 80, 84; of God, 152, 171–75; human, 26, 78, 83, 101, 110; in relationship, 83–84; and virtue, 82
Wippel, John, 75
wisdom, 23, 31, 126
Wittig, Monica, 60–61
Wojtyła, Karol. *See* John Paul II
Wolfe, Linda, 46

women, 76, 78, 83, 86, 211–213; as active, 168–70; and body, 27, 29, 76–78, 105, 143, 198, 207; definition of, 22–26, 105, 111–12; depiction of, 163–65, 168–71; dignity of, 79, 90–91, 101, 106; fallen, 122; and feminism, 28; importance of, 125–26, 139–40; rejection of, 61; virtues of, 170–71. *See also* action; contemplation; motherhood; passivity

Zdybicka, Zofia J., 84

The Complementarity of Women and Men: Philosophy, Theology, Psychology & Art
was designed in Minion with Maestro and Hypatia Sans display type and
composed by Kachergis Book Design of Pittsboro, North Carolina.
It was printed on 55-pound Natural Hi Bulk and bound by
Data Reproductions of Auburn Hills, Michigan.